IMAGES
of America

HARRODSBURG

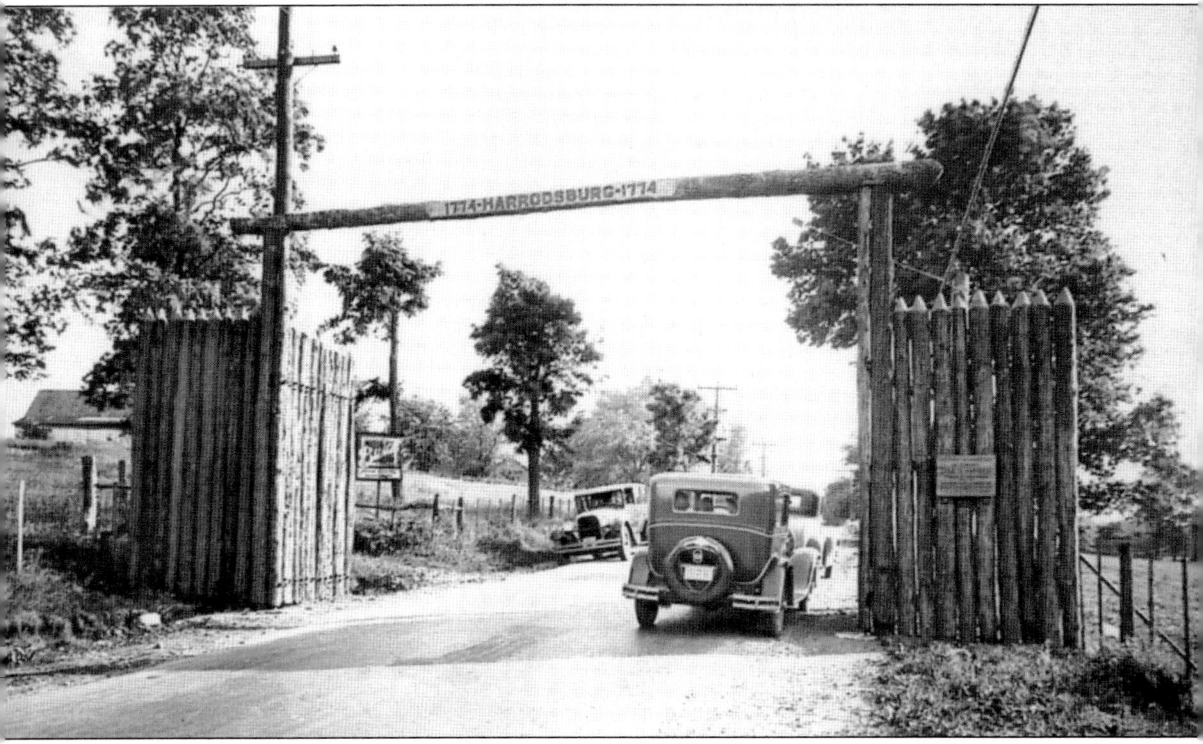

These stockade gates once greeted travelers to Harrodsburg via Lexington Road. A replica of the Fort Harrod entryway, the gates served as a reminder of the town's pioneer heritage. They were a gift from the Woman's Club of Harrodsburg and were erected in 1929 and removed in 1936. A plaque read: "As the friendly gates of Harrod's Fort were open to pioneers, so too these gates today are open to you—enter and abide."

On the Cover: Pictured around 1949 to 1950, Harrodsburg's Main Street was typical of small towns all across America, which still had bustling, booming downtowns of mostly mom-and-pop businesses.

IMAGES
of America

HARRODSBURG

Bobbi Dawn Rightmyer
and Anna Armstrong

ARCADIA
PUBLISHING

ISBN 978-0-7385-8210-8

Published by Arcadia Publishing
Charleston, South Carolina

Printed in the United States of America

Library of Congress Control Number: 2010937746

For all general information, please contact Arcadia Publishing:
Telephone 843-853-2070
Fax 843-853-0044
E-mail sales@arcadiapublishing.com
For customer service and orders:
Toll-Free 1-888-313-2665

Visit us on the Internet at www.arcadiapublishing.com

Dedicated to the memory of Andrew and Jesta Bell Armstrong,
providers of inspiration and materials for this book

Dedicated to my husband, Keith Rightmyer, for believing in me

Contents

FOREWORD

Thank you Bobbi Rightmyer and Anna Armstrong for giving us this pictorial treasure of my hometown—Harrodsburg.

Harrodsburg, Kentucky, is about four miles from the farm on Mount Pleasant Road where I was born and where I lived for 20 years before moving to Harrodsburg after World War II. Living here for these past 65 years has been a blessing to me.

Riding in the buggy with my mother into Harrodsburg from the farm was a joy. She drove that horse and buggy right to the livery stable on Greenville Street, where a nice gentleman took good care of the horses until we finished our shopping. This stable was in the rear of the Big Store, which had its wonderful entrance on Main Street and the nice stable off of Greenville Street. The Big Store had all kinds of most everything for sale: pots, pans, and many items that farmers needed.

Ben Franklin Norfleet had a hardware store with nuts, bolts, and other merchandise lining the walls. It was often said if Norfleet's did not sell a needed item, it simply was not available anywhere. The Bohon family had a buggy factory right here in Harrodsburg, and it was successful until horseless carriages came on the scene. Automobiles were sold in town (and they still are). Milt Whitenack, our farm neighbor, bought a new 1934 Chevrolet for $800 cash. He and countless others parked their cars on both sides of Main Street, and on Saturdays, Harrodsburg was full of cars. Folks felt free to sit in any of these cars, none was ever locked. Yes, Saturday was the heyday for the merchants when most of the "country folks," as we were called, came into town with crates of fresh eggs, cream in a can, and chickens in coops. These food items were sold at the grocery store. This was the first stop—a grocery store where the produce was taken. Townsfolk were happy to be able to buy these fresh items from the farm. To my knowledge, the C&T Food Market is the only one still in business today. I worked there for Page Bailey during World War II when there was rationing. Of course, staple items like salt, sugar, pepper, clothing, and everything needed on the farm could all be purchased in Harrodsburg.

Saturday in Harrodsburg was *the* social life of most of Mercer County. Most everyone knew everybody from Cornishville, Bohon, Duncan, McAfee, Salvisa, Burgin, and Dixville. It was a time to visit, find out what was going on, and to buy everything that would be needed on the farm until the next Saturday. There was no electricity, water, or telephone at our farm home until after World War II. It seemed like a miracle the first time I saw the lights on Main Street at night. The Great White Way was bright as day. The oil lamps in our home were only a glimmer. Being nine years old and able to see all that was available at night was a dream without sleep. Yes, Harrodsburg had it all for me.

It seems there were about three five-and-dime stores on Main Street. Many folks shopped in these—children especially liked the long candy counter and, after a careful decision, pointed to that special chocolate drop. Nice dress shops, men's shops, and stores for hats or anything needed or wanted lined Main Street. Clerks were there to help the customers in all their purchases; they had smiles that said, "Please come again." And so we did.

Bill Matthew had a restaurant on the corner where city hall is now. That building always looked so strong, as it does today. The Blue Ribbon Restaurant owned by Mr. Prewitt was on Main Street. It was once owned by Wiley Chumley before it closed. Was there a restaurant named the New York Café? It seems it had a parrot in a cage. Do you remember this? It was in the vicinity of Lawson Jewelry Store.

Mr. Isenberg was the owner of the great department store the Blue Front, located on the corner of Main and Poplar Streets. Each Christmas, he had a great party for all the local children. Santa Claus came with a noisemaker for every child. Have you seen the opera house on the second floor of this building? It was restored by the late Ralph Anderson to its original beauty. Many years ago, the opera came to Harrodsburg and enjoyed this fine house as did the folks here in Harrodsburg. The opera house was on the Christmas home tour three years ago, and it is a must-see. Thank you again to Ralph Anderson.

Another fine building is the Mercer County Courthouse Annex. It was known years ago as James Flats and was located on the corner of Main and East Office Streets. Many people lived in this apartment building. George Ann Sims Cross owned it, and then Hanley Ruby bought it. At the ground level on the East Office side was a small door that opened into a room, which was a wonderful little restaurant. It was known as the Hole in the Wall. Virginia "Miss Virgie" Pinkston was a marvelous cook, and she served delicious food for two or three years. Seasoning and serving good country food, she, too, formerly lived on a farm and learned the art of cooking early in life. She was a beautiful woman with twinkling brown eyes and a smile that I still remember. Anna Armstrong, coauthor of this book, is her granddaughter.

Of course, the president of the United States, Franklin Delano Roosevelt, arrived in 1934 to dedicate the wonderful Pioneer Memorial at Fort Harrod State Park to the men who paved the way for the great memories we now enjoy of our town—Harrodsburg, Kentucky.

To you James Harrod and to your men
Thank you, thank you, again and again
Thanks for coming in 1774
Thanks for memories we have in store.

Harrodsburg, named just for you
And our gratitude is ever true.
For these special memories,
Harrodsburg's Poet Laureate thanks again
Now and forever, Amen! Amen!

—Louise Isham Dean
Harrodsburg, Kentucky

ACKNOWLEDGMENTS

First and foremost, we thank the Armstrong archives, without which this book would not be possible. Unless otherwise noted, all photographs in this book are courtesy of these archives.

The authors thank the following people for their assistance, inspiration, and memories in the preparation of this book: Amalie Preston, Ron Reed, Jack Bailey, Gertrude Reed, Jim Miller, Don Rightmyer, Keith Rightmyer, Robin Ison, and Margaret Knapp. They also thank the following organizations: Harrodsburg Historical Society, James Harrod Trust, Mercer County Public Library, the Kentucky Historical Society, and the Arcadia Publishing team.

A very special thanks to Louise Isham Dean for writing the foreword and poem about Harrodsburg, and thanks to Tony Sexton for the use of his poem "Jimmy Taylor's Store."

Sincere, heartfelt gratitude is expressed to my coauthor, Anna Armstrong, for her knowledge, patience, and wonderful home-studio archives. There is no way this book would have been completed without her sacrifice and dedication

Introduction

A leisurely stroll down the streets of Harrodsburg is like time traveling through the historic past. Harrodsburg, Kentucky, is the oldest permanent settlement west of the Allegheny Mountains, and this town was just the beginning of the westward push that opened up the rest of this country. Founded in 1774 by James Harrod and a company of 32 men, the town was laid out with simple log cabins alongside the creek that came from what was called the Big Spring. When Fort Harrod was built, Kentucky had a huge Native American population, but when more pioneers began arriving in the mid- to late 19th century, most major Native American settlements had vanished from the region.

Harrodsburg is not a comprehensive history of the oldest settlement of the West, but it serves as a photographic companion to shine a light on the town's early history, churches, government, and businesses, and it offers a small taste of Main Street. This book will stir memories for Harrodsburg's residents, both past and present, and give tourists and other visitors a brief look at this historic community.

Referred to as the Birthplace of the West, Harrodsburg is well known for a long list of significant firsts in American history. The first courts and first elections in the new West were held in Harrodsburg.

When Harrodsburg was settled and more colonists arrived, with them came the need for spiritual teaching. Records indicate the first preacher in the settlement was an Episcopal pastor, Rev. John Lythe; he ended up being scalped by Indians. Records of Catholic influences in Fort Harrod date to 1775. A traveling minister would come through Harrodsburg every few weeks to present sermons to the early settlers. Soon, churches began to spring up almost faster than the town itself, with the first Presbyterian and Catholic churches located in the heart of Harrodsburg. The first Sunday schools in Kentucky also began in Harrodsburg.

The first school in Kentucky was erected in Harrodsburg at Fort Harrod, and the teacher, Jane Coomes, taught the children of the fort. Coomes was given a small cabin to use as a schoolhouse, and she used the Old English hornbook, a simple wooden paddle marked with the alphabet and numbers, to teach her young students. Bacon College (1839–1850) was the first institute of higher education, quickly followed by Daughter's College, Beaumont College (1856–1917), and the Academy (1847–1883).

During the first few years, Harrodsburg was still a dangerous wilderness area; births were few, but deaths were many. Harrodsburg was the birthplace of the first white child born in Kentucky, although the child's name is unknown. On the sad side, this was also the place where the first white child was buried. Although this name is also unknown, the Pioneer Cemetery inside Old Fort Harrod has a marker for this child, entombed in a small, raised sarcophagus.

Industry in Kentucky was established by Ann Poague McGinty, an early resident of Fort Harrod. When she decided to go with her husband to the new land, she was determined to bring her spinning wheel over the mountains. She soon began to teach spinning to other settlers, and the women helped to supply enough clothing for the fort. Ann's first husband, William Poague, made the first weaving loom in Kentucky, and Ann manufactured the first linsey-woolsey, using nettles and buffalo hair. (Modern readers can only imagine the itchiness of this material.) It became the first woolen fabric manufactured in Kentucky.

Soon, Harrodsburg began a period of rapid growth. Cabins and businesses began to spring up on the outside of the fort, and roads were laid out to develop a regular town. The first tavern in Kentucky was Harrodsburg's Old Wingfield Tavern, which was followed by numerous other saloons. Legends as to why Harrodsburg's current Main Street is on such a steep hill instead of the flat street Morgan Row occupies include the most believable one that says a discontented bartender from Morgan Row set up a grogshop (a saloon that sold cheaper liquor) at the foot of the big hill (now Main Street). The cheaper grade of whiskey soon attracted many wagoners and draymen to refresh themselves and their horses before going up the long hill. To cater to this growing business, several stores were quickly built around the saloon. Refusing to sacrifice the quality of the liquor at its taverns, Morgan Row forfeited the title Main Street. So the road used by the men wanting cheap whiskey became known as Main Street.

In the early 1820s, Harrodsburg became known as the Saratoga of the West because of the number of medicinal spas and resorts built near several area springs. Dr. Christopher Columbus Graham started the Harrodsburg Springs and then acquired the Greenville Spring; he combined them into the Graham Springs. People from all over would come to the resort to take the waters and minerals, seek quiet and relaxation, and enjoy the company of other people in the same social class.

Harrodsburg has always been centered on agriculture, especially tobacco, corn, hemp, and livestock. Farmers brought cured tobacco to town at the end of the season and left it at one of several tobacco warehouses to be sold. They transported corn to one of the gristmills to be ground into meal. A large portion of livestock was shipped out of Harrodsburg's train depot for auction.

One of the favorite attractions in Harrodsburg is the Old Fort Harrod State Park, which features a replica of the first fort. The cabins at the park are furnished with handmade utensils and furniture, and people dressed in period clothing offer tours and information. The park also has the Pioneer Monument (1932), which was dedicated by Pres. Franklin D. Roosevelt in 1934, the Lincoln Marriage Temple (1806), the Mansion Museum (1920s–present), and the Pioneer Cemetery. Tourists also enjoy the Beaumont Inn, previously Daughter's College (1855–1895), and touring the renovated Main Street area.

From this brief introduction, you can see Harrodsburg is full of many historic firsts of the West. It is impossible to include everything there is to tell. The James Harrod Trust, Harrodsburg's local historic preservation organization, is active in trying to preserve the unique and significant history of this place.

One

Old Fort Harrod

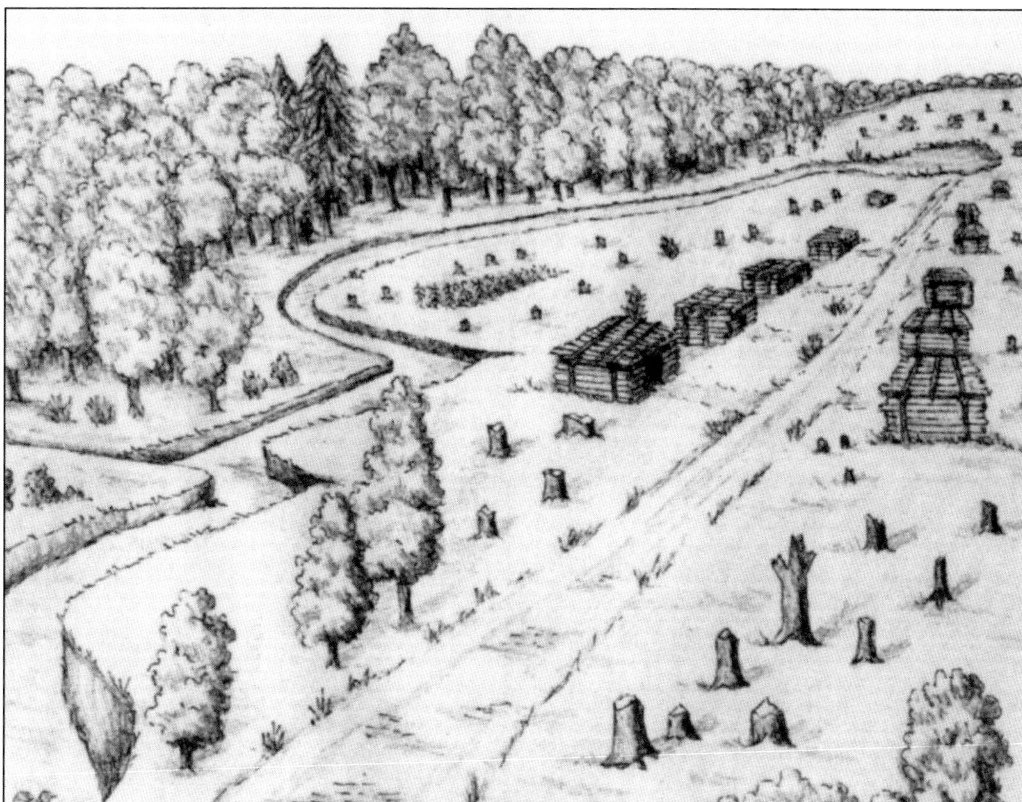

Local artist Ruth Beall (1913–2002) drew this sketch of what Harrodstown would have looked like in 1774. The first structures were simple log cabins close to the Big Spring near present-day East Factory Street behind the Mercer County School buildings. A wagon path was cleared following the course of Town Creek, which originated at the Big Spring and ran through town past the site where the first fort was built in 1775.

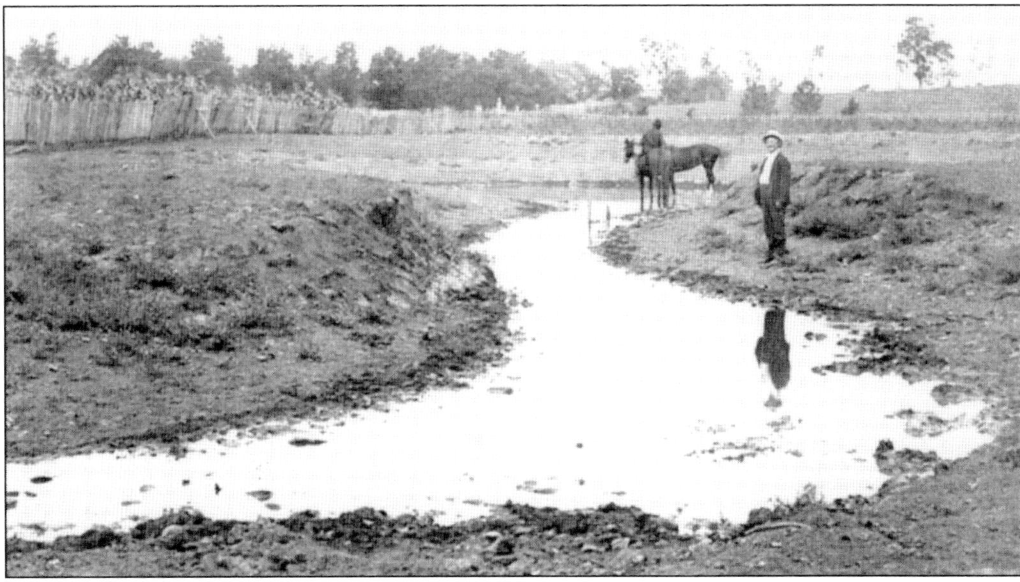

This photograph shows the Big Spring in the early 1900s. James Harrod and his men arrived here in 1774 and laid out a town site of simple log cabins alongside the creek. The cabins were abandoned briefly because of feared Indian attacks, but they were reoccupied in 1775. The construction of Fort Harrod began farther to the west, and the pioneers moved there when it was finished. (A.B. Rue.)

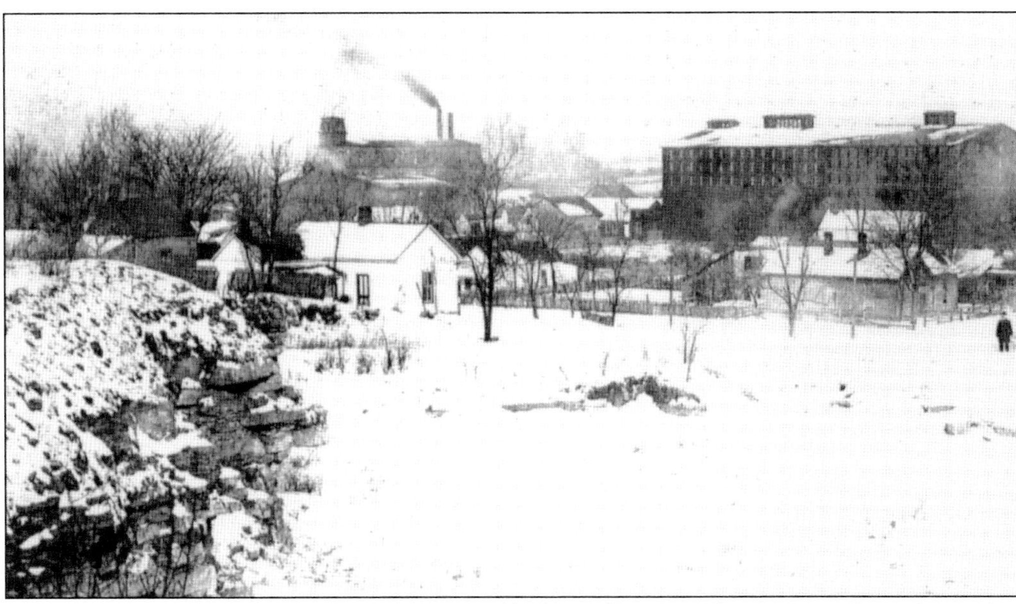

This is a view looking north from Old Fort Hill where the original Fort Harrod was located. A quarry opened there in the 1890s, and the site of the original fort was destroyed. The area has since been filled in for a fort parking lot. The large buildings are the J.B. Thompson Old Fort Distillery, which relocated from the Kentucky River near Oregon to West Factory Street. (A.B. Rue.)

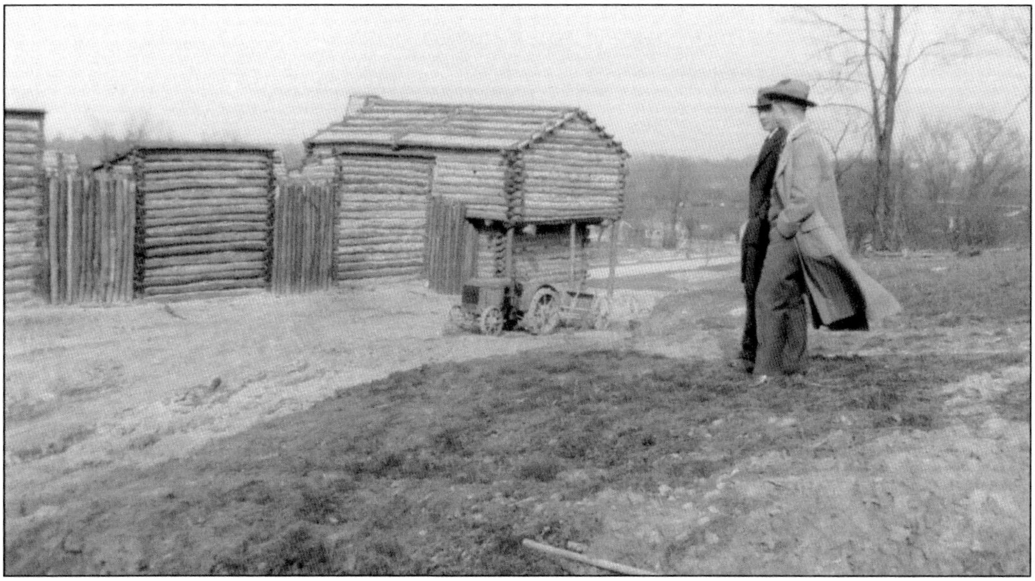

The above photograph shows the replica of Fort Harrod as it was being built in 1927, some 153 years after the original fort was constructed by James Harrod and his men. Court documents researched by local attorney and historian Hon. W.W. Stephenson give information on its accurate re-creation. This replica is slightly south of the original fort location. The photograph below is a 1953 view of an Osage orange tree planted in the 1870s in Fort Harrod State Park. It is the unofficial champion of its species because of its split trunk, even though it is taller and broader than Viginia's national champion Osage orange. Its height is 75 feet, and the circumference of the trunk base is 36 feet. Generations of children have been brought here to play and climb in this tree.

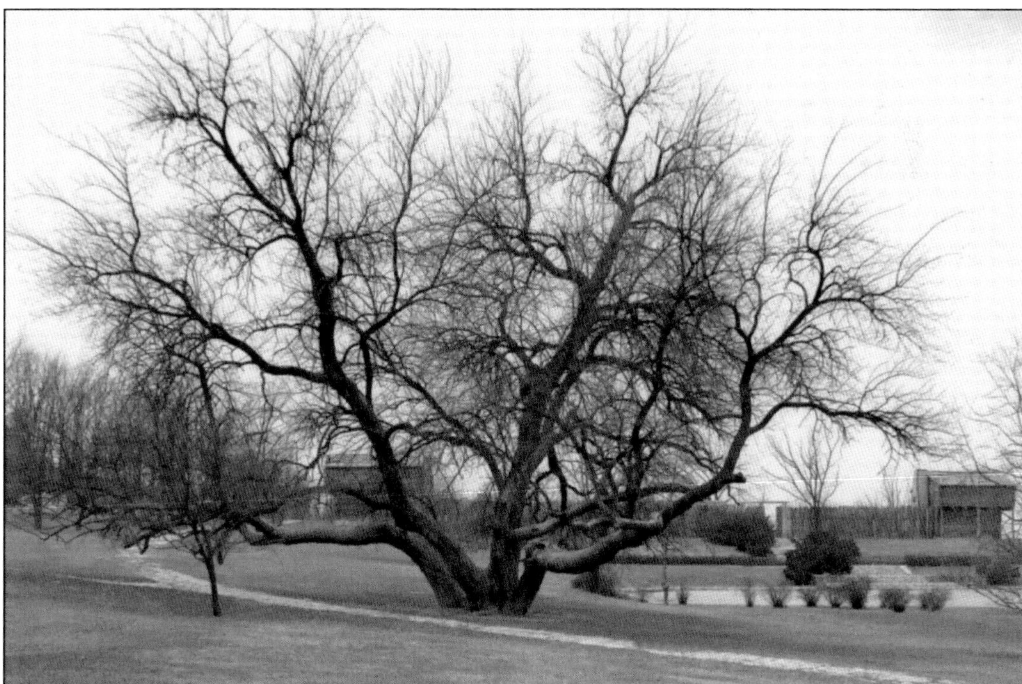

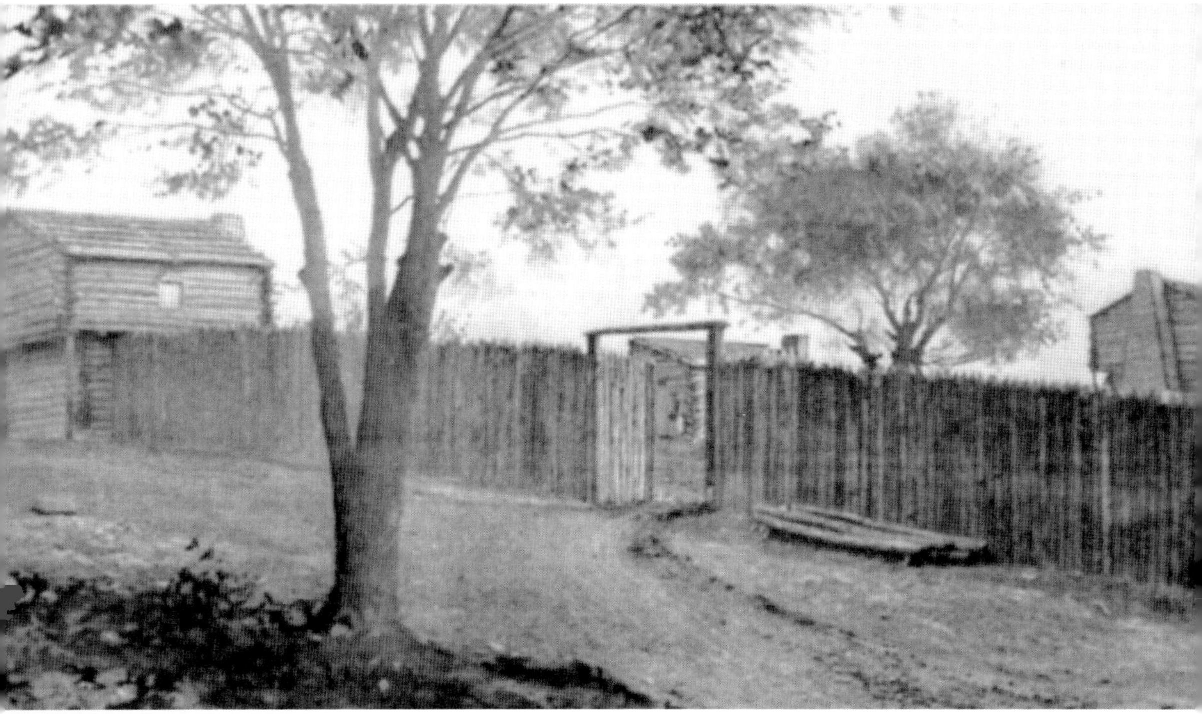

Old Fort Harrod State Park was the result of years of effort by members of the Kentucky Pioneer Memorial Association, organized in Harrodsburg and led by residents in 1923. Its goal was a tribute to the first permanent white settlement west of the Allegheny Mountains. The association selected the site of the present state park and raised support for the construction of a replica of James

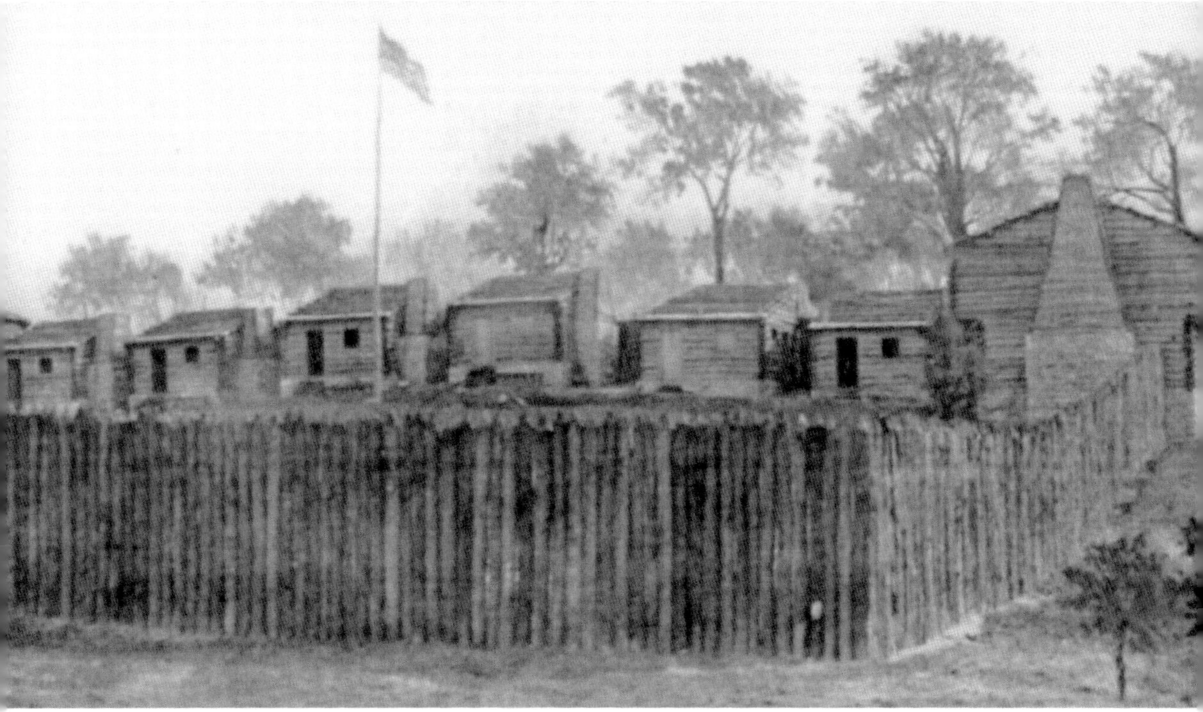

Harrod's fort. This "frontier cradle of advancing civilization of pioneer America" now preserves Kentucky's pioneer history through its displays of tools, furniture, and various other artifacts and its use of interpreters in period clothing to perform pioneer tasks such as blacksmithing, weaving, and woodworking.

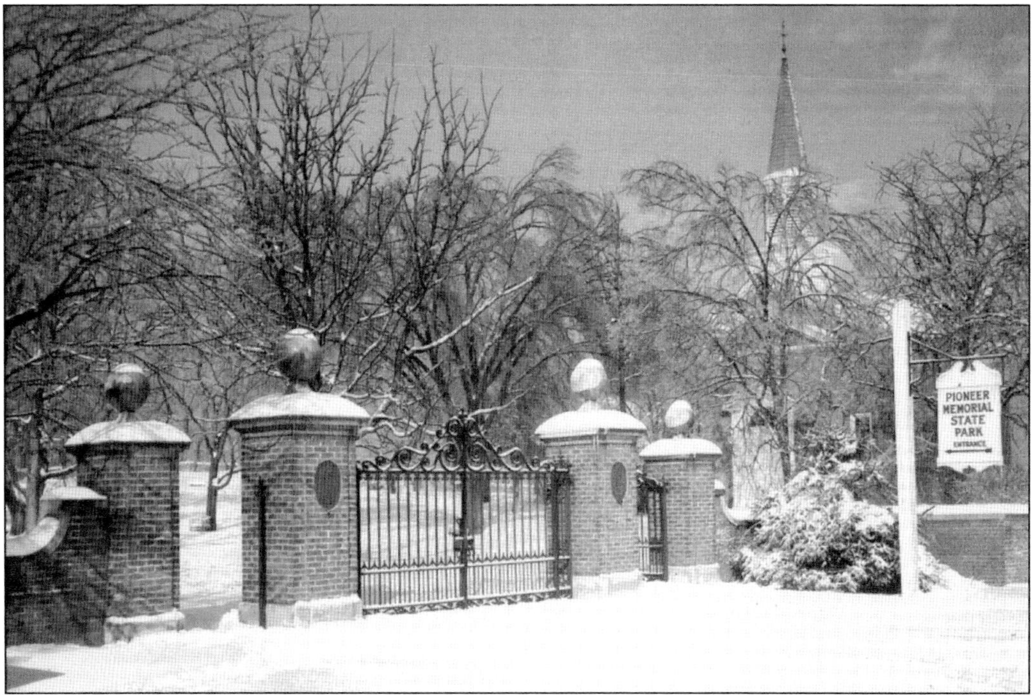

The beautiful handwrought iron gates forming the entrance to Fort Harrod State Park were a gift from the Society of Colonial Dames of America and the Society of Sons of Colonial Wars in the Commonwealth of Kentucky. These two societies recognized Harrodsburg, founded in 1774, as Kentucky's only colonial town and as being two years older than the Declaration of Independence.

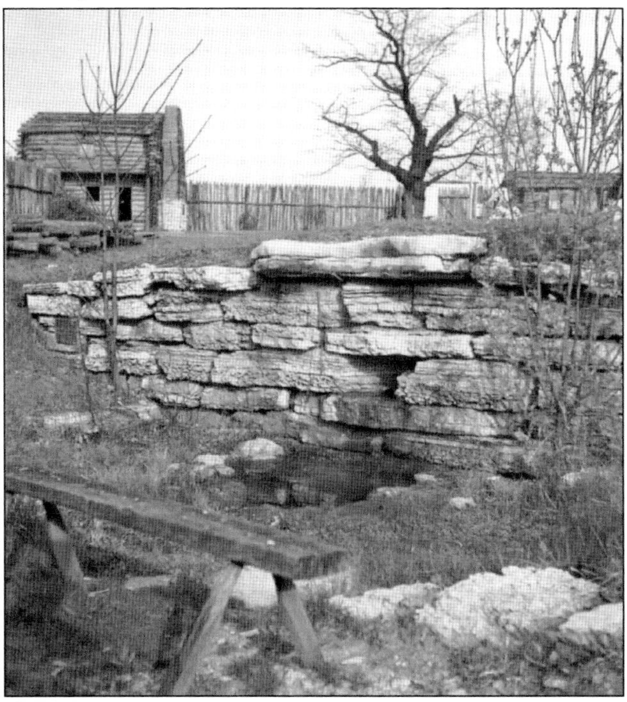

This spring inside Fort Harrod gave the settlers a safe supply of water. A trip for water to a spring located too far from cabins or outside a stockade often ended in tragedy for the settlers when Indians attacked. Some of the springs still run with water, but many have dried up due to disturbances of the underground streams by construction.

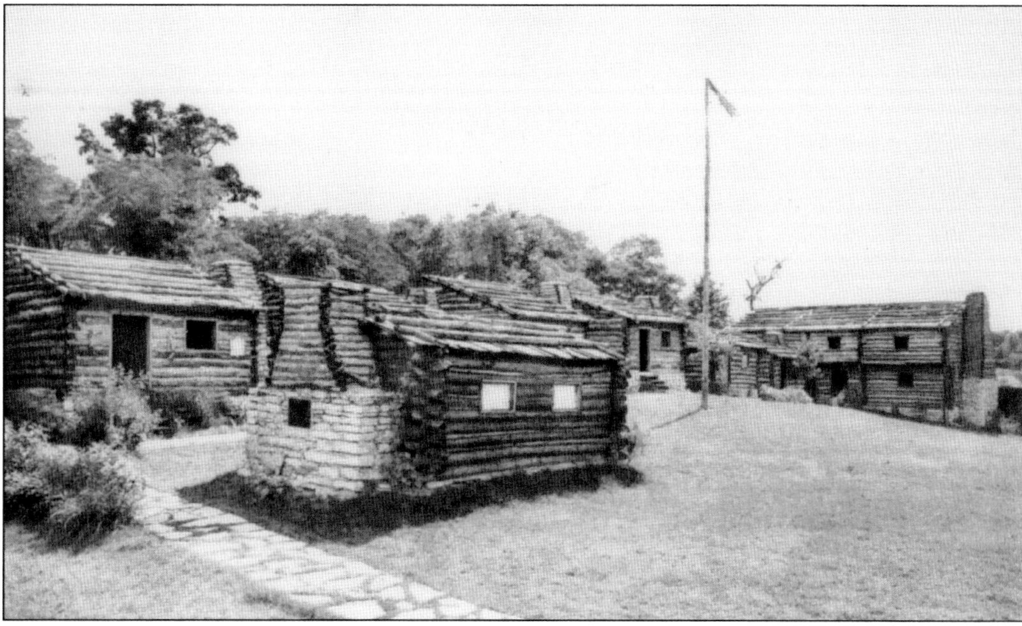

The photograph above is a 1934 view inside the stockade as it would have looked in pioneer times. The image below shows the interior of Ann Poague McGinty's cabin with a hearth equipped with everything a pioneer woman needed to prepare meals—cast iron footed kettles, griddles, a churn, and gourds for serving food and dipping water. Ann brought her spinning wheel on her horse over the Wilderness Road and taught the art of spinning to others. Her first husband, William Poague, made the first weaving loom in Kentucky, and Ann manufactured the first linsey-woolsey using nettles and buffalo hair. The famous pioneer woman was known as the first home economics demonstrator in Kentucky. She died in 1815.

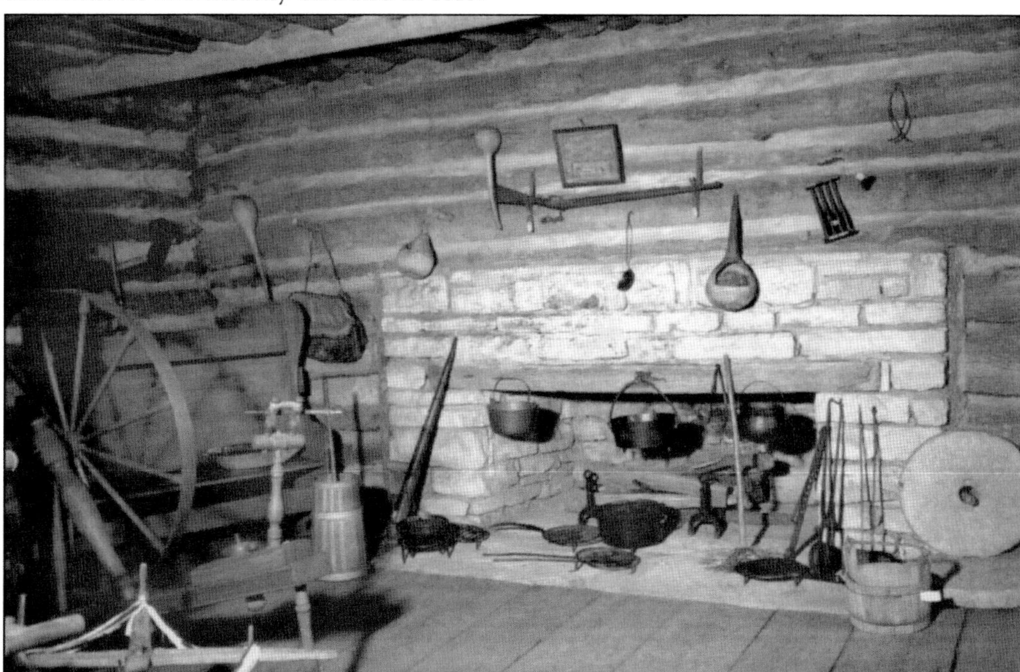

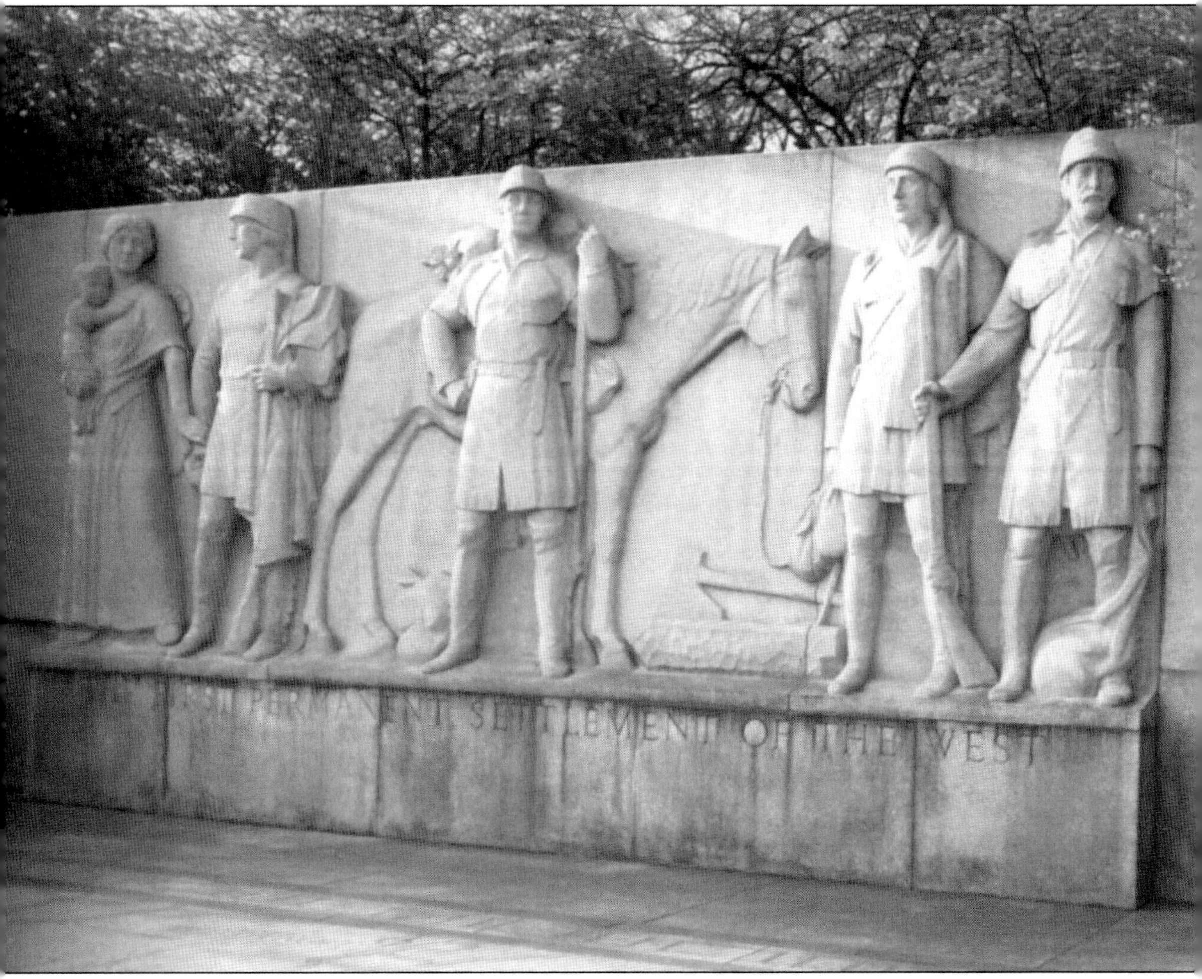

The Pioneer Memorial is a symbolic design representing the person, spirit, and era of the pioneers. Gov. Ruby Laffoon broke ground in June 1932, and in a tribute to the pioneers, he scattered some dirt in the Pioneer Cemetery. In June 1934, a monumental dedication ceremony featuring Pres. Franklin D. Roosevelt brought thousands to Harrodsburg. With this monument, the United States government recognized Kentucky for the important part it played in building and preserving the nation. Marking the crowning achievement of making Pioneer Memorial Park a national shrine, the monument divides naturally into three parts. The central section depicts George Rogers Clark, the pioneer statesman and military leader. The group to the right symbolizes youth and age, with the older man representing famous frontiersmen such as Harrod and Boone. The group to the left shows a frontier farewell and is symbolic of family life. The granite map in front shows the territory involved in Clark's campaign. Ulric Ellerhusen of New York was the designer and sculptor, and he completed the project in seven months.

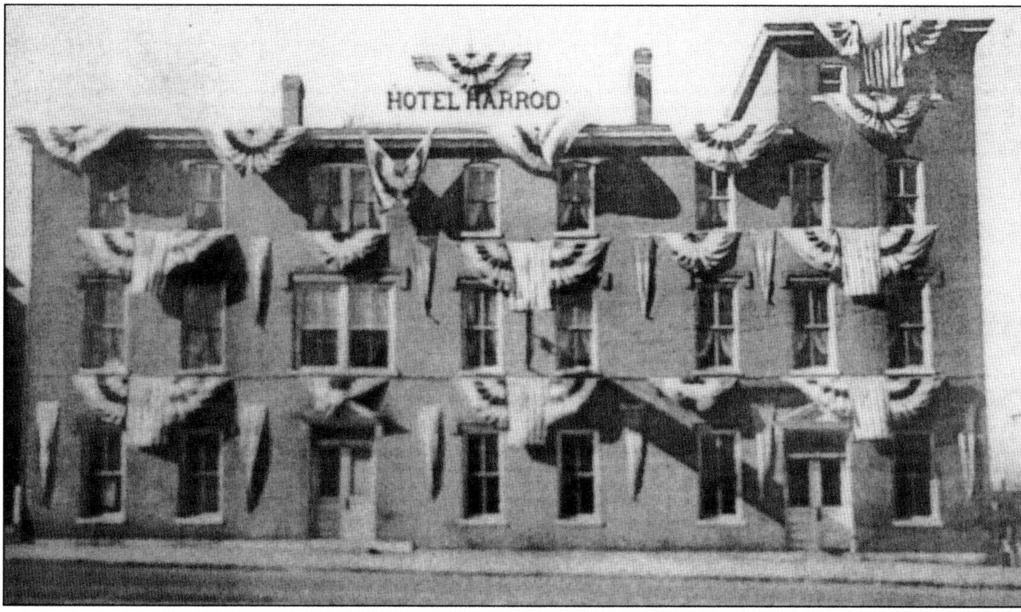

On November 16, 1934, before an estimated crowd of 60,000, Pres. Franklin D. Roosevelt came to Harrodsburg to dedicate the Pioneer Memorial. This was Harrodsburg's greatest day and its proudest celebration. All roads leading into town were choked with traffic. Special trains and buses had been arriving for several days prior, swelling the population to numbers that have never since been matched. The president and first lady Eleanor Roosevelt arrived by train and were welcomed by a town decorated with flags and red, white, and blue bunting everywhere.

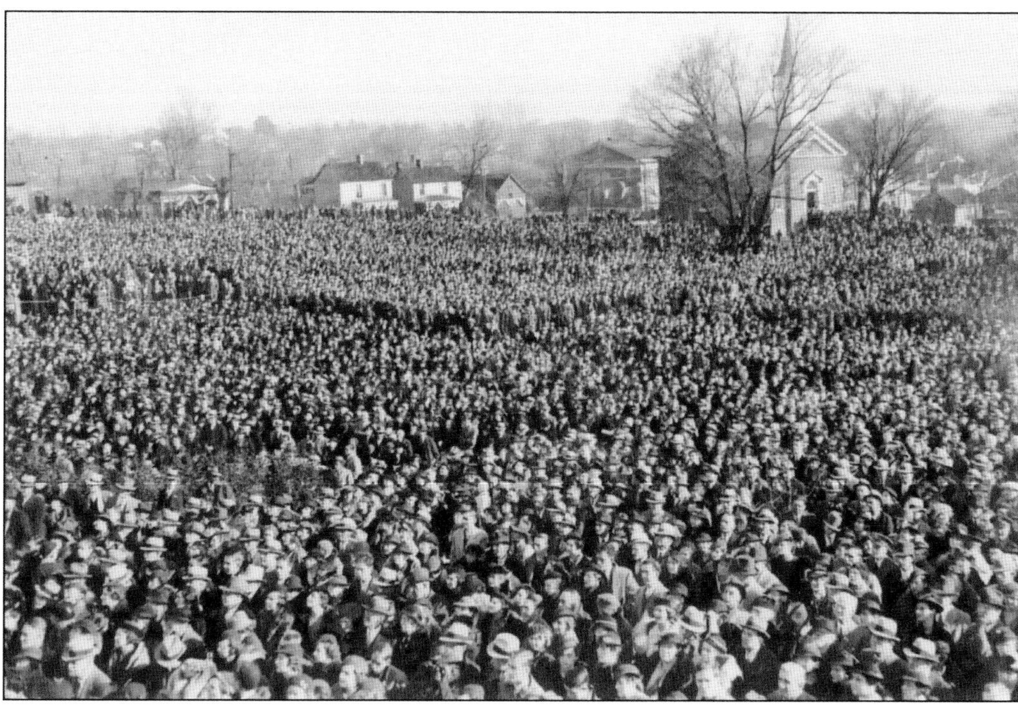

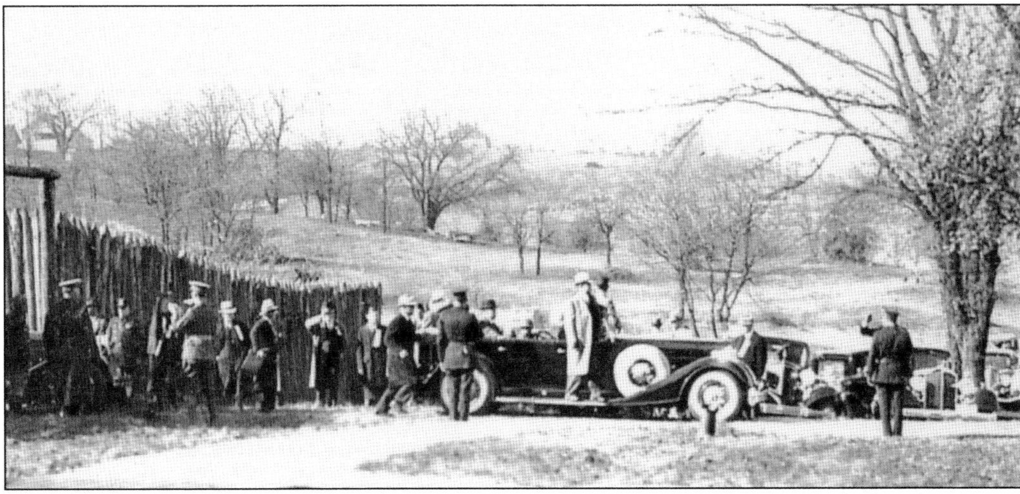

Pres. Franklin D. and First Lady Eleanor Roosevelt are seen leaving Fort Harrod after the Pioneer Memorial dedication ceremony. The preparation for this one day took months of work and hundreds of people, but President Roosevelt's speech only lasted about 10 minutes. He was quickly escorted back to the train that was waiting to return to Washington.

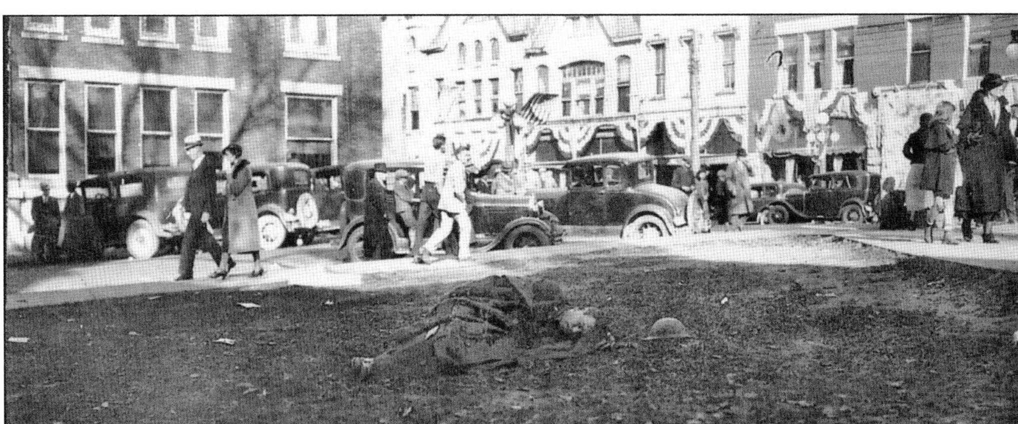

This photograph shows downtown Harrodsburg after the Pioneer Memorial dedication ceremony at Fort Harrod. People in the crowd are drifting back to their automobiles after a once-in-a-lifetime opportunity to see the president. Obviously worn out by an early-morning start and the excitement of the day, a soldier rests on the courthouse lawn in the foreground. The light-colored building in the center is the Blue Front on Main Street.

The Pioneer Cemetery is known as the first God's acre in the wilderness, although time and neglect have reduced the number of identifiable graves to a handful. Among those is the grave of the first white child buried in Kentucky, marked by a coffin-shaped stone. The photograph at right from the 1930s shows Jesta Bell Armstrong (left) with two unidentified friends visiting Fort Harrod. The photograph below is of "Uncle" Iverson Wilson, keeper of the Pioneer Cemetery for more than 20 years. He was a former slave who used a scythe so skillfully that he was selected to keep the grass trimmed. He died in 1939.

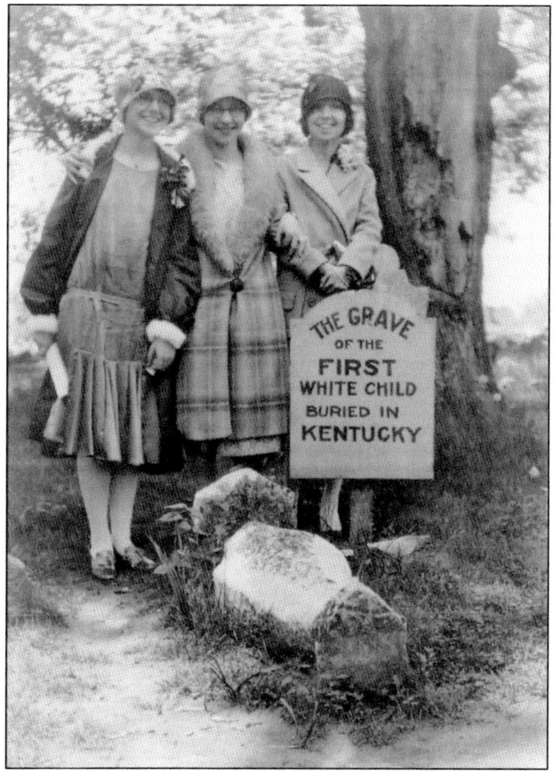

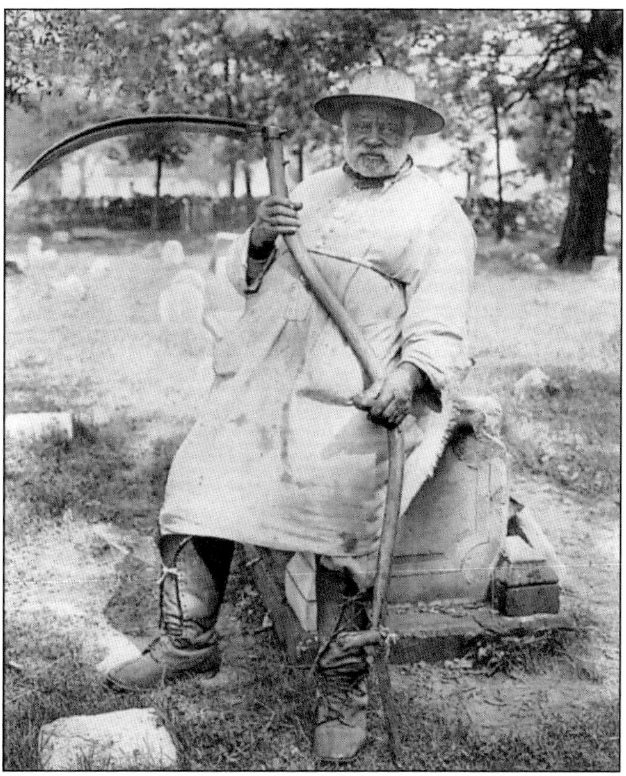

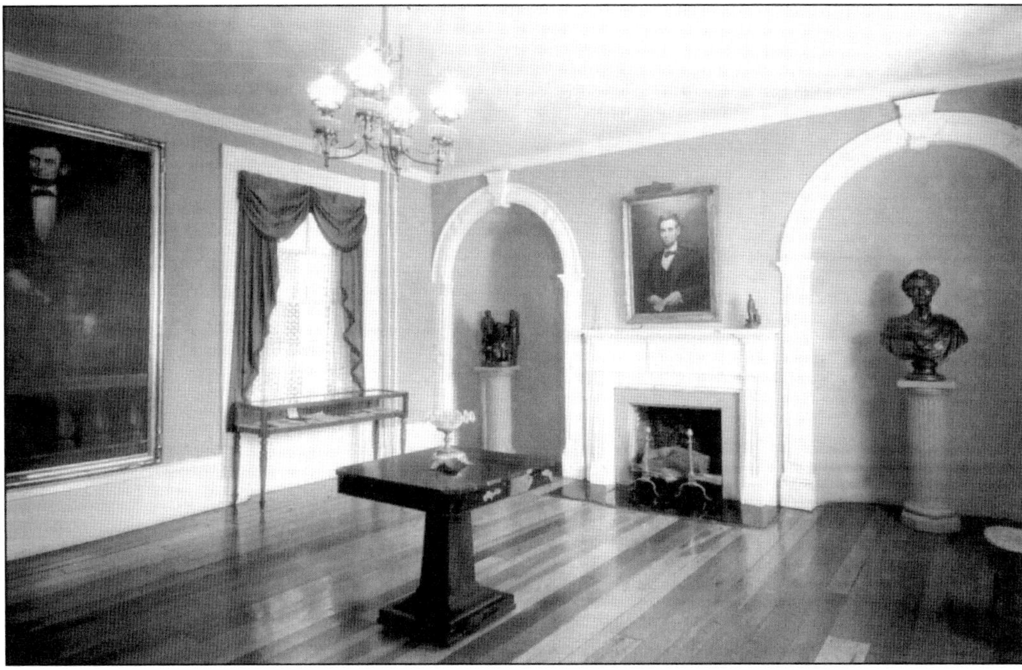

These two photographs are of rooms in the Mansion Museum, formerly the home of prominent Harrodsburg resident Maj. James Taylor and now part of Fort Harrod State Park. The above photograph is of the Lincoln Room, which contains mementoes of the Great Emancipator and his family. The Lincoln portrait above the mantle was painted by Italian American artist Ercole Cartotto of New York. It was gifted to the museum by Hon. George duPont Pratt of New York, whose generosity has benefited the mansion in many ways. The museum's Weapons Room in the photograph below contains implements of Indian warfare, flintlock rifles of the Long Hunters, dueling pistols, and powder horns. Most of the firearms collection was acquired through purchases by the State Park Commission.

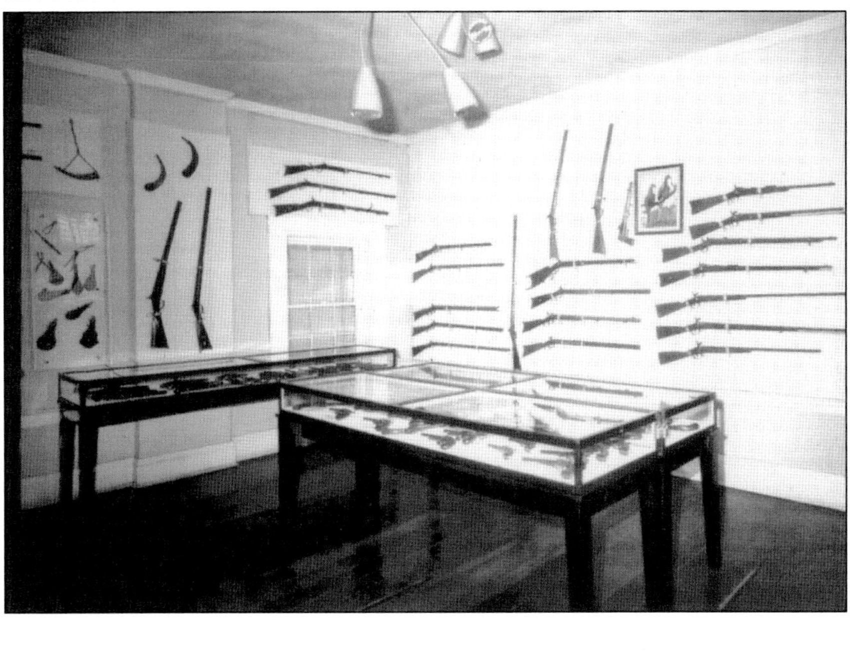

Two

CHURCHES

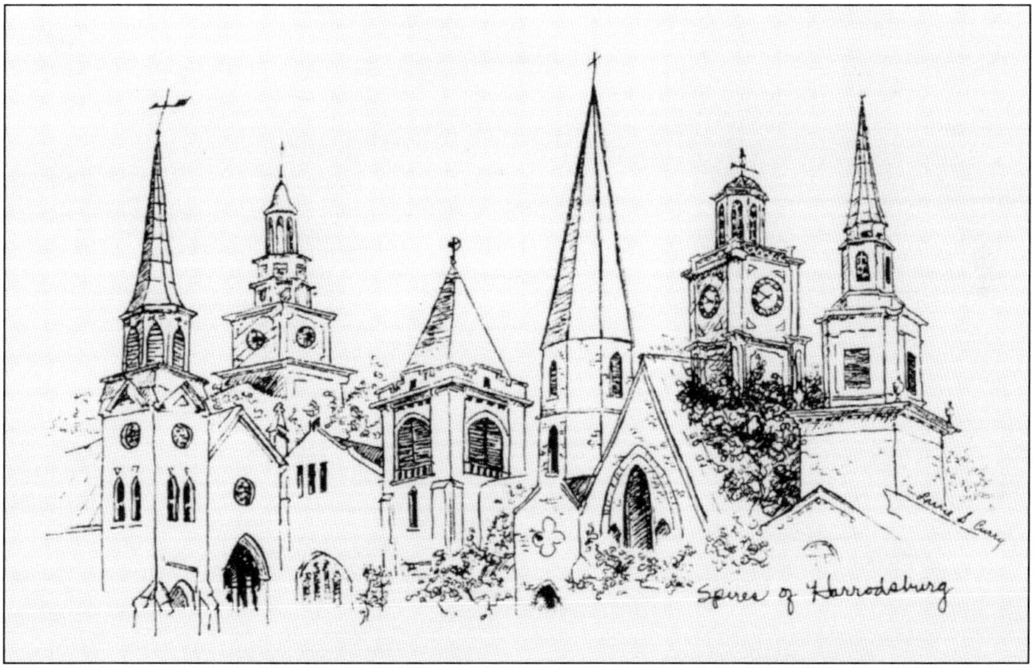

This drawing by Harrodsburg artist Larrie Curry shows the beautiful spires, which are all visible together from several spots in town. Shown from left to right are the Methodist church, the Christian church, the Presbyterian church, the Episcopal church, the courthouse (demolished 2009), and the Baptist church. The saying "a church on every corner" holds true here, as all these buildings are located within a three-block radius from the center of the business district.

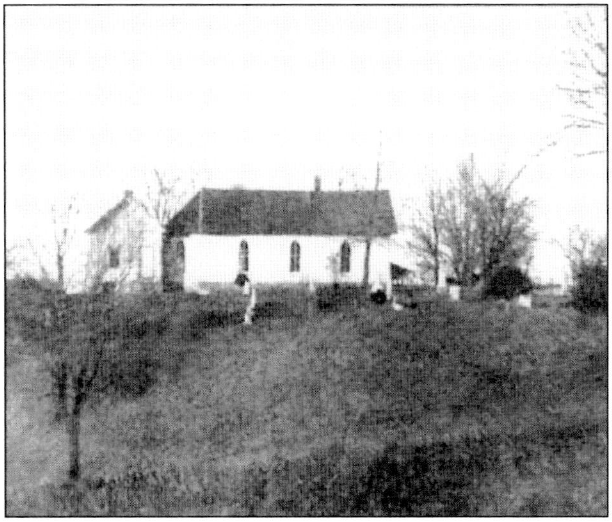

Built in 1894, St. Nicholas Catholic Church was the first Catholic church in the county and located on Irish Ridge Road, where numerous Irish Catholics had settled. During the same period, Catholics in Harrodsburg built a church on the corner of Mooreland Avenue and Chiles Street on land they acquired from Dr. Christopher Graham, owner of Graham Springs. Because travel was via horseback or horse and buggy, ministering to both churches put quite a burden on the priest, so St. Nicholas was closed. The building was demolished in 1944.

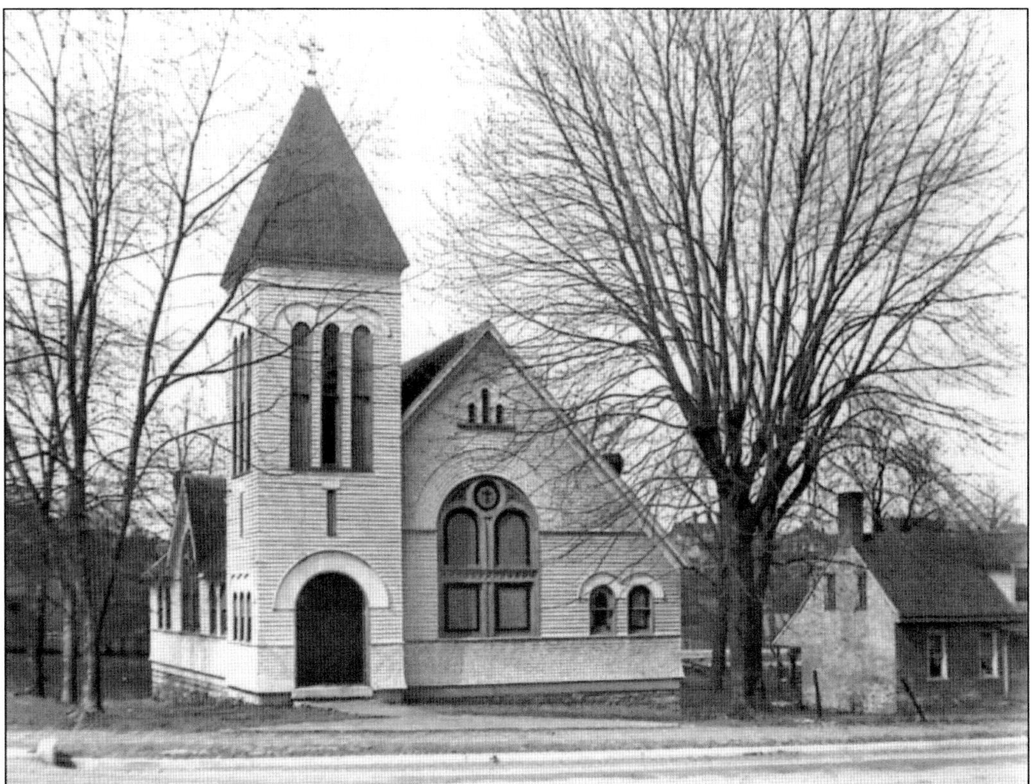

This is the attractive frame building that served the St. Andrew Catholic Church congregation for some 80 years between approximately 1894 and 1975, when it was replaced with a modern brick structure.

At right is a 1938 picture of Father Clarence Myers, the third resident parish priest of St. Andrew from 1934 to 1942. A 1934 article from the *Harrodsburg Herald* states his congregation numbered 50 and that he still traveled to St. Nicholas occasionally. Below is a 1940s photograph of the building known as the Hat Factory. Built in 1795 as an office for a hat factory on nearby Mooreland Avenue, it was sold by Dr. Graham to the church in 1893. The building was used for the St. Andrew parish house when Father Myers was there and later as a convent house for the school nuns. This historic house was the oldest brick building still standing in Harrodsburg and Mercer County until 2003, when it was bought by the Harrodsburg Baptist Church and demolished after 208 years of service to the community.

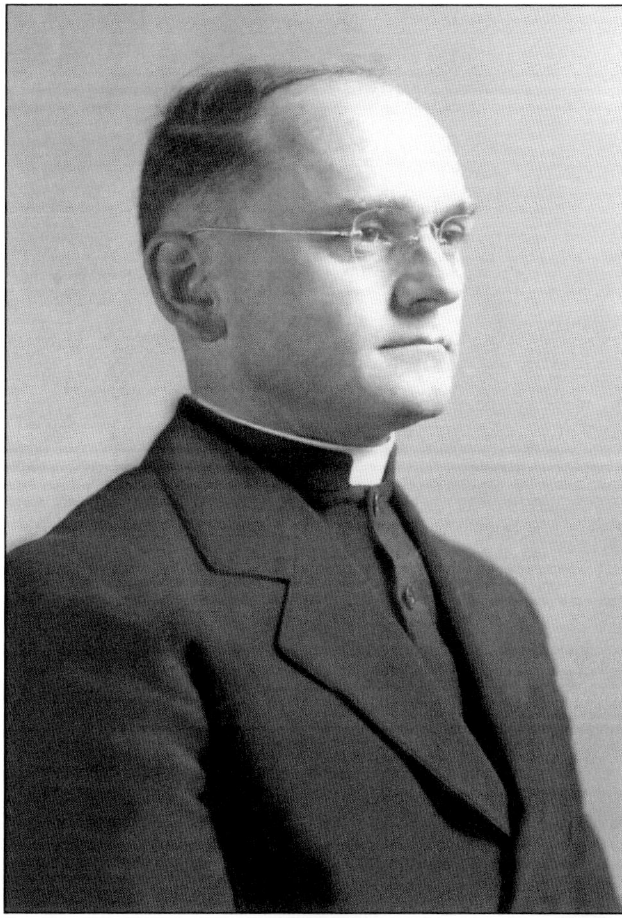

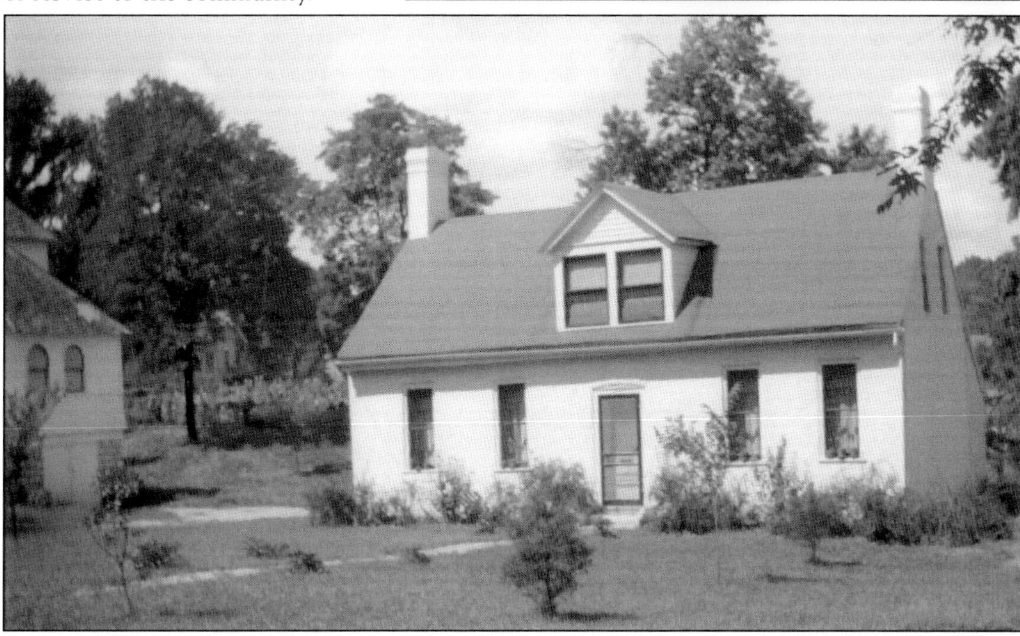

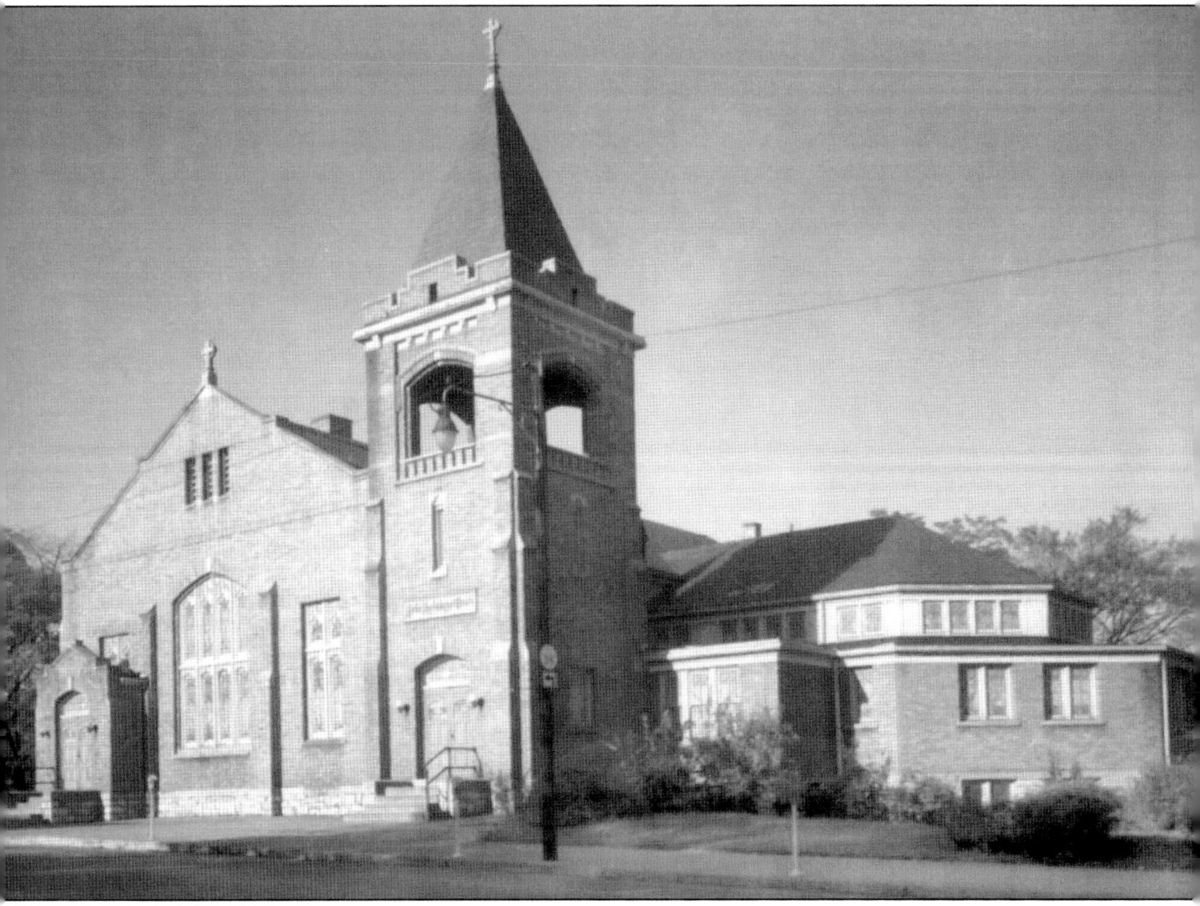

This photograph shows the 1853 version of the Presbyterian church, which started in 1783 as the Cane Run Church in a small log cabin near a stream of the same name. In 1816, the church moved to Harrodsburg, built a two-story frame structure, and changed its name to Harrodsburg Presbyterian Church. A storm demolished this building in 1818, and it was replaced with a brick one. By 1853, the congregation had outgrown the second building, and remodeling began. Harrodsburg experienced firsthand the terrible effects of the Civil War. The church was used as a hospital after the Battle of Perryville in 1862, with many from the congregation helping the wounded. The war divided the congregation, and it split into the Assembly Presbyterian Church under the USA (Northern) Synod and the First Presbyterian Church under the US (Southern) Synod. In 1911, the two churches reunited to become United Presbyterian Church.

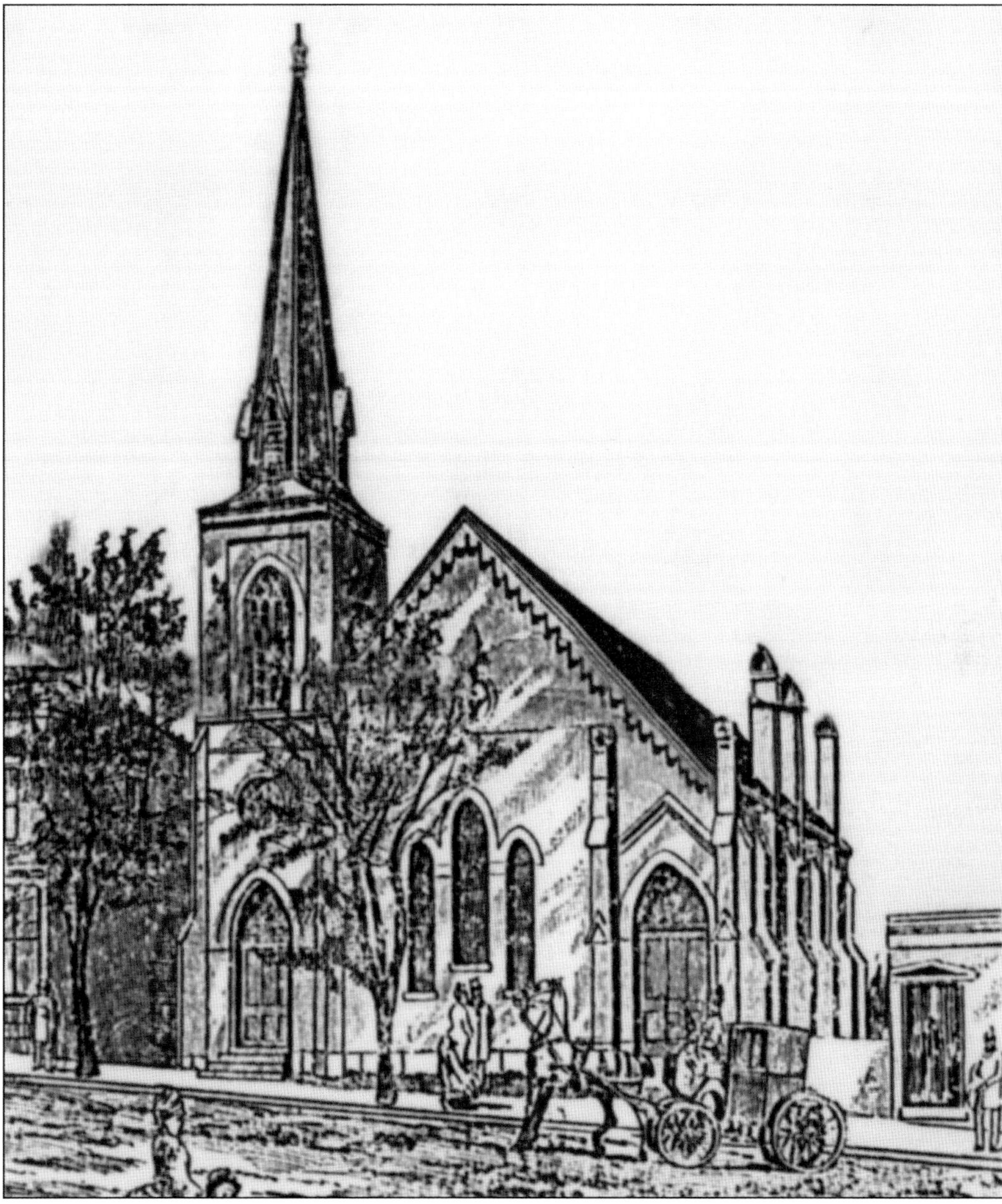

This is a drawing of the Assembly Presbyterian Church on East Poplar Street as it looked in the late 1800s. Harrodsburg experienced a year of devastation from fires in 1883, with a total of 35 buildings in the Main Street business district being either totally destroyed or partially wrecked. On May 14, fire broke out on the corner of East Poplar and Greenville Streets, and when the flames were finally extinguished, 27 buildings were left in ruins. By the daylight of May 15, the partially burned Assembly Presbyterian Church (located on East Poplar Street where Lanham's Accounting Office is now) could be seen through the smoke. A wide plank had been used to bridge the space from the roof of the building next door (then the post office) to the church tower. Water was passed over this precarious bridge, and the church tower and surrounding buildings were saved. After the two factions of the Presbyterian church reunited, this structure was used for various purposes; it was eventually sold privately and replaced by a residence.

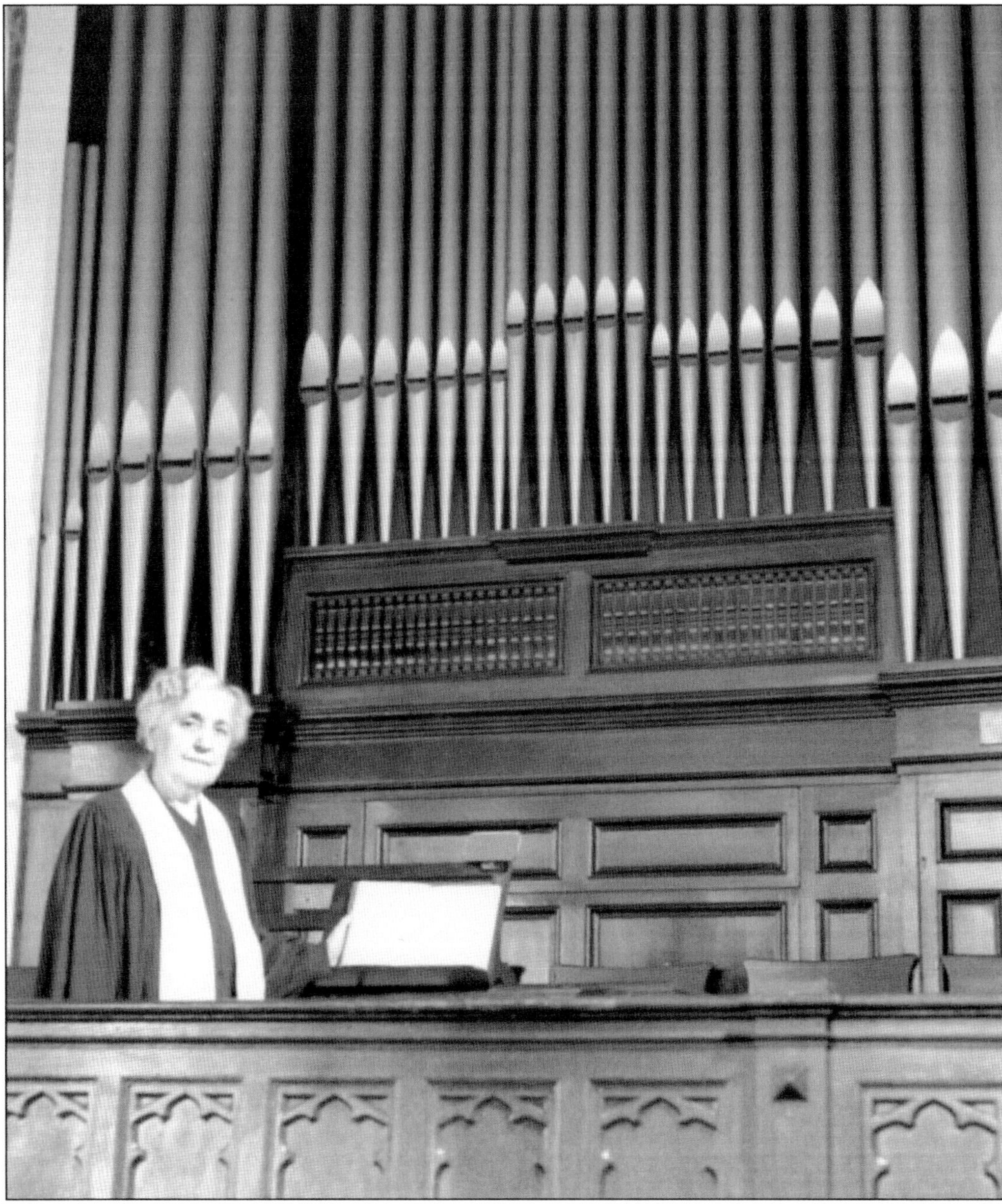

This photograph shows Sophia Hardin Grimes and what was probably the second pipe organ installed in a Harrodsburg church (1901). It was taken at the First Presbyterian Church (later renamed United Presbyterian Church) located on South Main Street. "Miss Sophie," as she was called, was born in Harrodsburg and educated at Daughter's College. She was the church pianist and organist from 1890 to 1960. In a newspaper interview shortly before her death at age 91, she is quoted as saying, "I know that my musical ability is a gift from God and I have been happier giving it back to Him by playing for individuals, civic clubs, and most of all for my church, than if I had gone on the concert stage and used it only to make money." In her 70 years of playing, she missed fewer than a dozen services and played on 3,640 Sundays. Upon her retirement in 1960, stories of her unique record of service appeared in both *Presbyterian Survey* and *Presbyterian Life*, official magazines of the national Presbyterian Church.

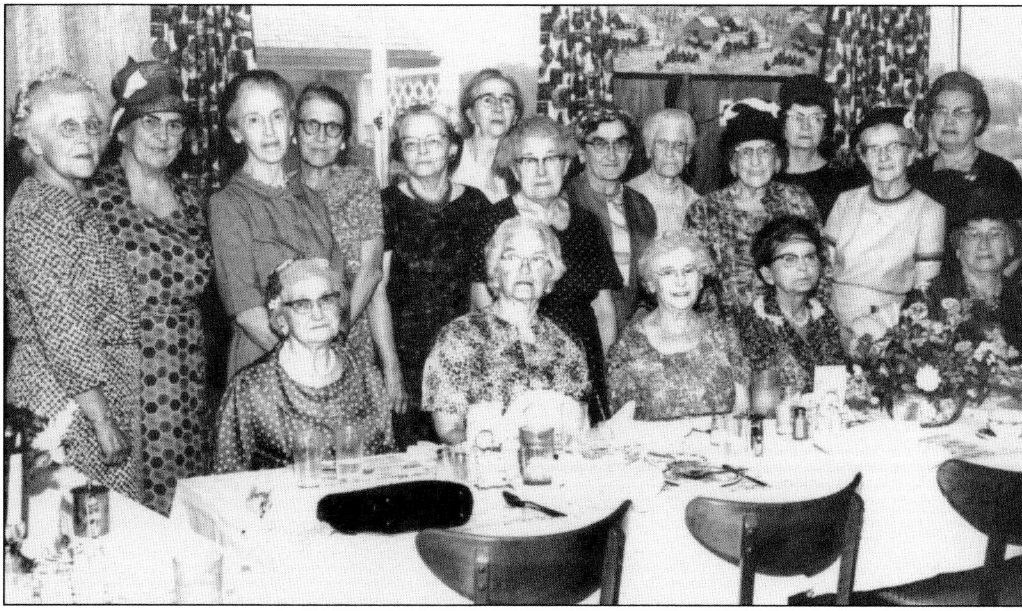

The above photograph shows a group of United Presbyterian Church women at a luncheon, probably in the 1950s. Included in the image are, in no particular order, Mrs. William (Kate) Riker, Mrs. Buck, Mrs. Hervey, Mrs. Williams, Mrs. Leon Davis, Mrs. Ransdell, Anne Sharpe, Carrie Woods, Lillie Hunter, Mrs. Nelson Davenport, Mrs. Les Crutcher, Mrs. Marshall Lawson, Mrs. Allen Edelen, Carrie Tucker, Mrs. Walker Latta, Mrs. Reynolds, and Margaret Kennedy. The picture below is another group of Presbyterian women at an annual Christmas luncheon at the Beaumont Inn, probably in the late 1990s. They are, from left to right, Mary Mitchell Gravely, Betty Nichols, Gertrude Reed, Ann Hemphill, and Mary Weber.

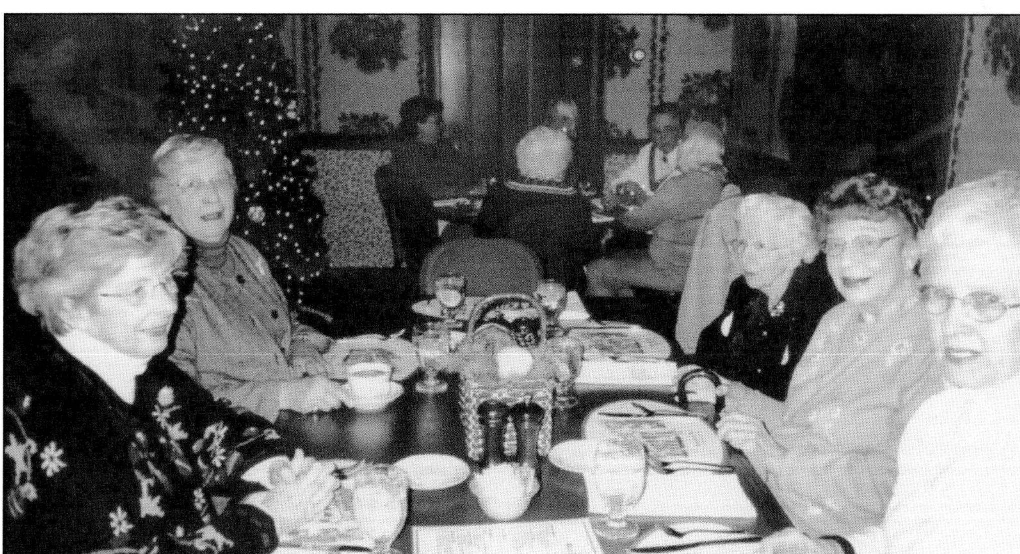

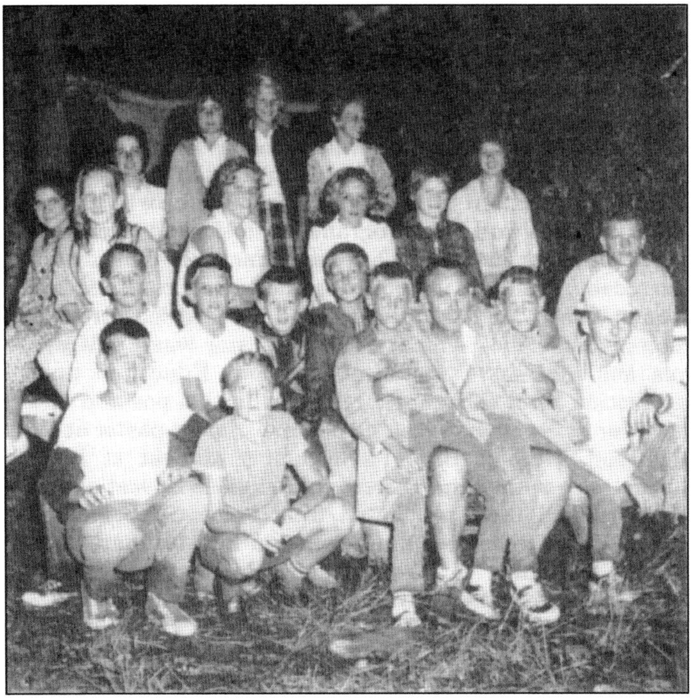

This group is attending a 1961 Presbyterian Youth Camp. Pictured, from left to right, are (first row) Tommy Young, Ronnie Young, and Bill Dean holding Nick and Chuck Dean; (second row) Curry Woods, Steve Cummins, William Gravely, Bill Wickliffe, and Jim Keightly; (third row) Paula Boughter, Ann Howells, Mary Gay Sebring, Kathy Reed, Darcie Dorwart, and Julie Dean; (fourth row) Pat Shewmaker, Kathy Shaw, Ann Dedman, and Kathy Graham.

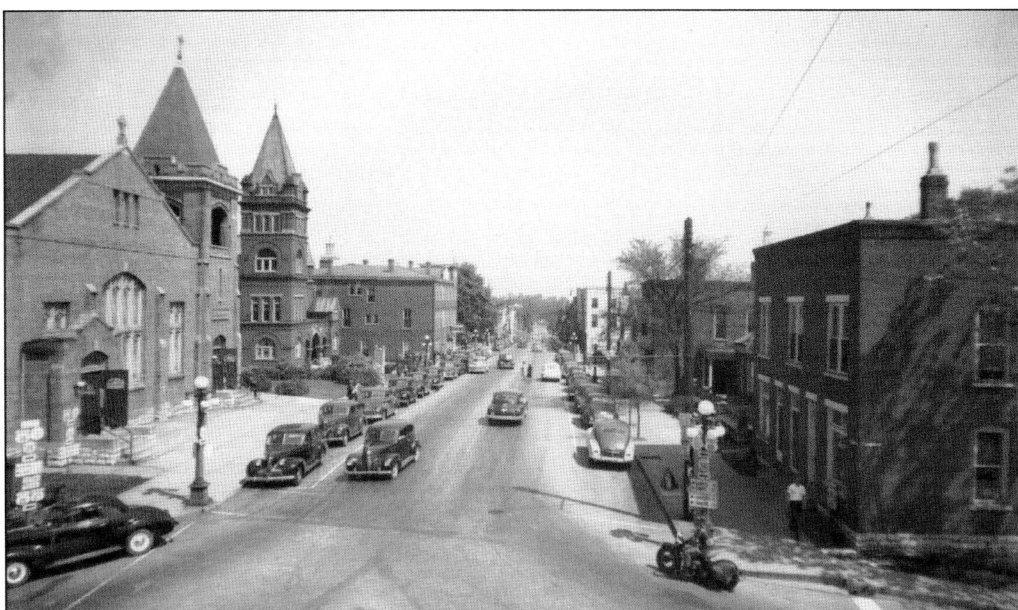

The many cars parked on South Main Street indicate this photograph was taken on a Sunday morning in the 1940s. Three of Harrodsburg's churches are still located there. On the left are the Presbyterian church, the Baptist church, and the last building is Avalon Inn, which was *the* place to eat Sunday lunch. The Christian church is out of sight on the right.

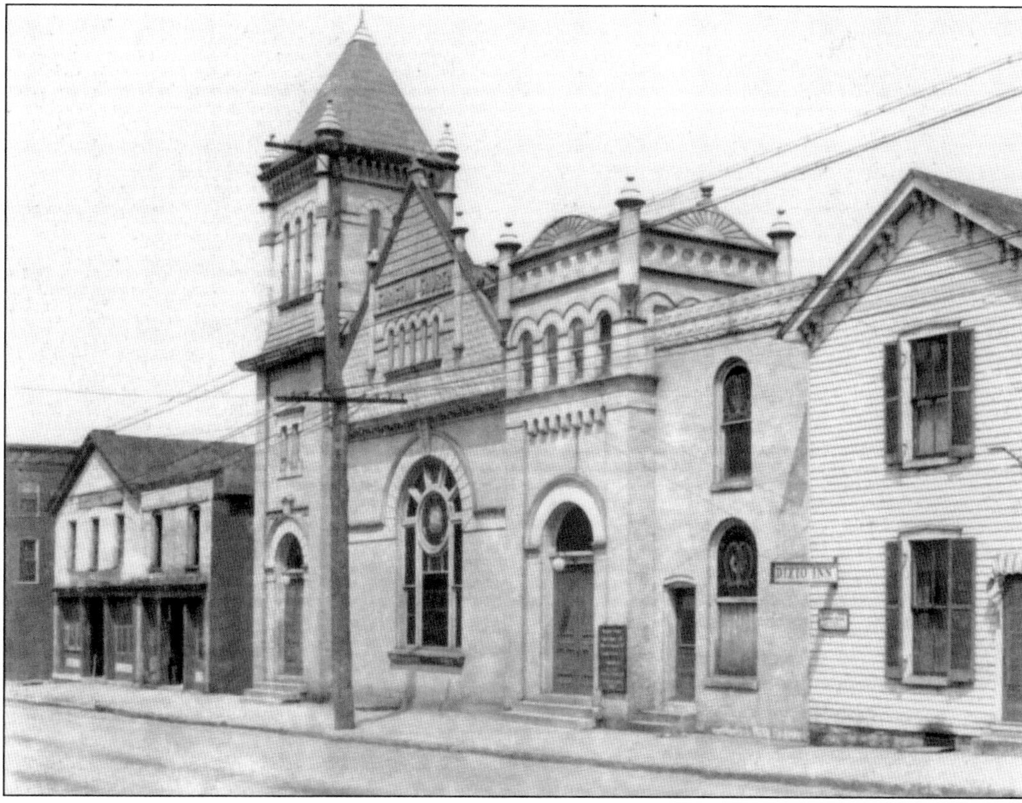

This photograph from the 1920s shows the first Christian Church building (1848–1926) in Harrodsburg. A group of 10 responsible subscribers agreed to fund $4,500 for a lot and the construction of a church on this South Main Street location. The structure to the left is the George Bohon Buggy Company. On the right is the Dixio Inn, a boardinghouse that served delicious meals to both boarders and locals.

This 1930s image shows a group of young people posing in front of the second (and current) Harrodsburg Christian Church. By 1926, the congregation had outgrown the original building. Under the leadership of Rev. T. Hassell Bowen, the old church was razed and a new one built; it was dedicated in June 1927. The new sanctuary had a seating capacity of 1,100.

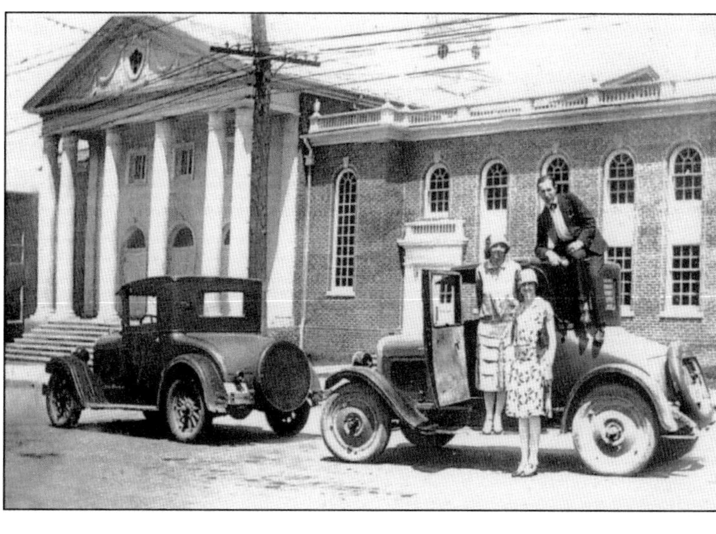

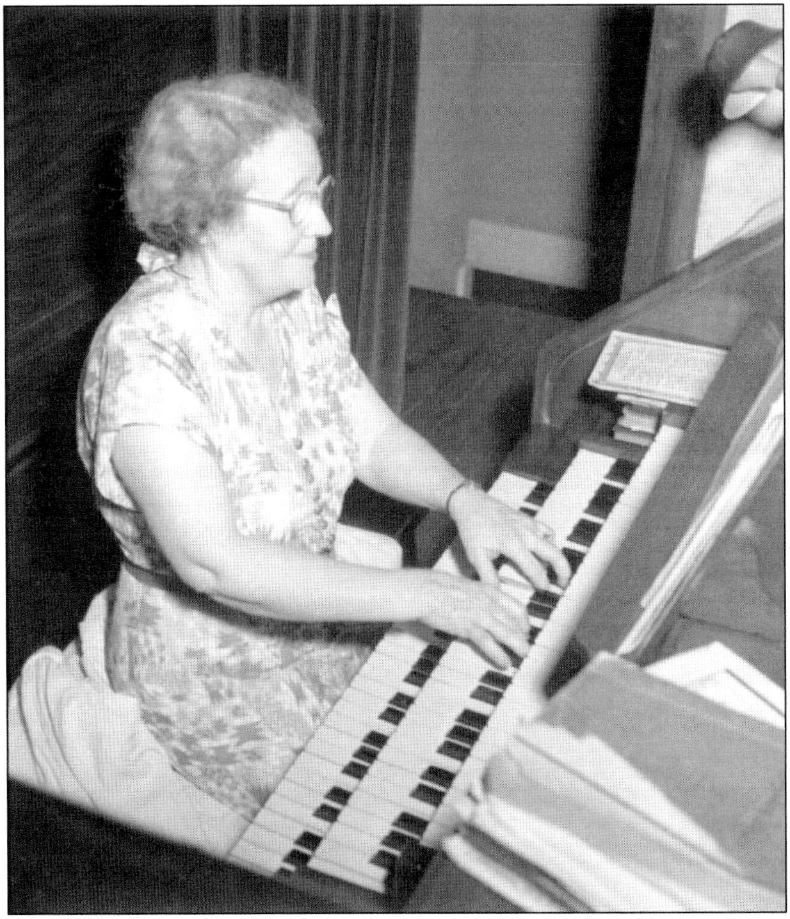

Virginia Givens Alexander served the Harrodsburg Christian Church with grace and dedication during her 53 years as the church organist. She played her last service on July 1, 1973. Alexander is quoted as saying, "I always wanted to play a pipe organ, and I did for 53 years. It was such a pleasure." In honor of her service, the Alexander Foundation was started for repairing or replacing the organ.

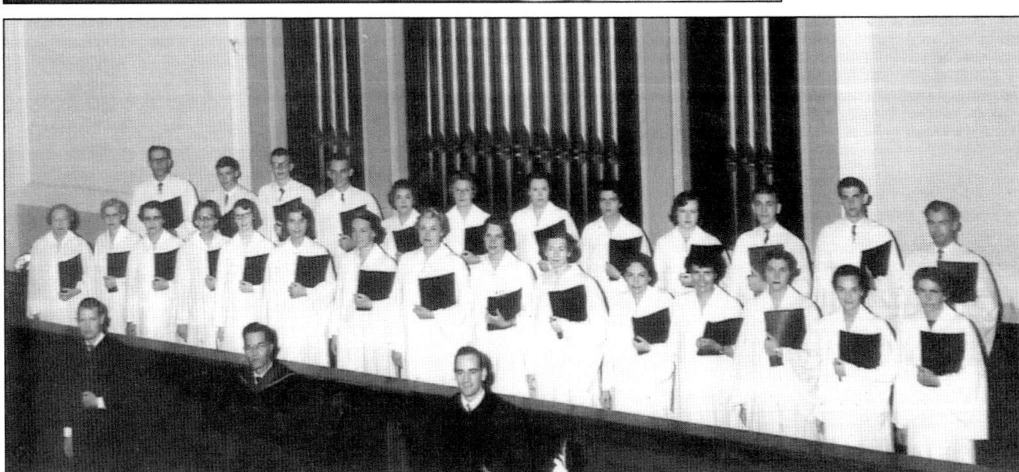

This photograph of the Harrodsburg Christian Church sanctuary dates to the late 1950s or early 1960s. The choir loft was always full of some of the finest singers in Harrodsburg and Mercer County, and they looked wonderful standing in front of the pipes of the organ. The three men in front are music director Bill Gravely (left), minister Jim Kelly (center), and an unidentified youth minister.

Members from 30 churches of all denominations in Mercer County joined the congregation of the Harrodsburg Christian Church in a service of tribute to its pastor, the Reverend Dr. T. Hassell Bowen, and his wife, Margie. On July 4, 1952, after 28 years of service, Rev. Bowen retired from preaching to teach at the College of the Bible in Lexington, Kentucky. He was highly respected and loved for his wisdom and kindness both inside and outside the church community. The photograph at right shows Rev. and Mrs. Bowen with the silver bowl and candelabra they received for their many years of service. In the image below, people wait in line to pay their respects to the Bowens after the reverend's last sermon.

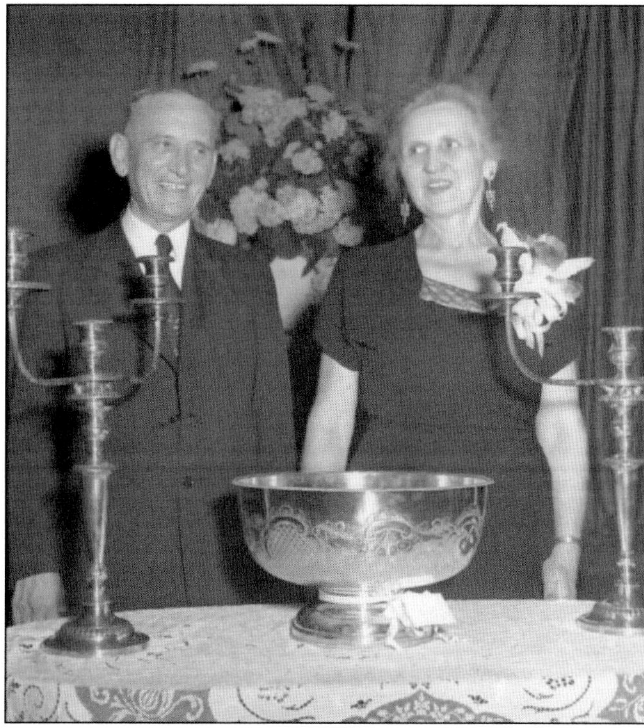

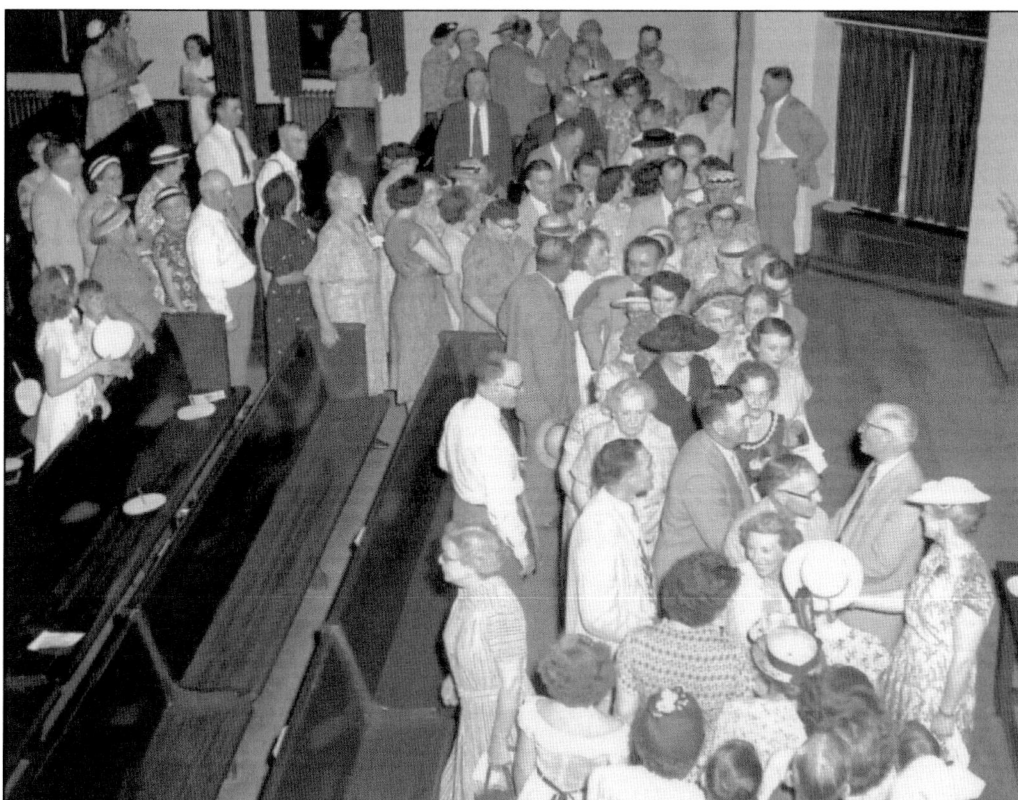

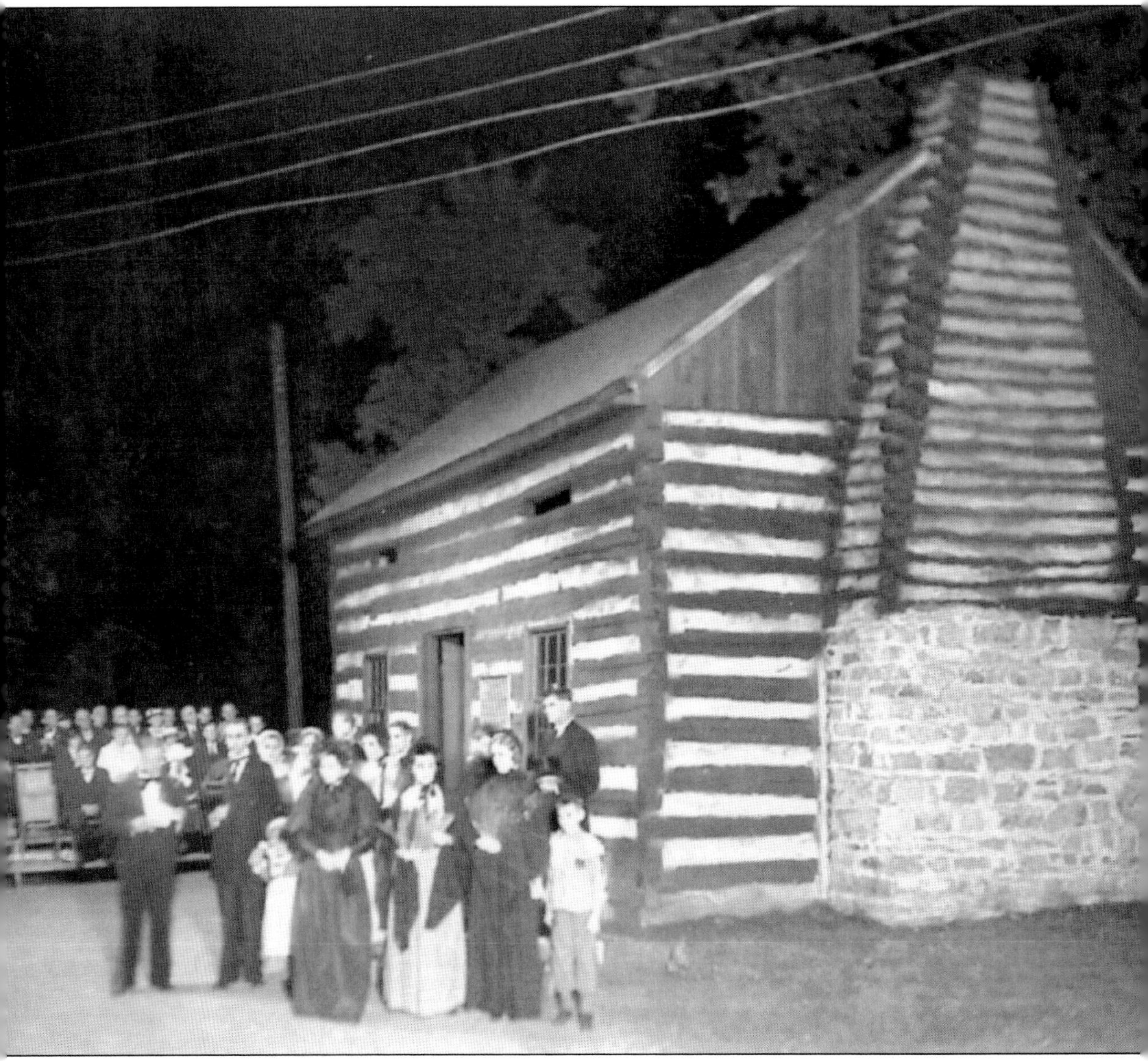

This log cabin was the home of Rebecca Hart and the site of the first Methodist prayer meetings held in Harrodsburg in the early 1800s. In 1828, an official Methodist society was organized, paving the way for the future establishment of a Methodist church in Harrodsburg. This 1935 photograph shows a pageant reenacting a gathering of early Methodists for an old-time prayer meeting at the Hart cabin. The cabin was located on the corner of West Broadway and North College Streets. Because of its history, the Stoll Oil Company of Louisville, which had bought the property in the early 1930s, decided to restore it, furnish it with period pieces, and open it as a museum. The exact date of its demolition is not known. These very cabins were Harrodsburg's oldest buildings, constructed outside the fort at a time when the threat of Indian attacks had lessened but close enough to the stockade to get back inside in case of trouble. The settlers, anxious to escape the confines of the fort, wanted to establish their own places to raise their families and plant their crops.

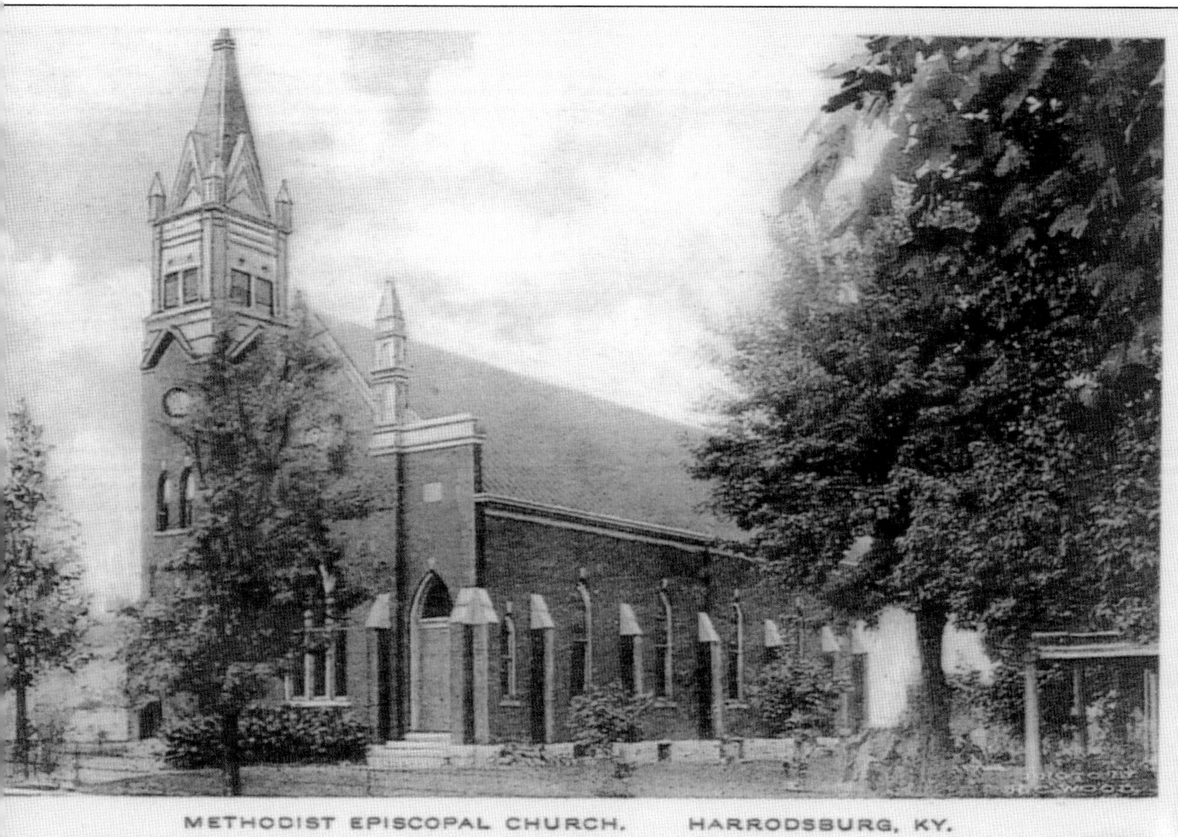

This first church of the Methodist congregation was built in 1840. In the late 1830s, they were able to buy the lot where the first and all successive churches were built. Handmade bricks were used in the construction of this handsome building. Wanting to make a contribution of their own, the women of the church decided the bell would be their focus. They did not want an ordinary bell, but one with personality, so they donated their coin silver and other silver ornaments to be used with the base metal in casting the bell. It was said to have a very sweet tone. This building served the congregation for 49 years until 1889 when it was torn down and a new church built on the same foundation. The original bell was again hoisted to the tower and called the faithful to worship. This early photograph was taken by H.C. Wood, local historian, writer, artist, and photographer. His pictures were often reproduced for the popular postcard market in the mid-1800s.

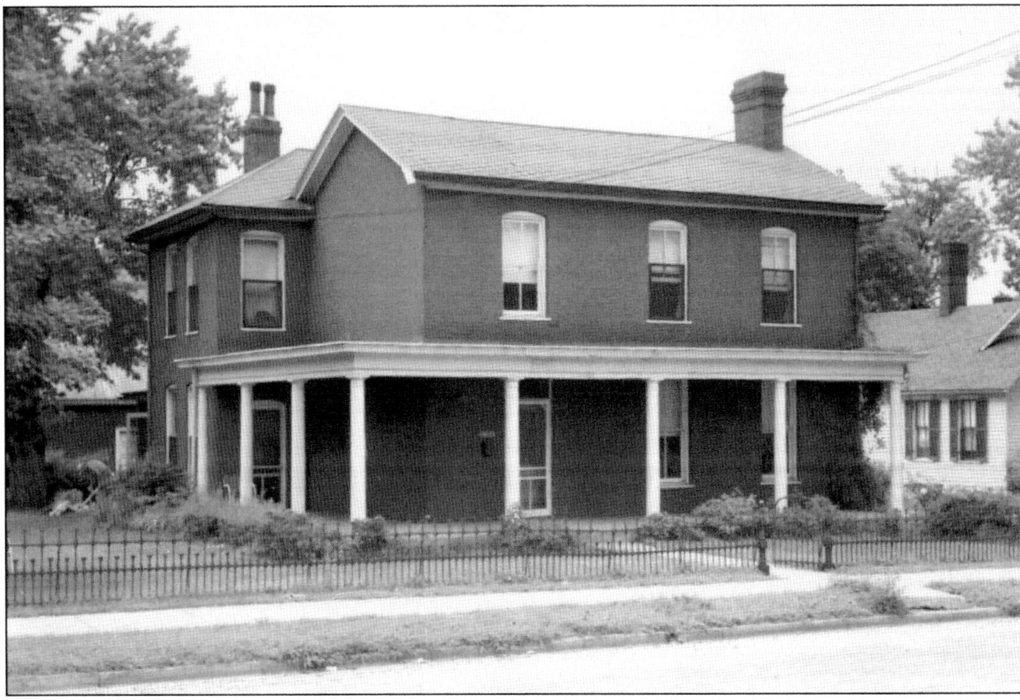

The Methodist parsonage located next to the church is thought to have been built at the same time as the first church in 1840. According to tradition, it is the oldest continuously used Methodist parsonage west of the Allegheny Mountains. After the Civil War Battle of Perryville on October 8, 1862, the parsonage and church were used as a hospital for both Confederate and Union troops. The picture above shows the house as it originally looked. The image below is how it currently appears. In 1910, the wraparound porch was taken off, and a Greek Revival portico and reworked entrance were built.

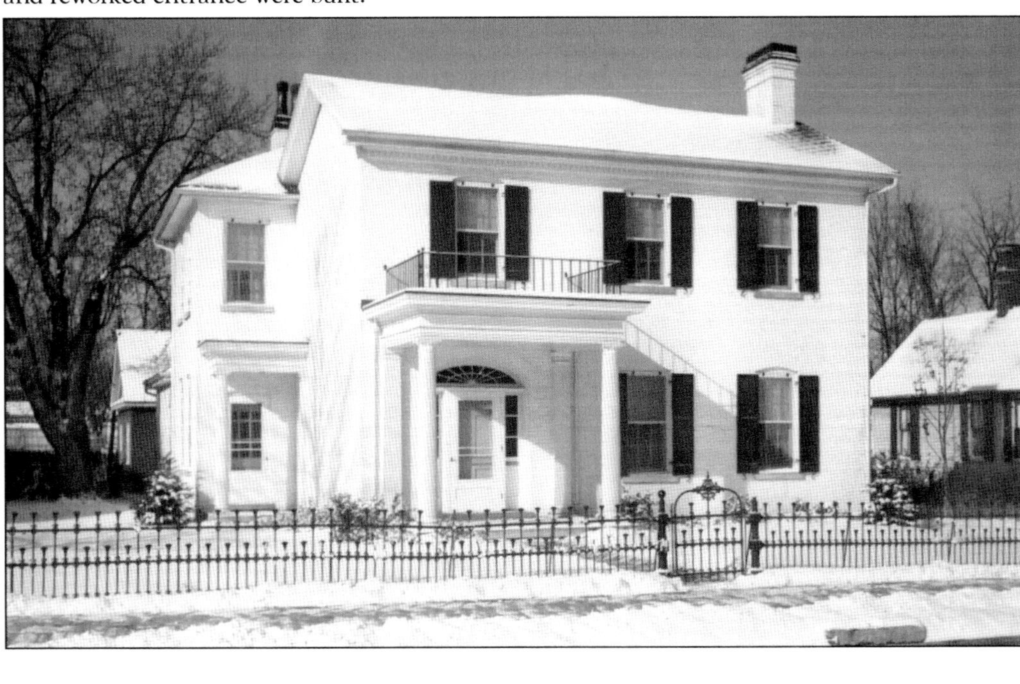

The photograph at right was taken by either Jesta Bell Armstrong Matherly or her brother Andrew Armstrong in 1939 and was used by Mrs. G.R. Tomlin, the Methodist pastor's wife, as an inspiration for a painting. The painting, along with Tomlin's interpretation and comments on it, was used to illustrate the cover of a Methodist magazine, shown in the photograph below. The scene was a Sunday school room in the church. Tomlin's interpretation of the picture was, "The light shines upon the Word, and on the floor is the cross in shadow form, remembering that in order to walk in the light properly, we must keep the vision of the shadow of the cross."

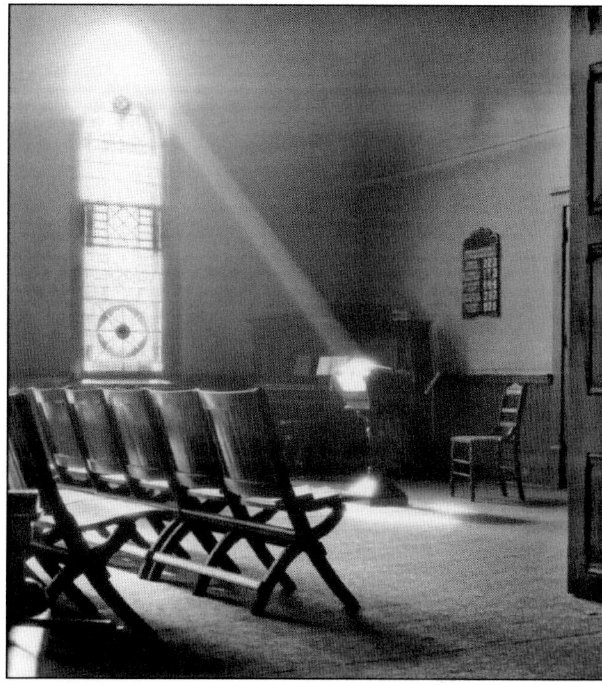

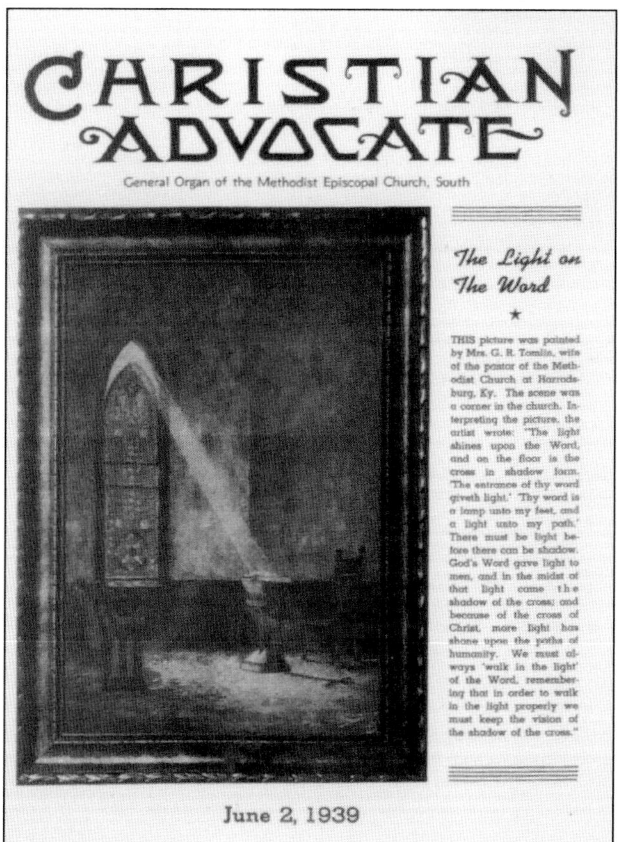

CHRISTIAN ADVOCATE

General Organ of the Methodist Episcopal Church, South

The Light on The Word

★

THIS picture was painted by Mrs. G. R. Tomlin, wife of the pastor of the Methodist Church at Harrodsburg, Ky. The scene was a corner in the church. Interpreting the picture, the artist wrote: "The light shines upon the Word, and on the floor is the cross in shadow form. 'The entrance of thy word giveth light.' 'Thy word is a lamp unto my feet, and a light unto my path.' There must be light before there can be shadow. God's Word gave light to men, and in the midst of that light came the shadow of the cross; and because of the cross of Christ, more light has shone upon the paths of humanity. We must always 'walk in the light' of the Word, remembering that in order to walk in the light properly we must keep the vision of the shadow of the cross."

June 2, 1939

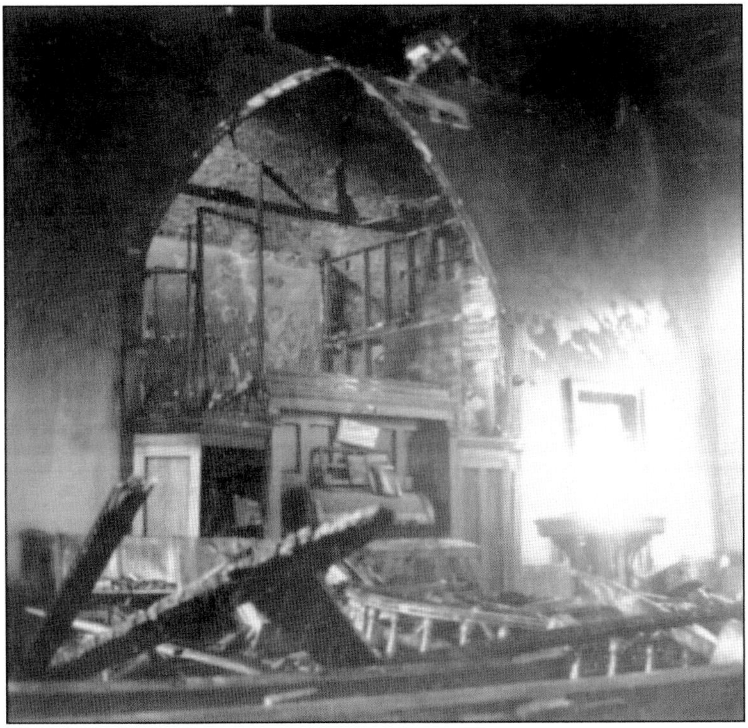

This photograph shows the charred remains of the Methodist church interior after a devastating fire in January 1940. The pipe organ's motor box was believed to have been the cause, and the loss was estimated at $50,000. Bibles, church records, and several stained glass windows were destroyed. Although the firefighters arrived on the scene promptly, they were able to do little more than contain the fire.

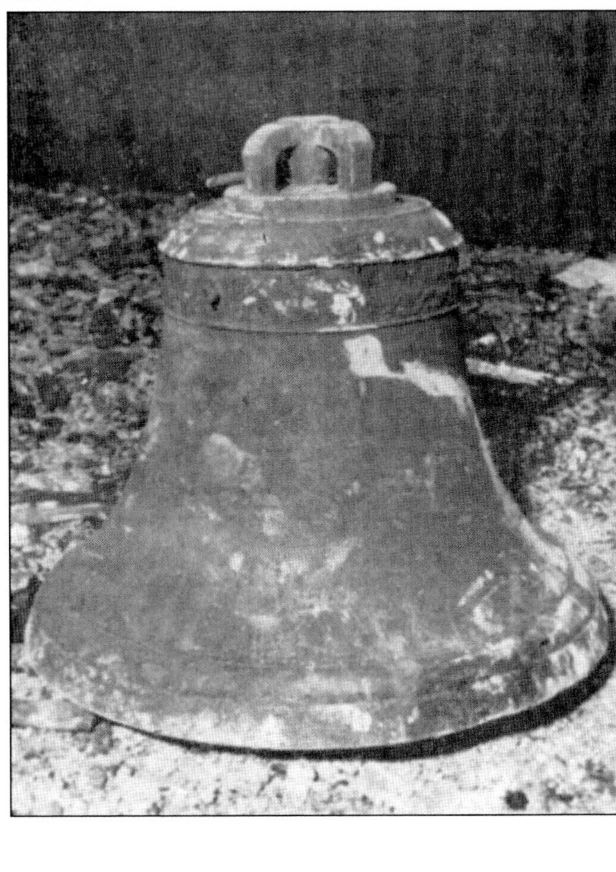

This is the charred, but still intact, bell. When the bell tower was engulfed, the *Harrodsburg Herald* reported the steeple blazed up like a huge candle and looked like a flaming torch against the sky. When the church was rebuilt soon afterward, the bell was reinstalled in the new bell tower.

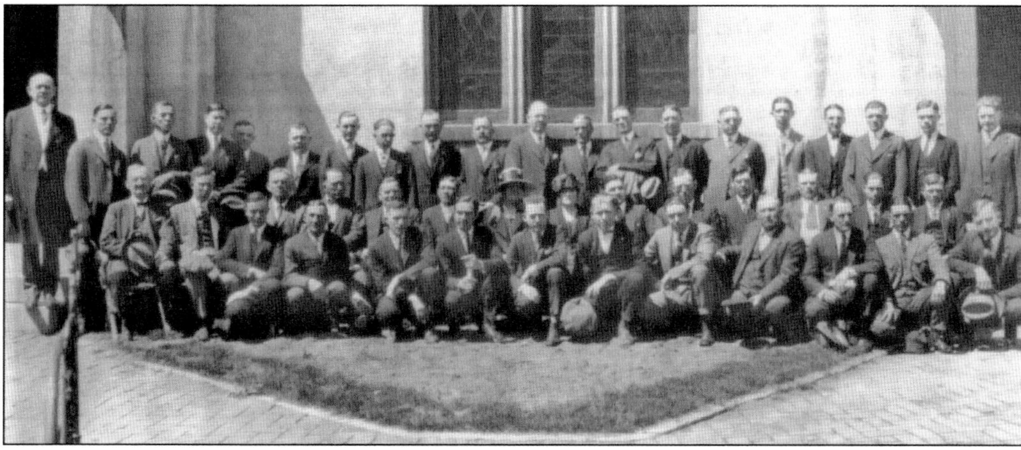

Above is a 1922 photograph of the Humble Workers. They are, from left to right, (first row) David Walters, Virgle White, Elmo Robertson, John Wesley Kays, Ruben Curd, Marshall Wickersham, Mr. Burdett, Jim Harve Laer, James Cook, James Baker, and Mr. Moss; (second row) D. Lee Curry, J.G. Scanlon, Ed Marksbury, Dr. Sutherland, Mike Conn, Elmer Anness, Mrs. Spilman, Mrs. Humble, Jim Farley, Otho Mitchell, W.V. Daugherty, Leonard Freeman, Harvey Sharp, and A.D. Freeman; (third row) Brother Jones, J. Mitchell, Mr. Webb, Mr. Tucker, Carrol Smith, Tom Squifflet, Cecil Brown, W.B. Purdom, Allen Bunnel, J.D. Baxter, Robert Graham, Bill Johnson, Lewis Woods, Walter Hopper, John Brewer, Fred Wilder, Walter Crews, Paul Key, Onie Kays, and Andy Moore. The photograph below is of a 1952 vacation Bible school class. Standing from left to right are: Barbara McGlone, Patsy Noel, Mrs. Everett Warner, Christine Siler, Jimmie Clay, Gene Germain, Bonnie Sims, Bill VanArsdall, Charles Matherly, Elizabeth Sale, and unidentified others. Both photographs show Methodist church groups.

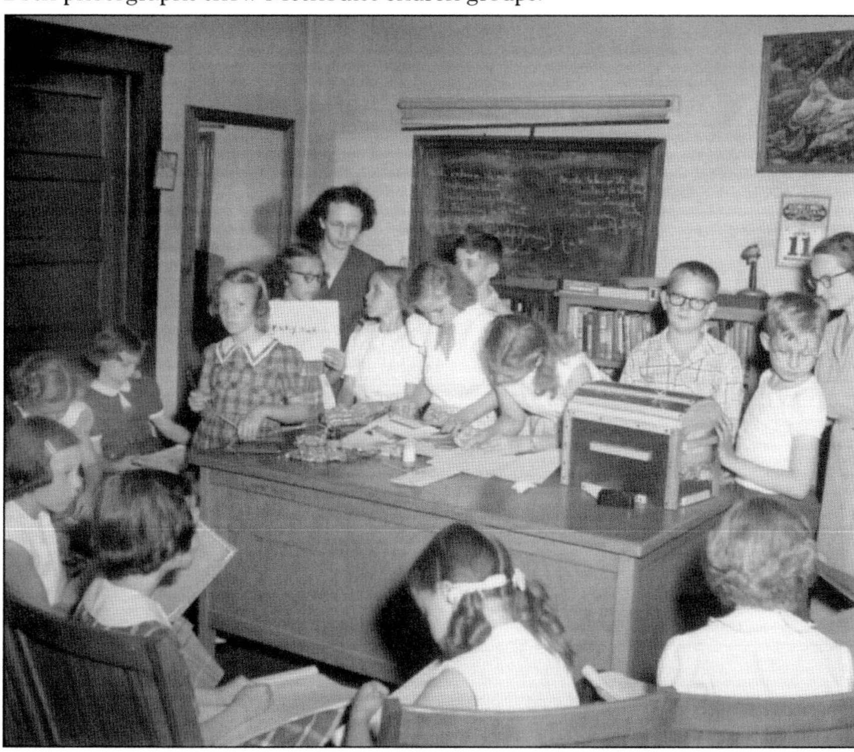

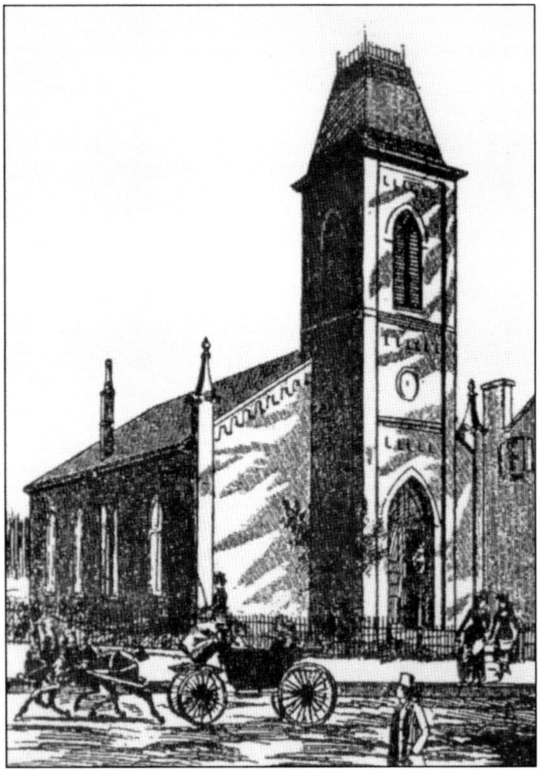

The drawing to the left shows the Republican Meeting House on West Office Street across from the Mercer County Courthouse. Bought in 1840 from the Methodists, it was the first home of the Baptist congregation that had been sharing Sundays with the Methodists. The picture below was captioned by the photographer, "Laying the Baptist Church foundation in 1899" and was taken by William Reed, a local businessman whose hobby was photography. This is the foundation of the first of two buildings; it served the congregation for over 100 years. The brick building with the steeple next to the foundation is the Republican Meeting House, which was demolished in 1948 to clear a lot for parking between the VanArsdall Apartments and the rear of Hotel Harrod, thus ending its 121 years of service to the religious community.

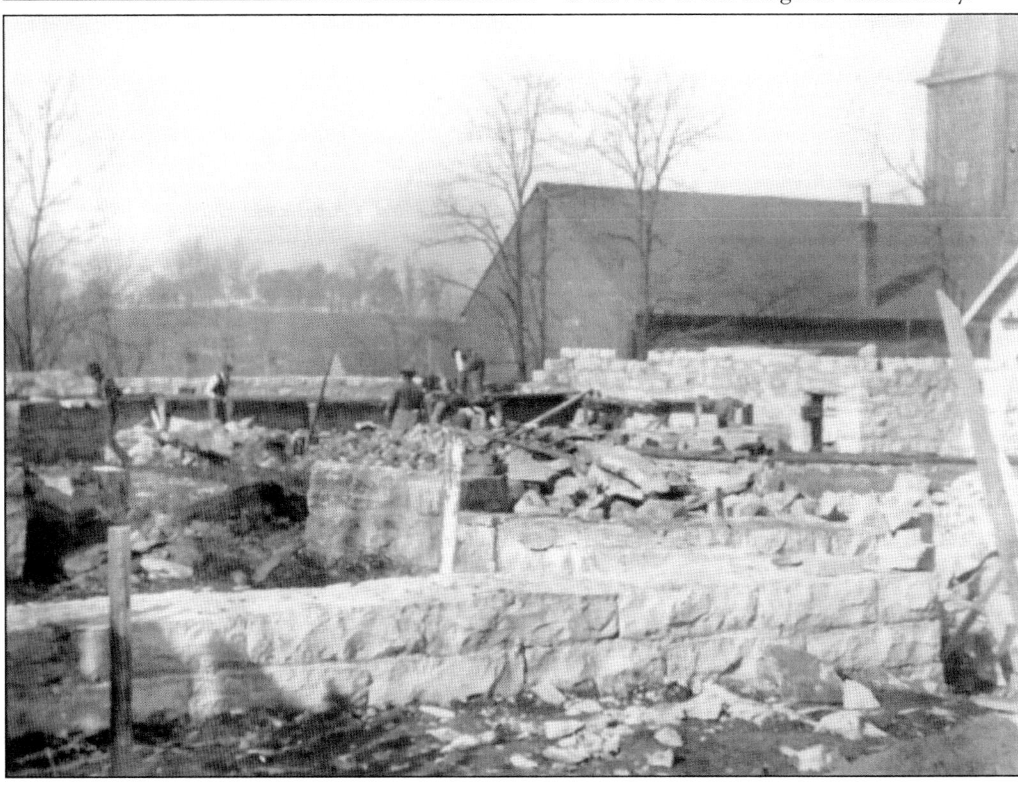

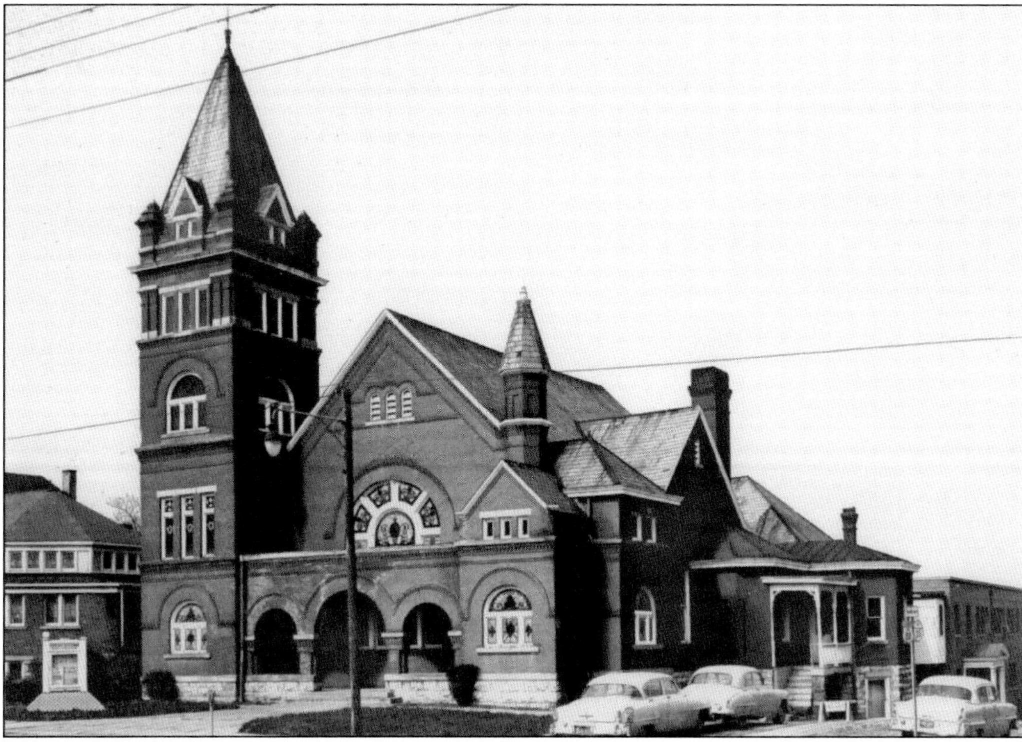

The above photograph is of the first Harrodsburg Baptist Church, in use by the congregation from 1900 until 1961. The photograph below shows the sanctuary adorned with many ferns, palms, and other large plants, as was the custom of that era. Records of the church minutes of July 18, 1899, read that the architect is requested to furnish plans for the new church "to cost not over $12,000 complete and furnished with lights, pews, furnace, etc., ready for occupancy." The final cost was $15,700.93. The dedication was reported as "a grand affair" and the *Louisville Courier-Journal* called the new church "the town's finest building and a monument to the enterprise of its pastor and congregation."

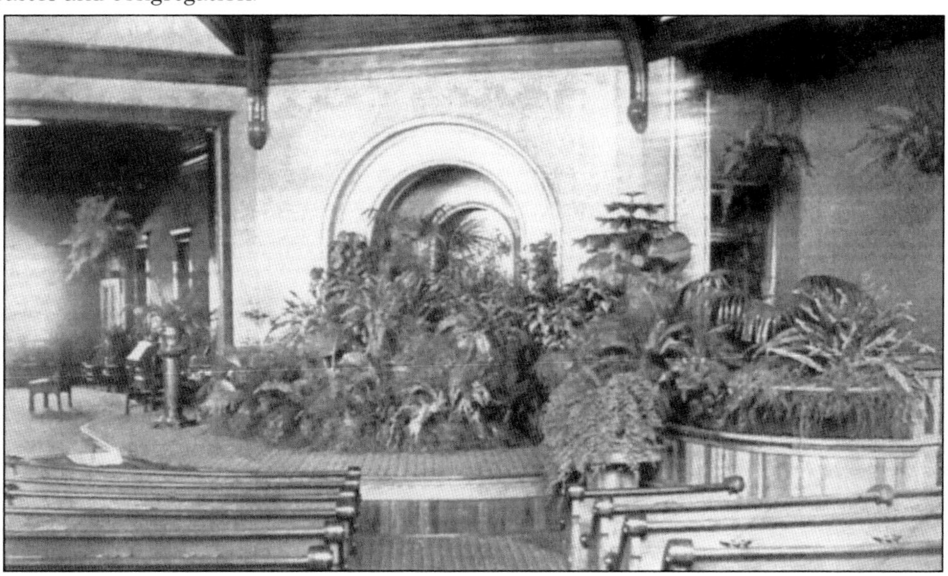

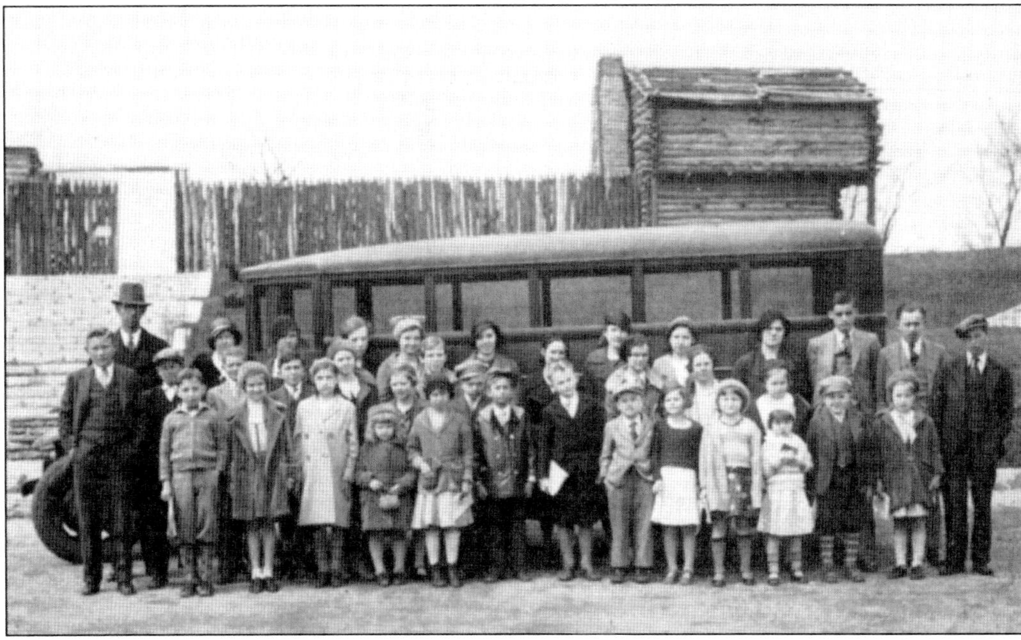

This large bus, shown in the parking area at Fort Harrod, was one of two used to provide transportation for the children of rural Mercer County to and from Sunday school and church services at the Harrodsburg Baptist Church. A copy of this photograph was published in a 1933 church yearbook.

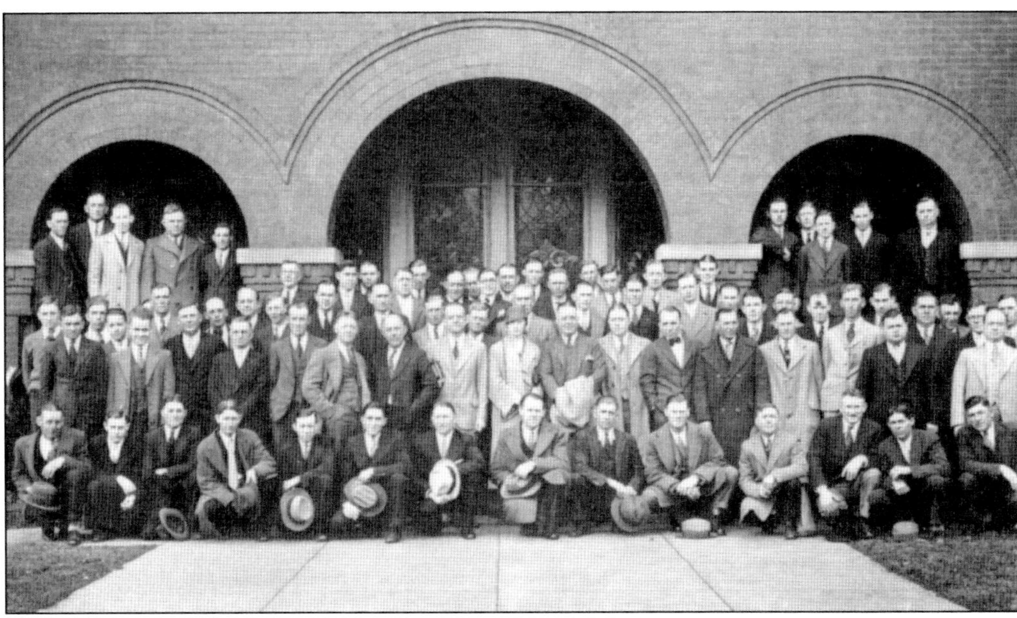

The Gland Hand Bible Class is shown posing in front of the church in 1933. Officers and leaders of the class were Otto Redwiz, president; W. Atkinson, attendance director; Dr. William Hynes, social director; Graydon Clark, spiritual director; Fred Martin and Dudley Lacefield, secretaries; William Reed, chorister; Edna Ison, pianist; and G. Whitcomb Ellers, teacher.

The right photograph shows one whole Main Street block of churches. On the left is the United Presbyterian Church, next is the old Baptist church, and on the right is the new Baptist church under construction in 1961. When the new building was partially completed, the dismantling of the old one was begun. The present church was built at a cost of $554,262.38, quite a difference for a 60-year time span. The picture below shows the new sanctuary, which seats hundreds more, during the week of dedication. The cross in the baptistery was made by John Cardwell from a piece of poplar wood from the 1900s sanctuary.

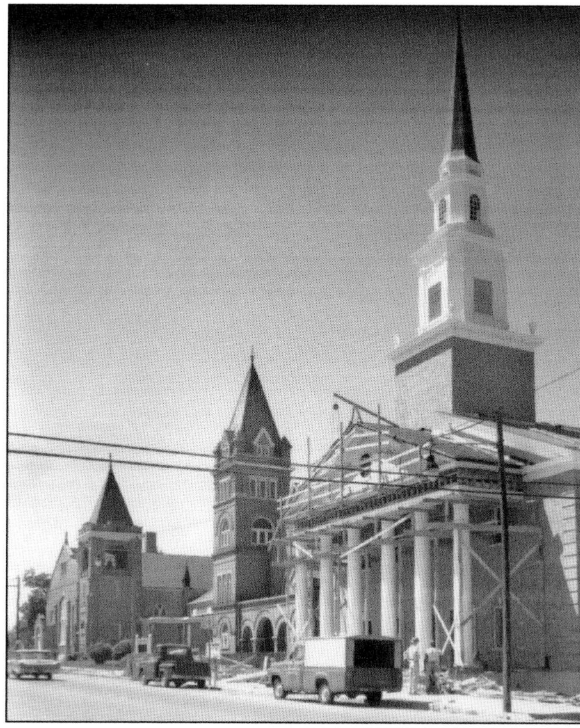

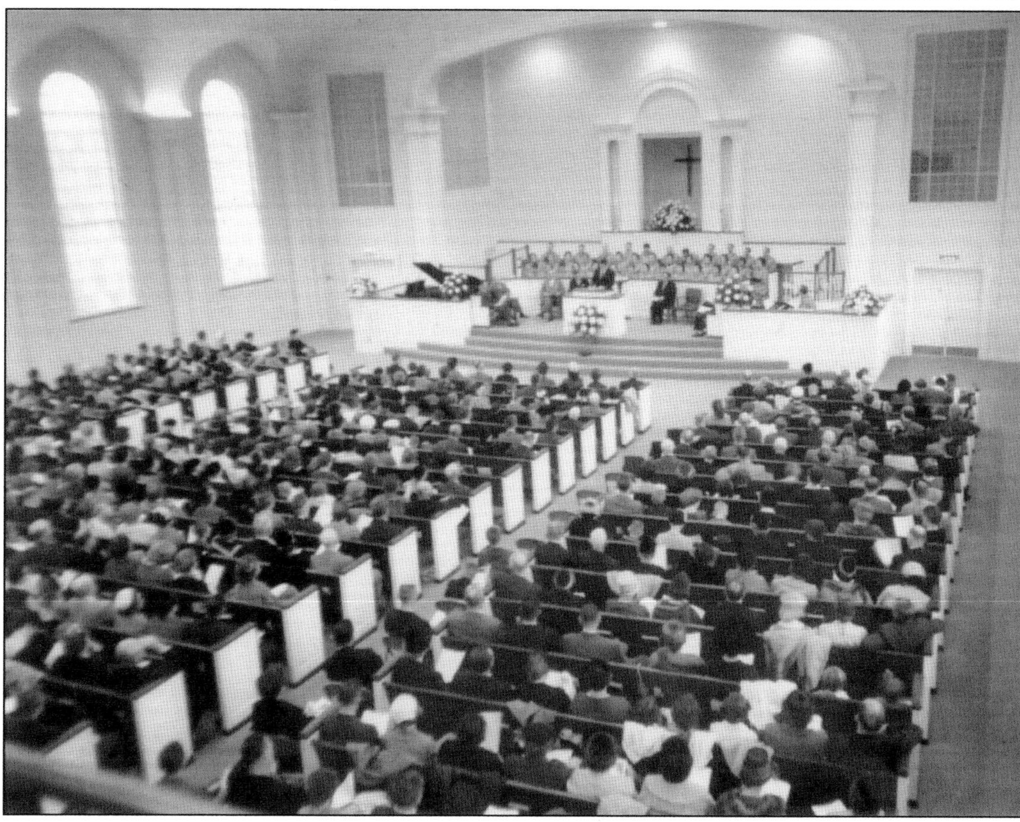

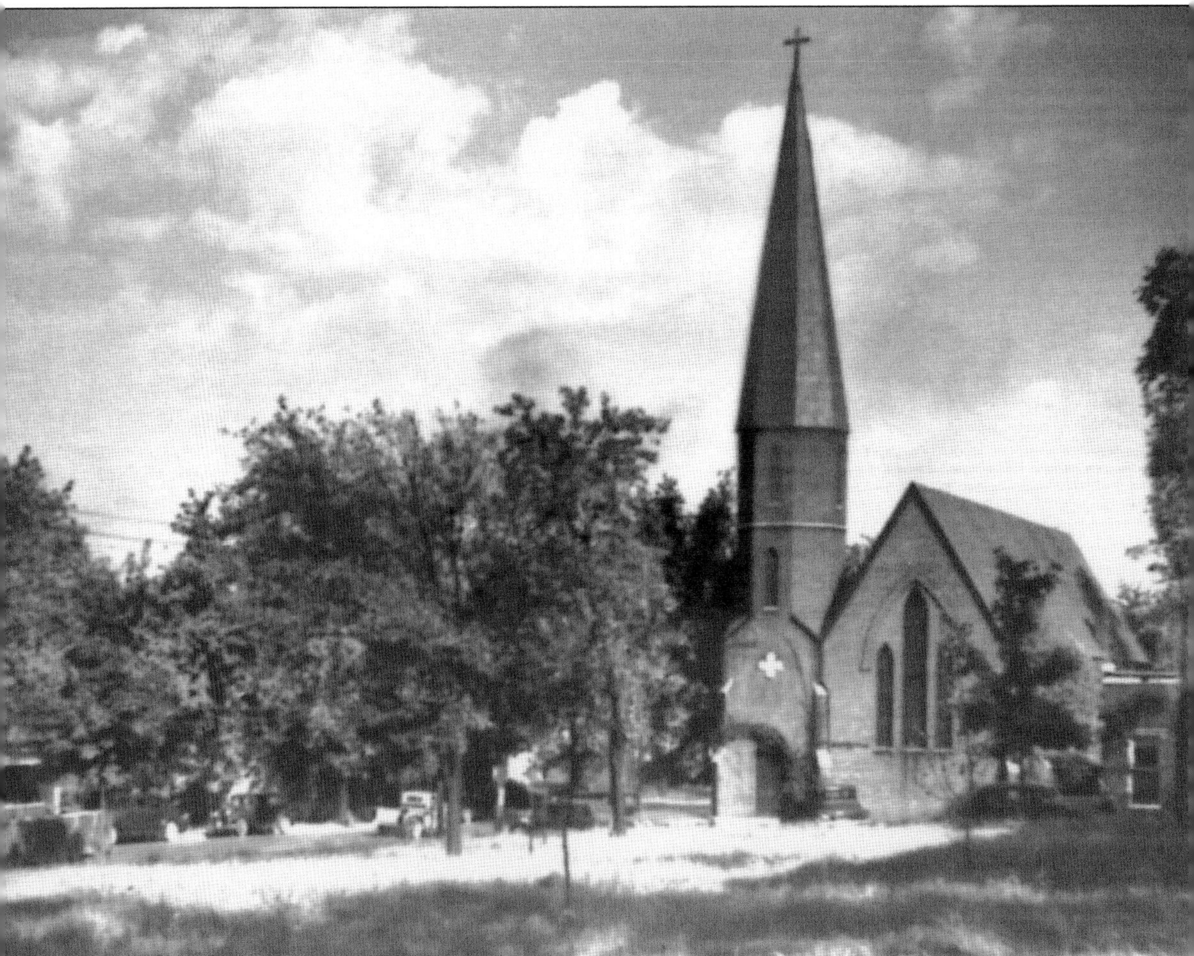

St. Philip's Episcopal Church is the only church in the central business district that stands as it was originally built. The Gothic architectural design was the result of Bishop Smith's desire to create something "worthy of the town." Harrodsburg was known at the time as "the Saratoga of the South" because of the throngs of wealthy Southerners, many of whom were Episcopalians, who came here for the benefits of the medicinal spring water. The church was described by Rexford Newcomb, architecture professor at the University of Illinois, as "the most perfect specimen of pure Gothic, exterior and interior, of its size in Kentucky." It was dedicated in 1861 by its designer, Bishop Benjamin Smith. The church sits on land rich in history, from Indian fights to the horrors of the Civil War. The property was also the site of skirmishes in the late 1700s between pioneers, including George Rogers Clark, and Indians. After the Battle of Perryville in 1862, the church was where Gen. Leonidas Polk made an impassioned prayer for blessings on friend and foe alike.

The right photograph is of a view from the sanctuary showing the stark simplicity and beauty of the St. Philip's, a small version of the English cathedrals after which it was patterned. Bishop Smith not only designed the building using a carved wooden model he made himself, but he also carved a freestanding alter, three ecclesiastical chairs, and the communion rail shown in the picture below. All the pews were handmade by locals using wooden pegs, as were the cross beams in the large doors. The stained glass windows were imported from Italy. Incorporated into one window behind the alter are symbols of the church, a golden crown, and a blood-red cross—the Cross of St. Philip.

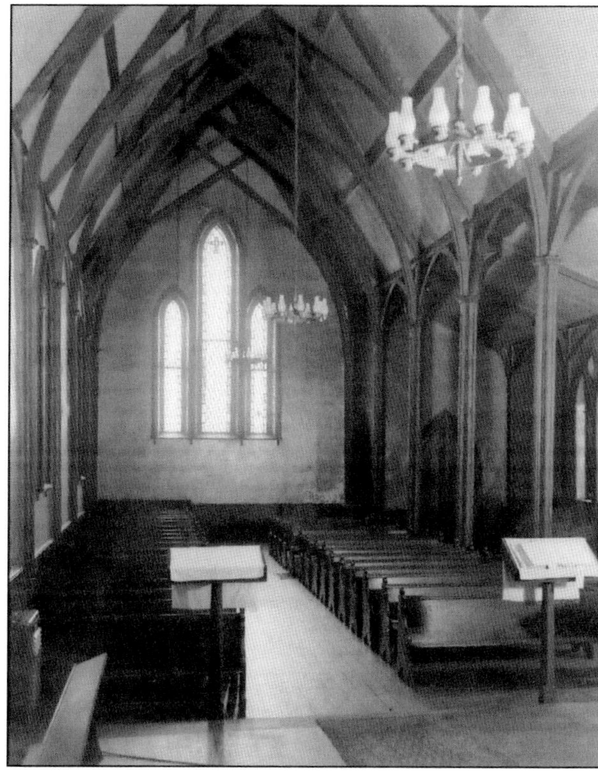

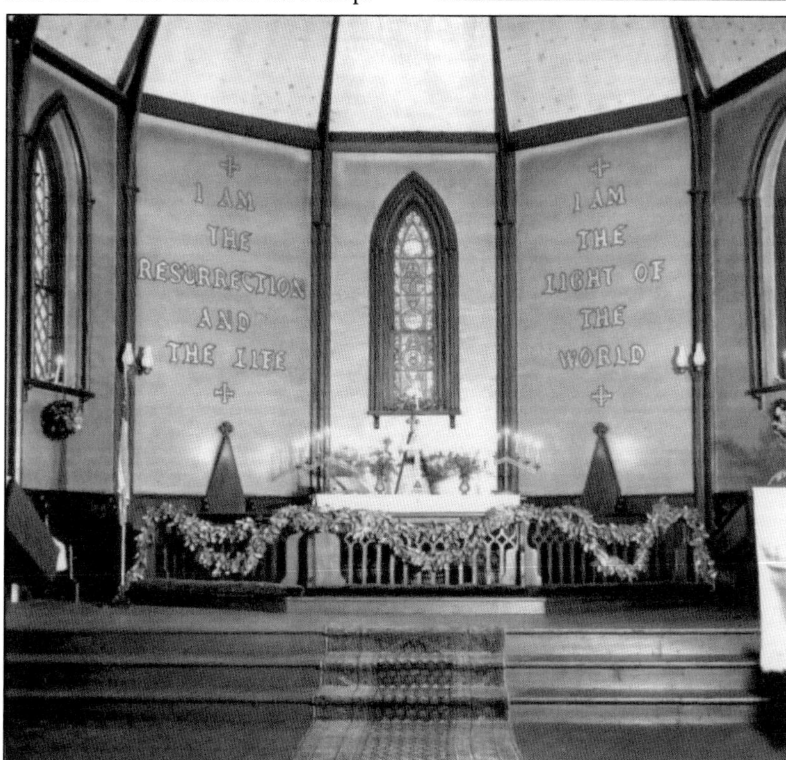

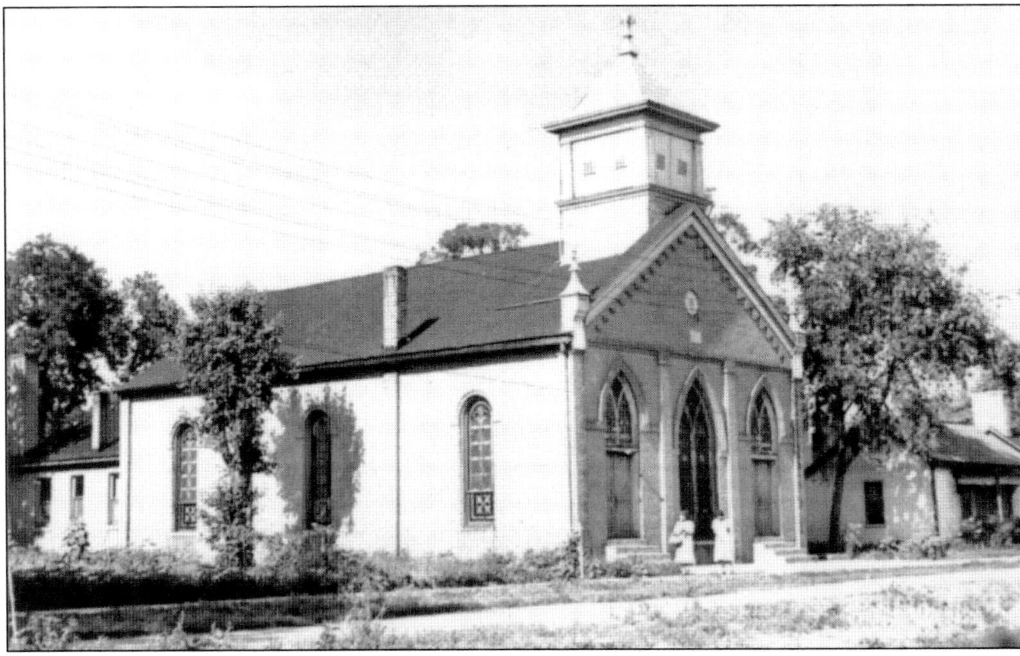

The First Baptist Church on West Broadway Street, Kentucky's oldest street, was built in 1873, but its history dates to the 1840s when it was organized as the African Baptist Church. The original building, also on this site, was both church and school. In 1897, a split in the congregation caused the organization of a new church, Centennial Baptist. The remaining members reorganized under the current First Baptist name.

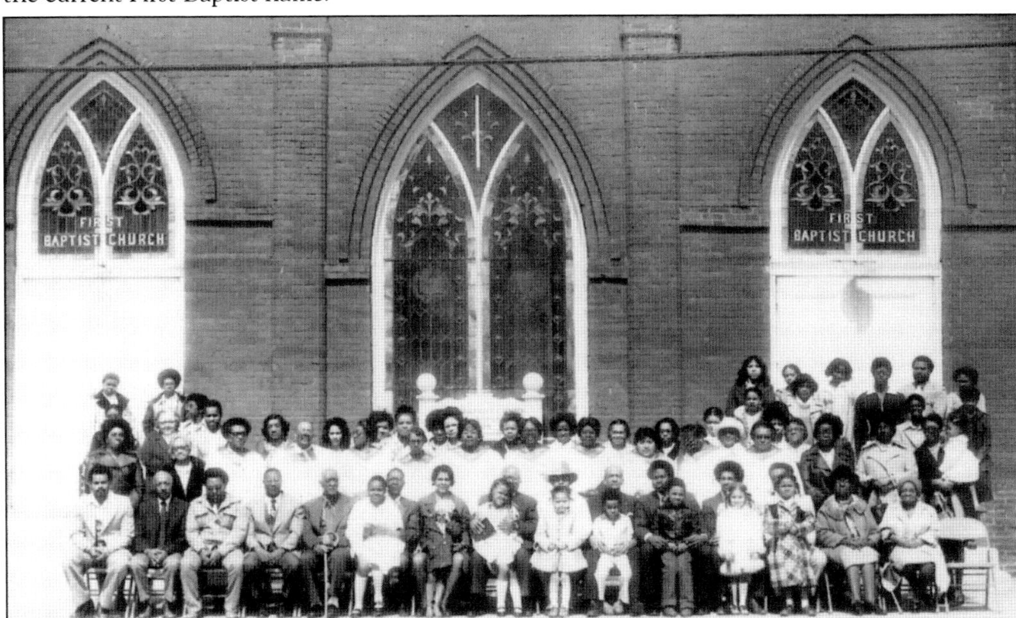

The occasion for this photograph from the 1960s was probably a homecoming or anniversary celebration. First Baptist Church appears to have been thriving at that time with a congregation of over 60. Now, many of the older members have passed on, and their children have moved away, making pictures like this just a memory of better times.

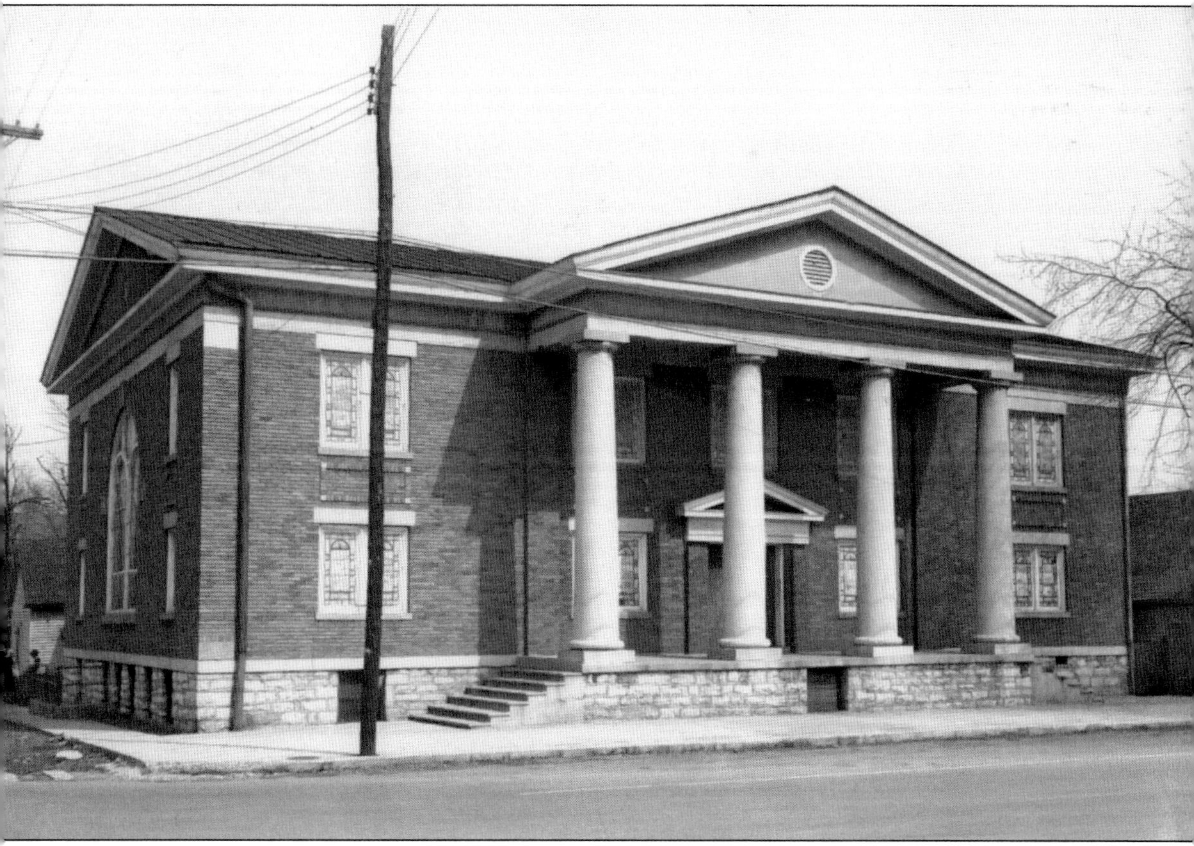

St. Peter African Methodist Episcopal (AME) Church, on the corner of West Lexington and College Streets, was built in 1917 at a cost of $25,000. The first opportunity for Harrodsburg's black Methodists to worship publicly dates back to 1839. Enslaved Methodists built their first church on a lot that was located on the corner of North Greenville and East Broadway Streets and purchased for $1. Nat Wilson's undertaking establishment once stood on that corner, and funeral homes have occupied the lot since then. The congregation stayed 19 years until 1858 when it moved to a larger site on the corner of East Broadway and East Streets. While at the second location, the congregation founded the Wayman Institute in 1885 to provide higher education for the local black children. After 59 years, this second church was condemned, and in 1917, the church began this third structure pictured above. Church members hauled rock for the foundation and helped with construction whenever needed. The congregation has been pastored by some of the most prominent ministers in the Kentucky Conference.

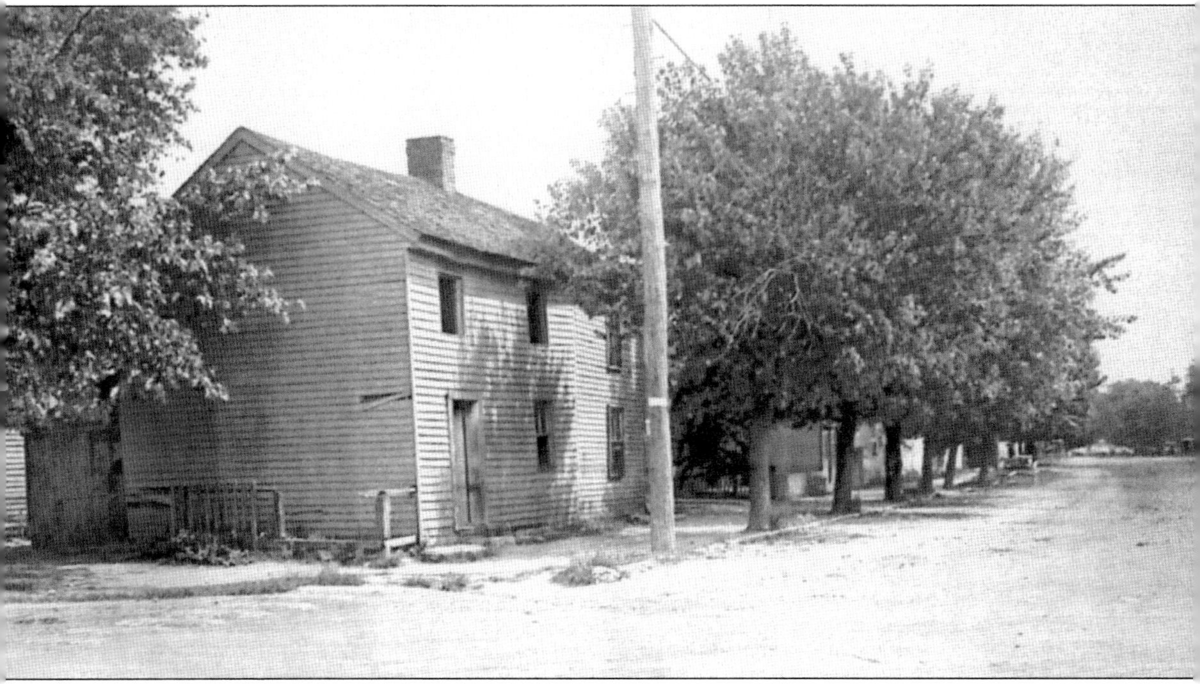

This photograph dates to the turn of the century and shows the St. Peter AME Church site at that time. This corner of West Lexington and College Streets—so close to Fort Harrod—is rich in history. This home, known as the Askew house, is said to have enclosed a log structure, one of the "lottery cabins" thrown up by James Harrod and his men in 1774. These were built quickly to establish the pioneer's claim on the best land. Many of the cabins were later improved by the addition of siding and extra rooms, as was the Askew house. In 1840, Prof. Eyre Askew is listed in the census as a schoolteacher with 30 students, which he taught at this site for a time. The house was torn down after St. Peter AME Church bought the lot in 1917, and three of its logs were used to replace rotted logs in the cabin housed in the Lincoln Marriage Temple at Old Fort Harrod State Park.

Three

GOVERNMENT

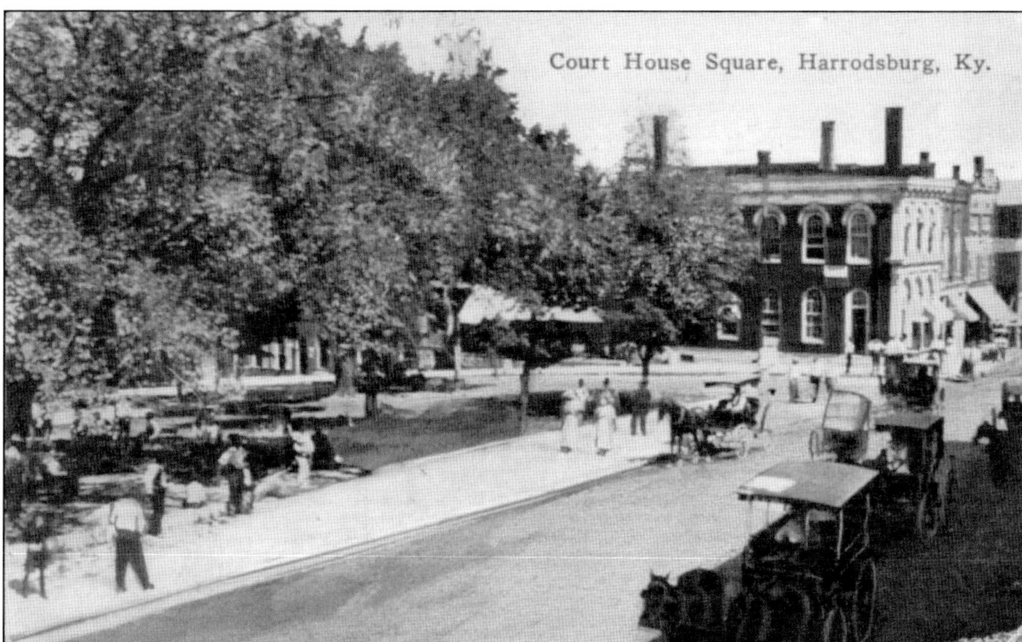

This late-1800s photograph shows the courthouse square, which was the center of activities for the town. It was located centrally in the business district, which was originally just several acres of land known by pioneers as the Woods on the Hill. The courthouse, clerk's office, jail, market house, and stray pens (to hold livestock wandering the streets) were all located there.

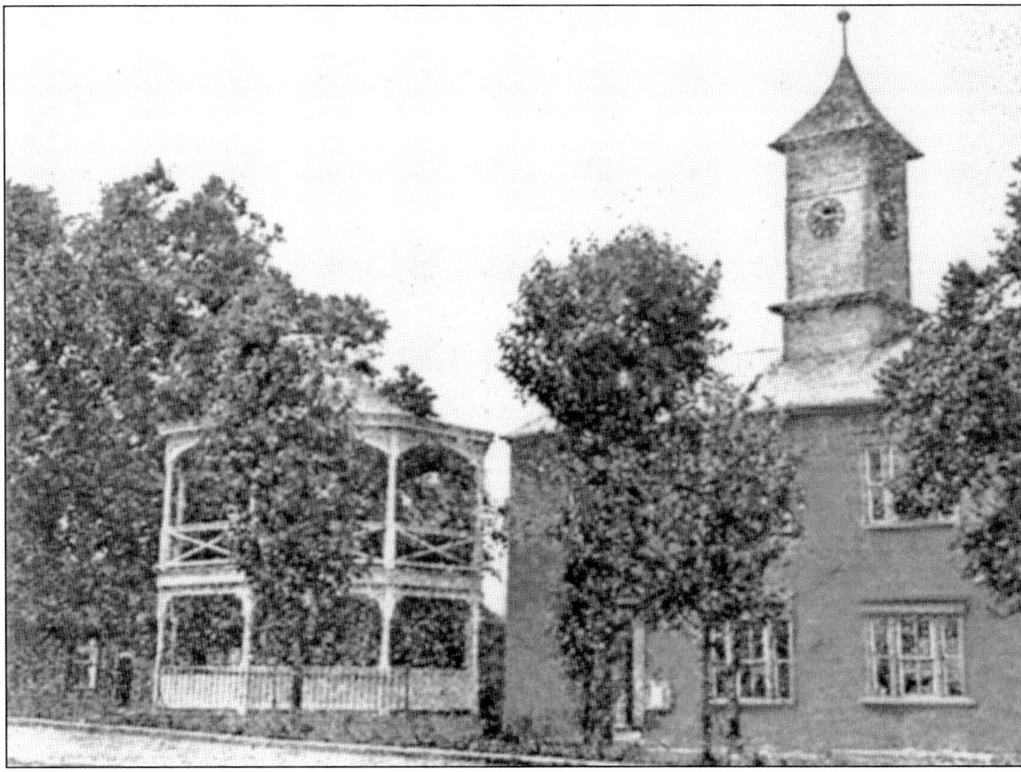

These two photographs show uses for the courthouse square in the early 1900s. Above, a 1902 image shows a large, two-story bandstand on the courthouse lawn. The early 20th century was a time when people enjoyed family outings for concerts, and bandstands were common in public areas at the time. Harrodsburg had several bands that provided entertainment locally and in surrounding towns. When the courthouse was replaced in 1912, the bandstand was torn down and not rebuilt. The photograph below is of a crowd of men gathered on the courthouse lawn for county court day. On these days, the public square was the trading center and gossiping place for rural Kentuckians. Everything was for sale or trade—livestock, food, farming and household goods. Itinerant vendors and hucksters of every sort worked the crowds for business.

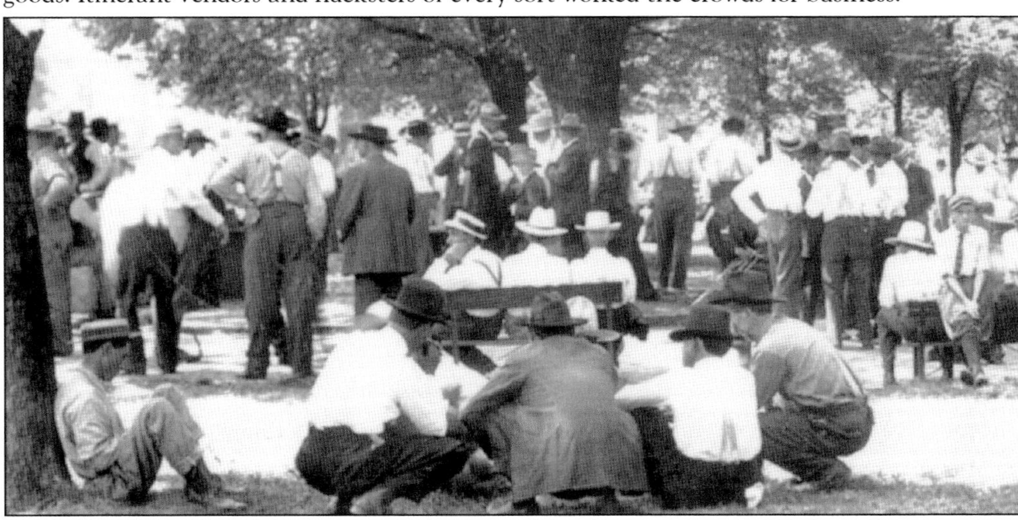

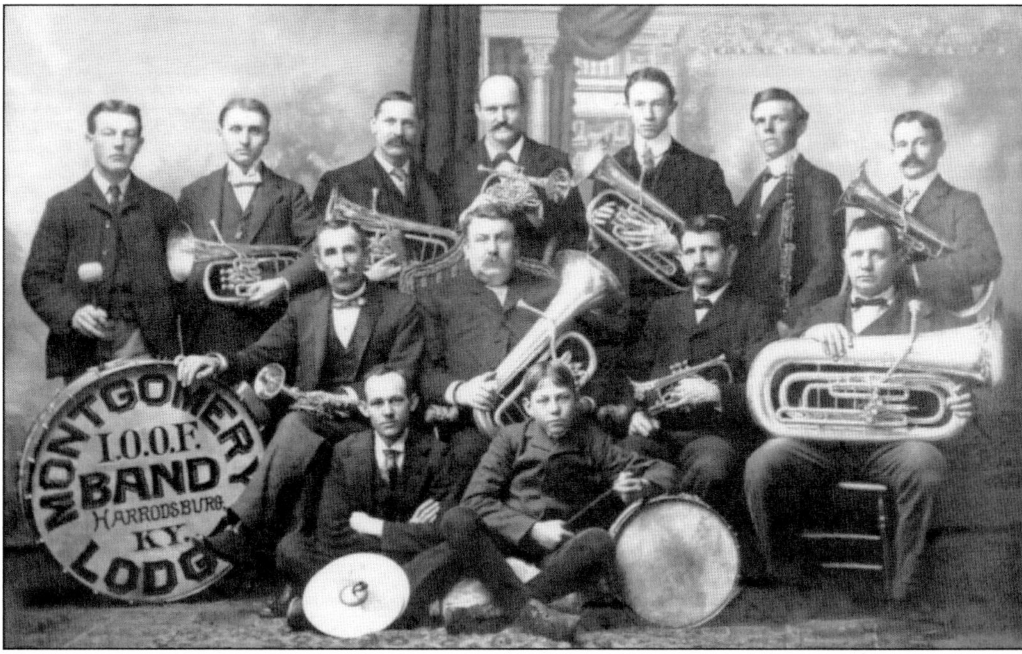

Pictured is one of several bands formed by members of local organizations in the early 1900s. This group of 12 men and a young boy make up the band of the Harrodsburg Independent Order of Odd Fellows (IOOF), Montgomery Lodge No. 18. These were prominent businessmen and civic leaders; they were not musicians but people who had time to become skilled enough to perform at concerts in the local bandstand.

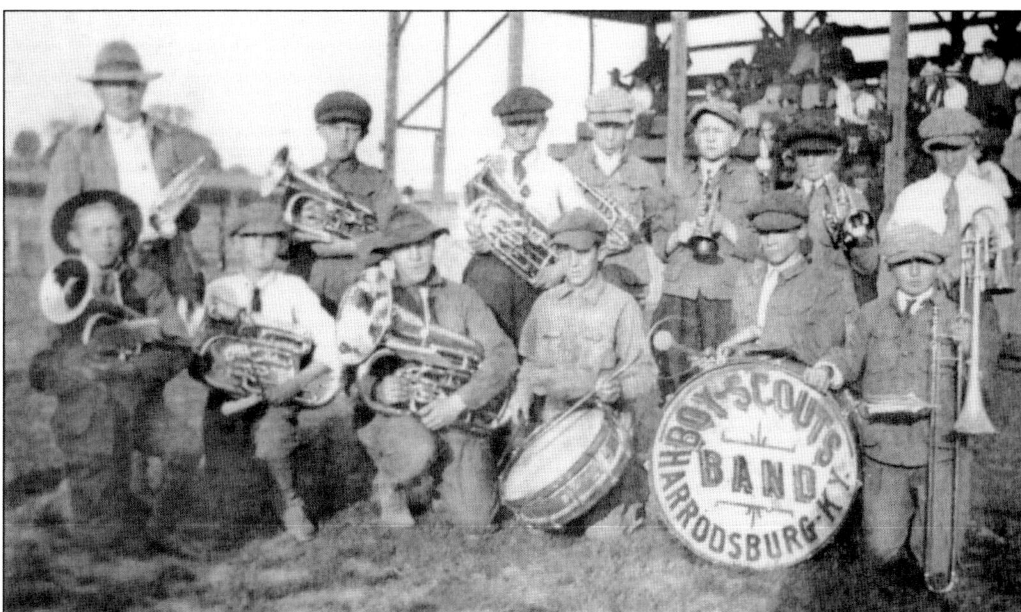

Musical training started young, as shown in this Boy Scout Band of 12 boys posing with their leader at the Mercer County Fairgrounds in the early 1900s. The band traveled in addition to performing locally for bandstand concerts, and a newspaper account tells of its appearance at a large political rally in Nicholasville in 1915.

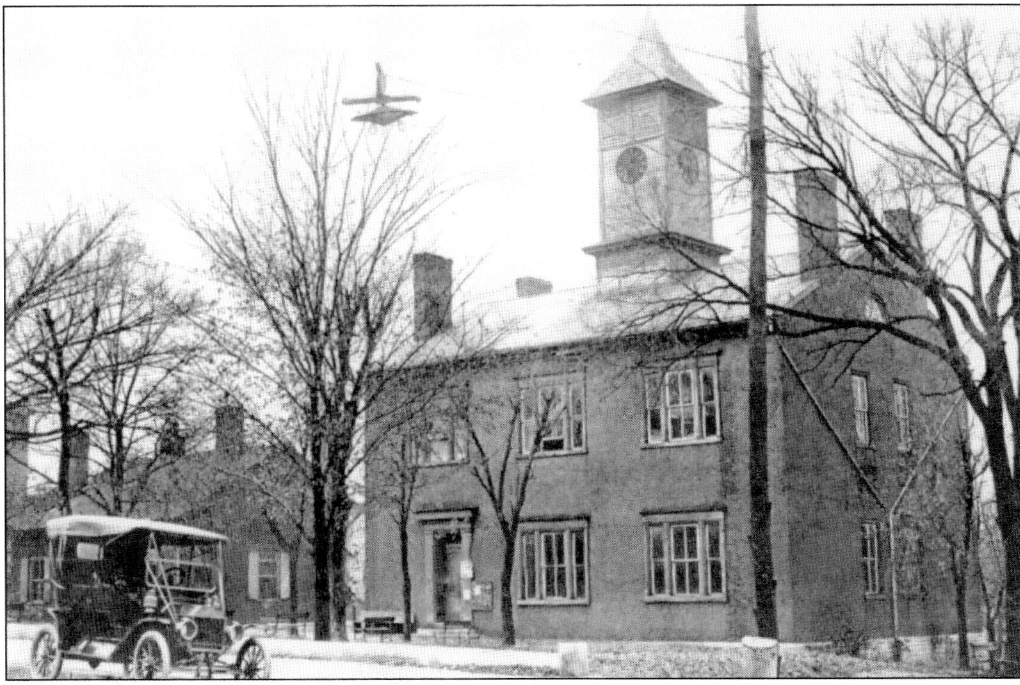

The above photograph is the second Mercer County Courthouse (in use from 1818 to 1912), described in an article in the *Harrodsburg Herald* as a respectable brick building with a slate roof, a town clock, and having every convenience for the furtherance of business. It also housed the town's first library, described as "excellent but not fully appreciated." A mass killing occurred at the courthouse on November 26, 1873, when three men died in what became known as the Thompson-Daviess tragedy. The picture below shows an early-1900s group of prominent Harrodsburg residents posing in front of the county clerk's office next to the Mercer County Courthouse. The men seated in front are, from left to right, W.W. Stephenson, Ben Hardin, Dr. Yeamon, and judges Charles Hardin and Charles Corn. Others identified in the photograph include Meriweather Smith, James VanArsdall, Dr. Robarbs, Ben Casey Allin, Lew Brown, Ora Adams, and Mr. Poteet.

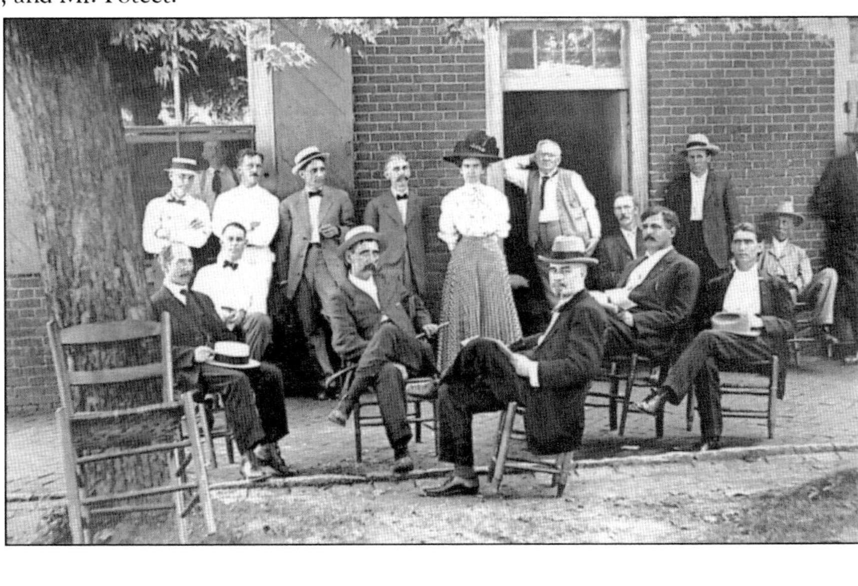

At right, construction on the new Mercer County Courthouse was underway by 1912. Parts of the old courthouse walls were incorporated into the new building. The identity of the two men on the rafters is not known.

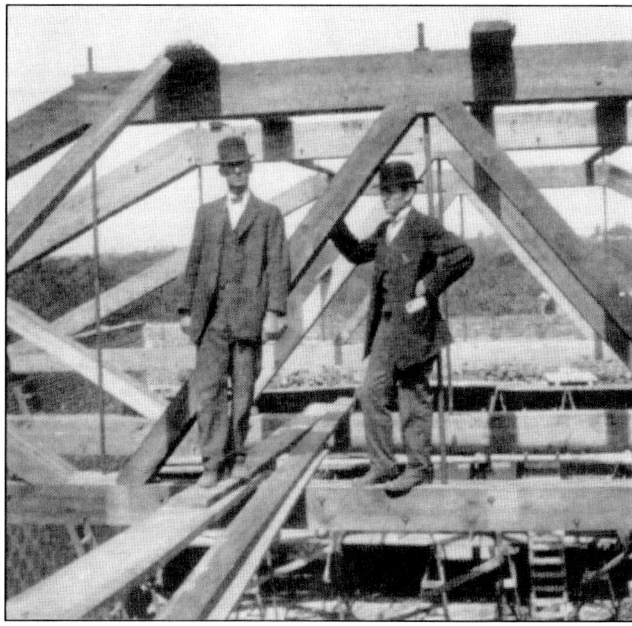

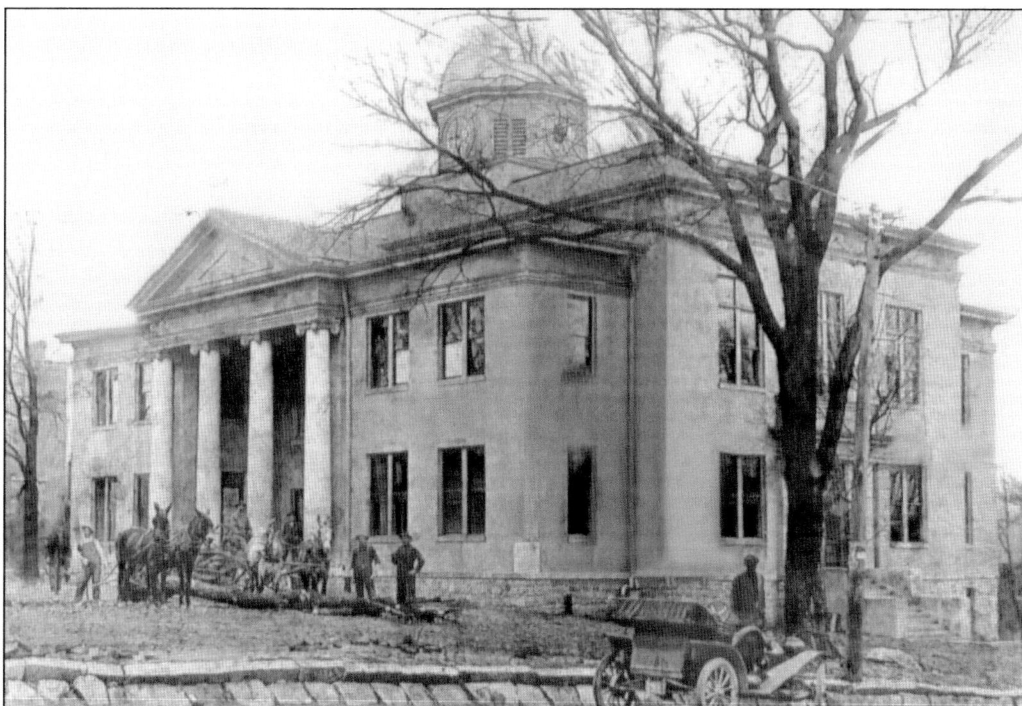

This is the third courthouse (1912–1929), described by Col. George Chinn as a "pure Southern Colonial" building. Built at a cost of almost $25,000, it was equipped with fireproof vaults and a fireproof room to house the Harrodsburg Historical Society's valuable collections. In 1928, an electrical fire in the clock tower did much damage, and the decision was made to rebuild. A plan for an "almost totally new courthouse" was accepted. The light-colored block in the corner of this building is the cornerstone, which contains a time capsule.

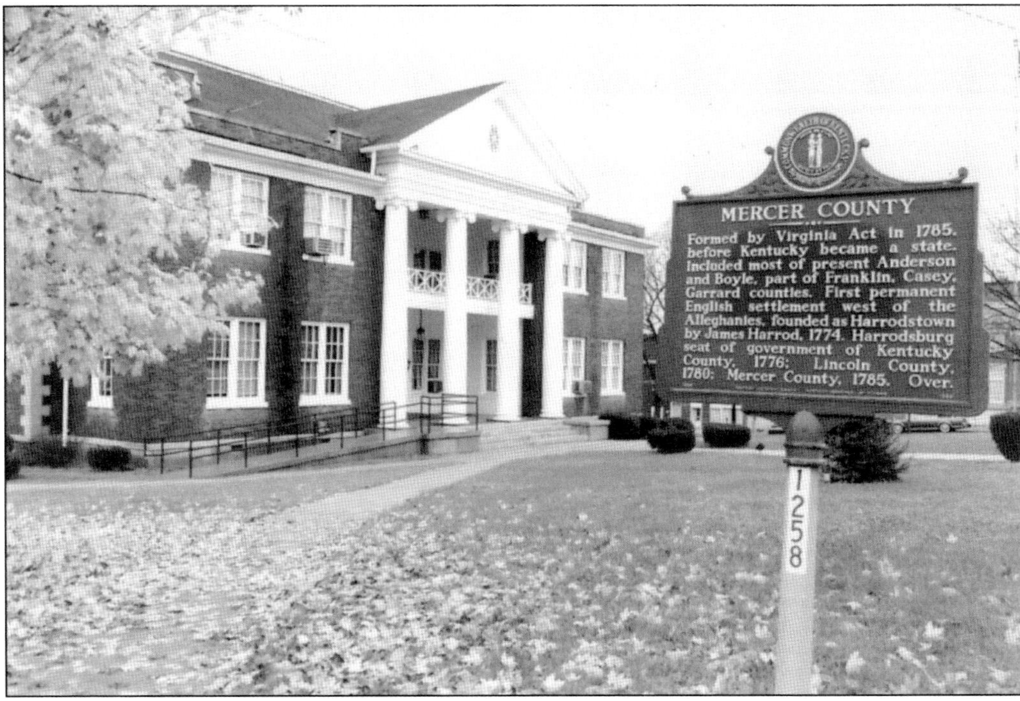

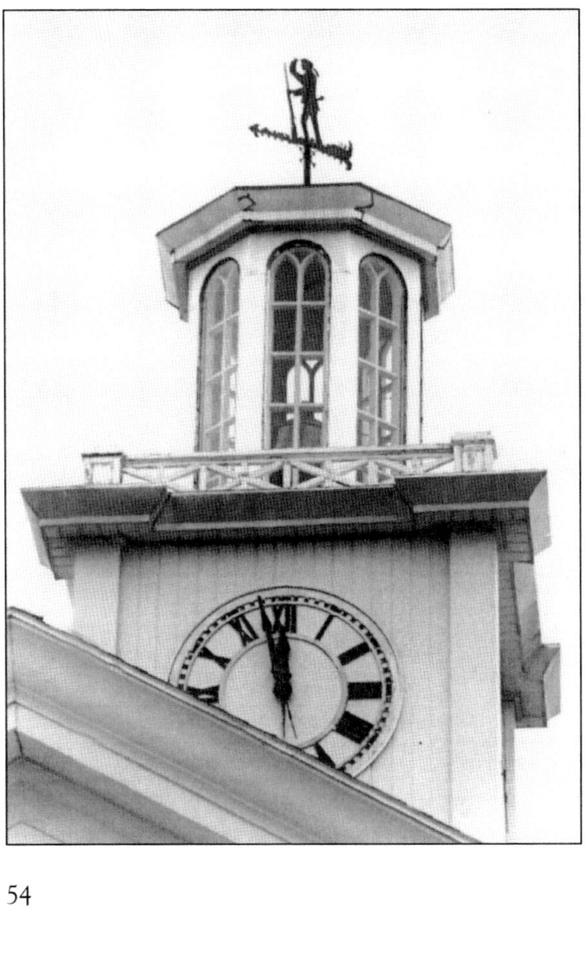

These photographs are of the fourth Mercer County Courthouse (1929–2009), which served the community for 80 years. A comparison with pictures of its predecessor shows a generally similar Southern Colonial–style building. It was believed, as stated on the cornerstone, that materials from the three previous courthouses had been incorporated within its walls. In 1980, it was listed in the National Register of Historic Places, but that was not enough to save it from demolition in 2009. By decrees of the Kentucky Administrative Office of the Courts, the fourth courthouse was deemed "unsafe and unsound." Because the historic courthouse was completely demolished, no materials from past courthouses will be incorporated within the walls of the new courthouse. Although it will still sit upon the land once known as the Woods on the Hill, the new judicial center will leave no room for green space.

The photograph to the right shows the marble cornerstone originally placed in the 1912 Mercer County Courthouse. When it burned, the cornerstone was salvaged and placed in the new 1929 building. When that building was torn down in 2009, the cornerstone was located, safely removed, and stored until a plan for opening and preserving its contents was decided upon. The picture below was taken just after the top of the copper time capsule was pried open. The contents were in remarkably good condition and consisted of newspapers, bills, receipts, pamphlets, postcards, photographs, and coins. Some words to a song written by Henry Cleveland Wood for the 1912 cornerstone ceremony include, "we have gathered here today at the passing now away, of a landmark and a relic of the past. May our newer courthouse see Mercer's full prosperity, and a country's peace and freedom that will last."

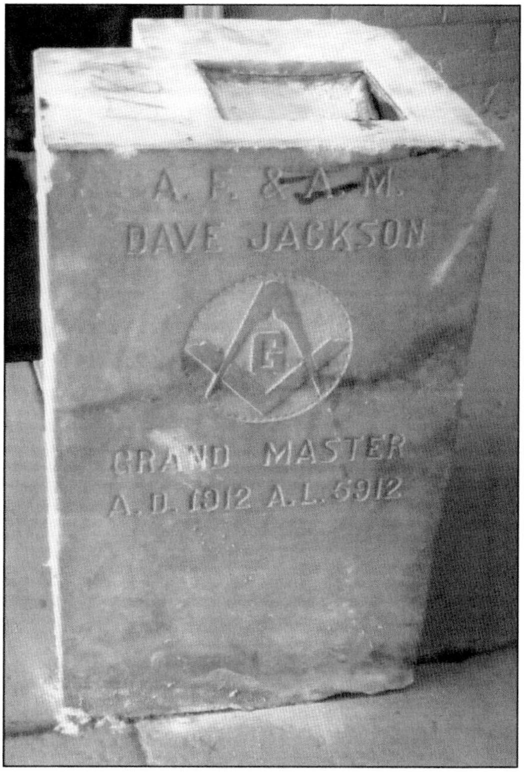

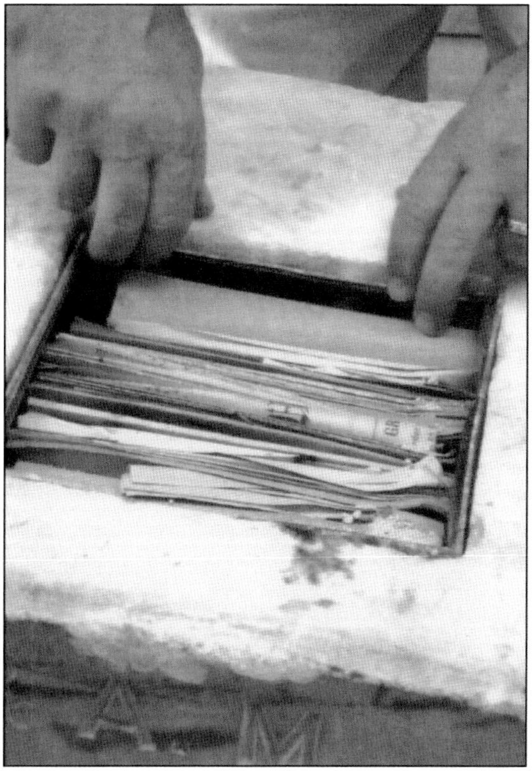

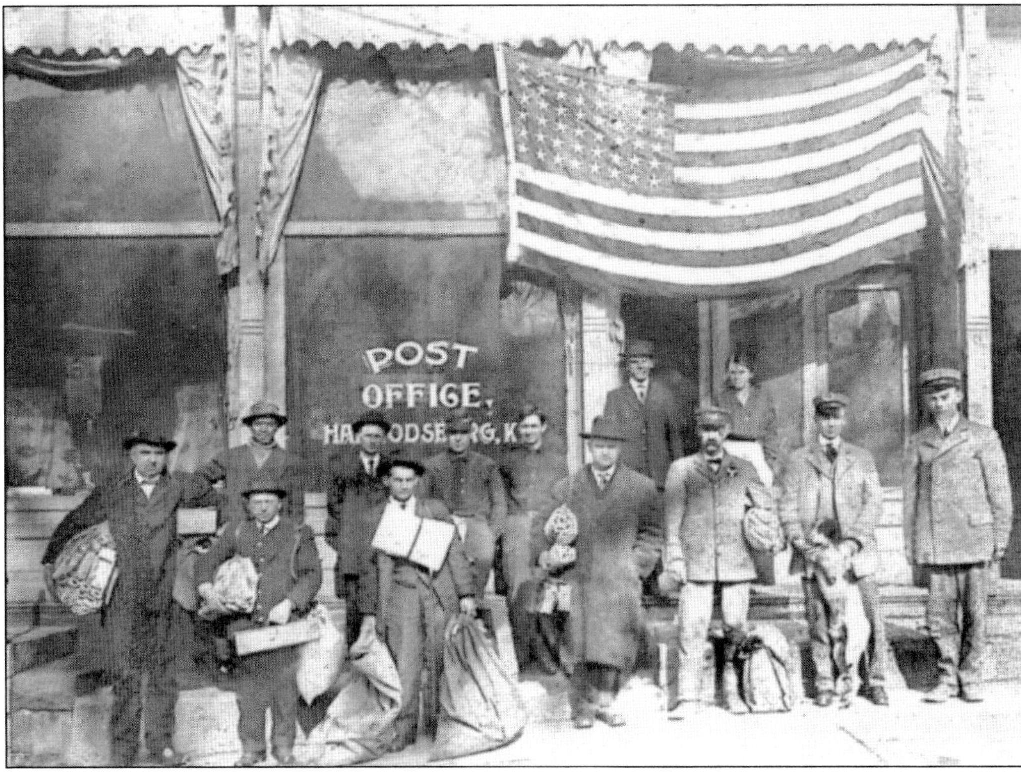

This photograph above of Harrodsburg's post office on Short Street would have been taken sometime between 1913 and 1921, when J. Hal Grimes, standing at left in the doorway, was postmaster. The employees are, from left to right, (first row) J. VanDivier, Finis Smalley, Thomas Hawkins, Henry VanDivier, Lee Coleman, Paul Clemmons, and Frank Conner; (second row) Bill Yads, Minor Ransdell, Tub Alderson, and Frank Davenport; and Ossie Tatum is at right in the doorway. The picture below shows the lot that is the present site of Harrodsburg's post office. In 1927, the United States government purchased the lot and razed all the buildings, but did not have the money to start construction. According to Gertrude Reed, "My first recollection of that area was an empty lot with Chautauqua tent shows coming every summer."

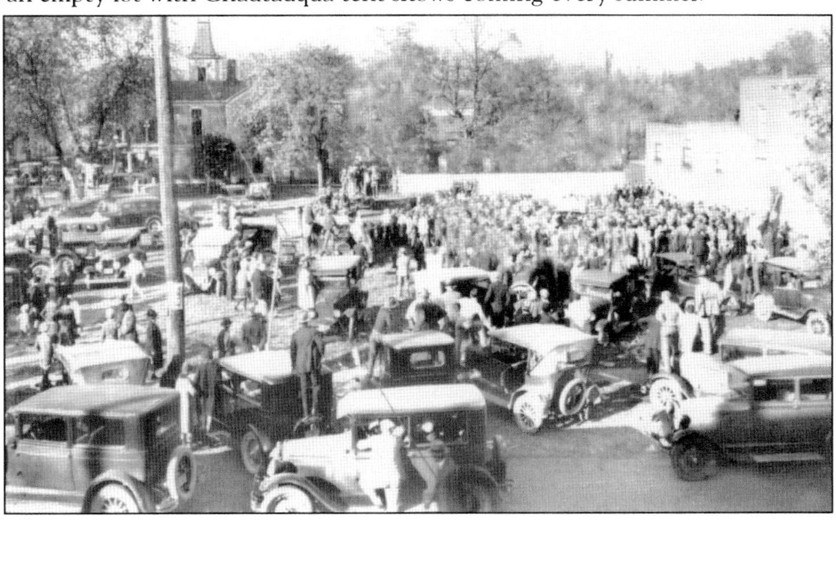

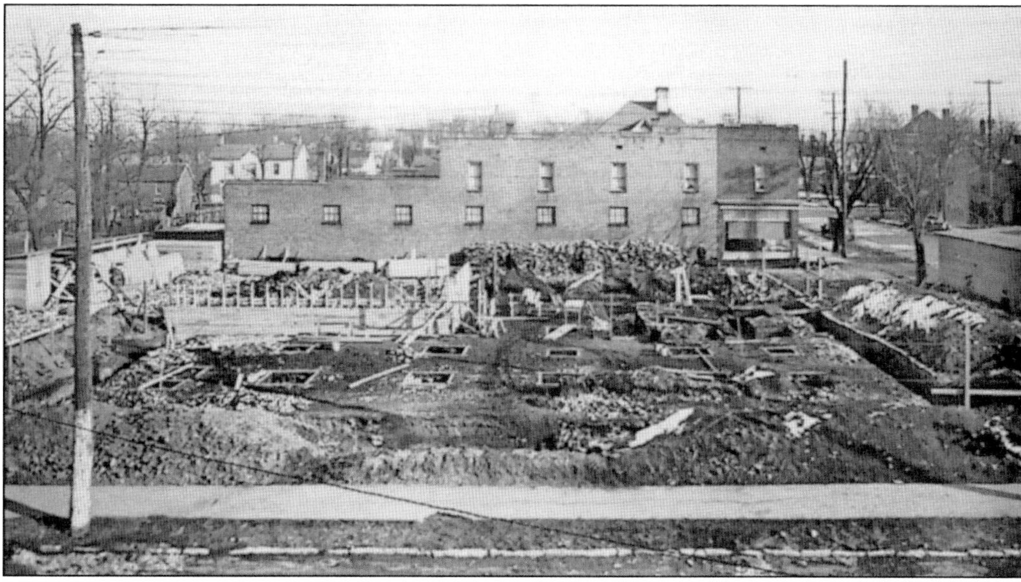

This photograph was made in January 1931 at the start of construction on Harrodsburg's new post office. The deed for the land was made in 1916, but the money to build was not appropriated until 1930, some 15 years later. The building was completed early in 1932.

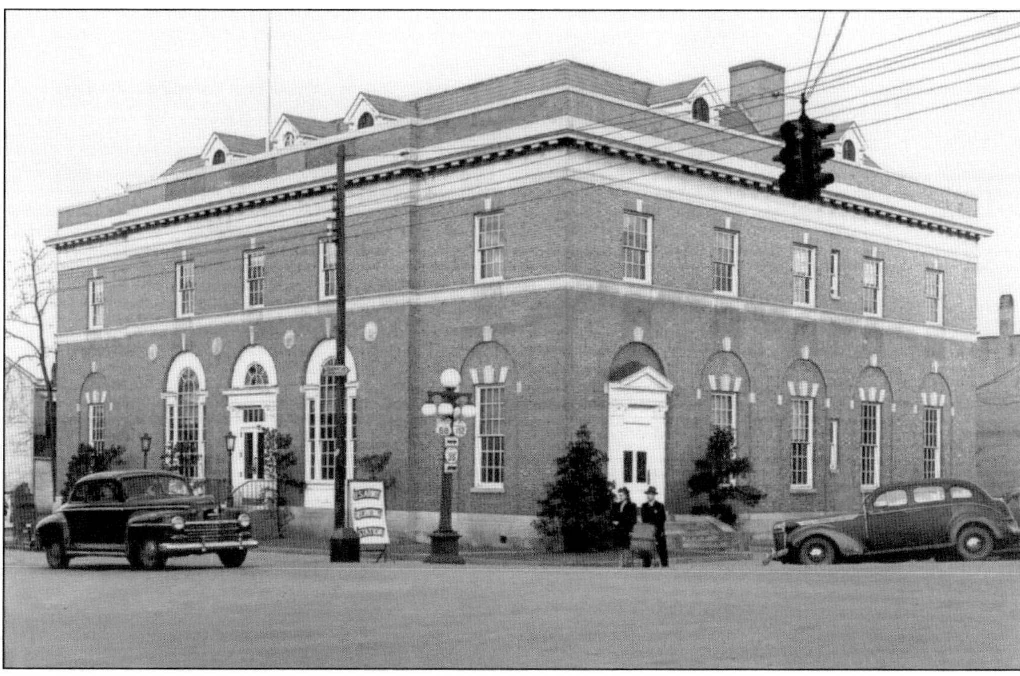

The new Harrodsburg post office opened its door to the community on April 6, 1932. The town owes a debt of gratitude to some residents interested in how the new building would fit into its historic surroundings. They convinced the officials to design a Colonial-style post office building that would conform to the age of the town.

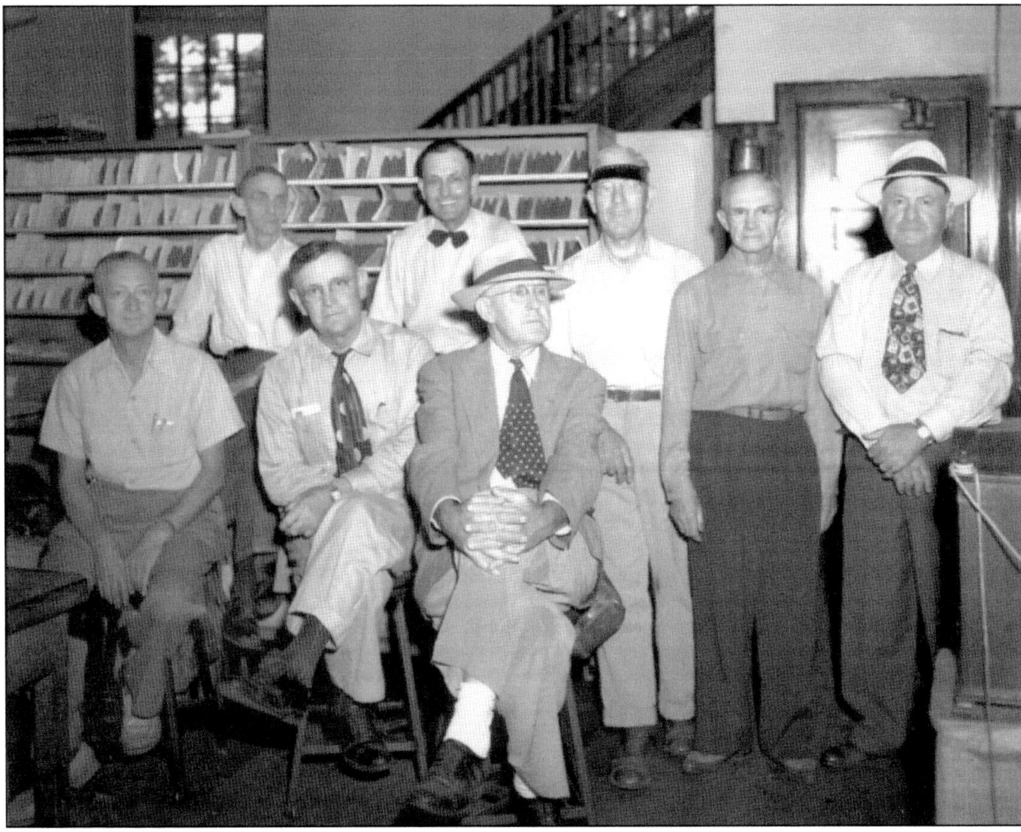

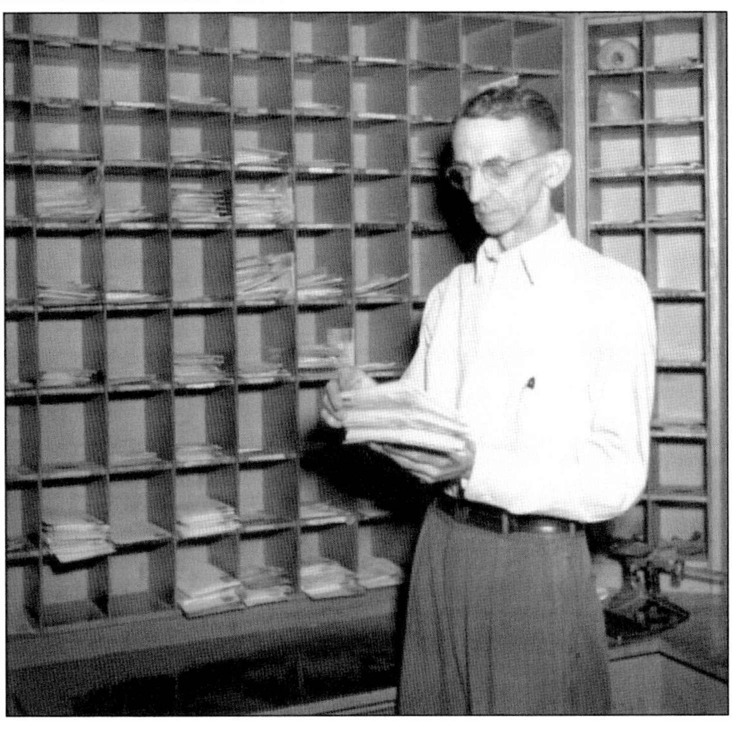

The 1951 photograph above is of employees of the Harrodsburg Post Office with more than 25 years of service to the postal system. Pictured, from left to right, are (first row) F.L. Ransdell, L.M. Reed, and W.R. Penny; (second row) J.P. Williams, Lucien Brewer, B.G. Alderson, James Graham, and M.S. Claunch. Interestingly, men with the surnames Alderson and Ransdell appear in this image and in the photograph that dates to 1913–1921 at the top of page 56. The picture at left shows J.P. Williams sorting mail by hand.

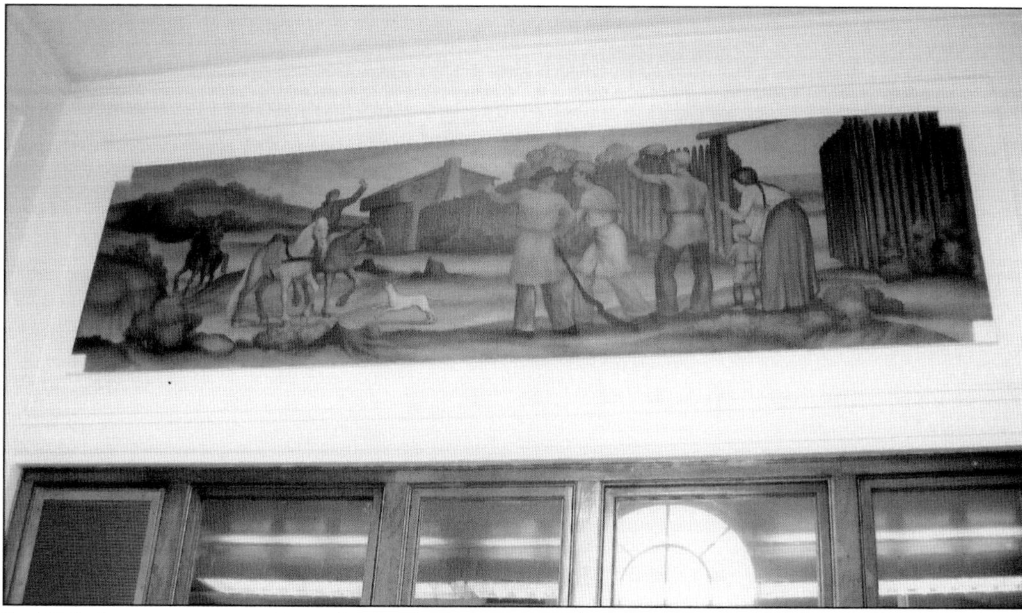

In 1938, the congressman from the Sixth Congressional District gave Harrodsburg the opportunity to secure murals depicting the town's history for the post office lobby. This project was part of the Works Progress Administration Federal Art Project (WPA/FAP). During this period, the WPA completed numerous art projects in public buildings around the country. A committee from the Harrodsburg Woman's Club aided in the selection of the subject matter, and in 1941, the murals were dedicated. Even though the murals are large, they are just below the ceiling and usually go unnoticed by the customers. Pioneer scenes of Harrodsburg grace all six of the murals. The above photograph shows a scene depicting pioneers as they welcome travelers to the fort, and the image below depicts settlers collecting water at the spring.

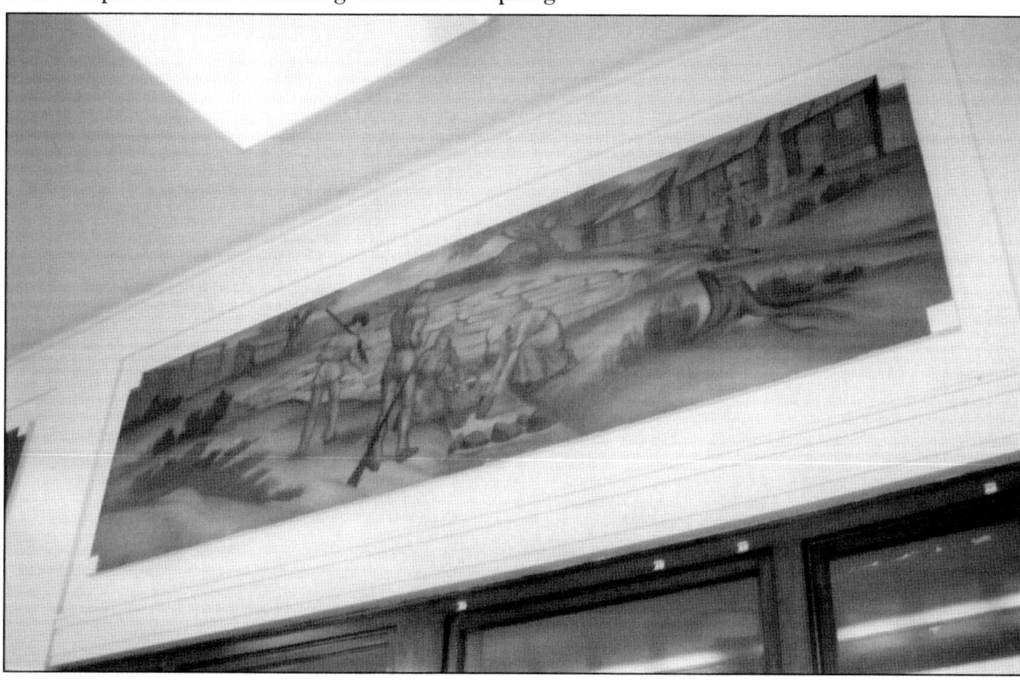

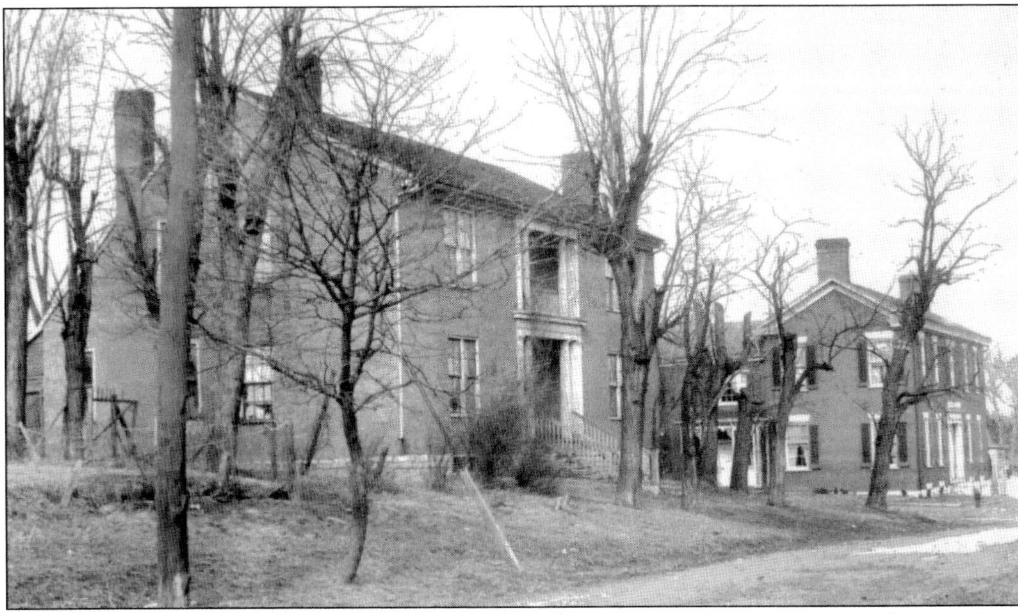

As early as 1876, the Dr. Smedley house on South College Street is shown on a map of Harrodsburg. John Smedley was a successful druggist and physician who saw patients in his home and also made house calls. In 1914, this grand, old brick house was torn down to make way for the construction of the A.D. Price Memorial Hospital.

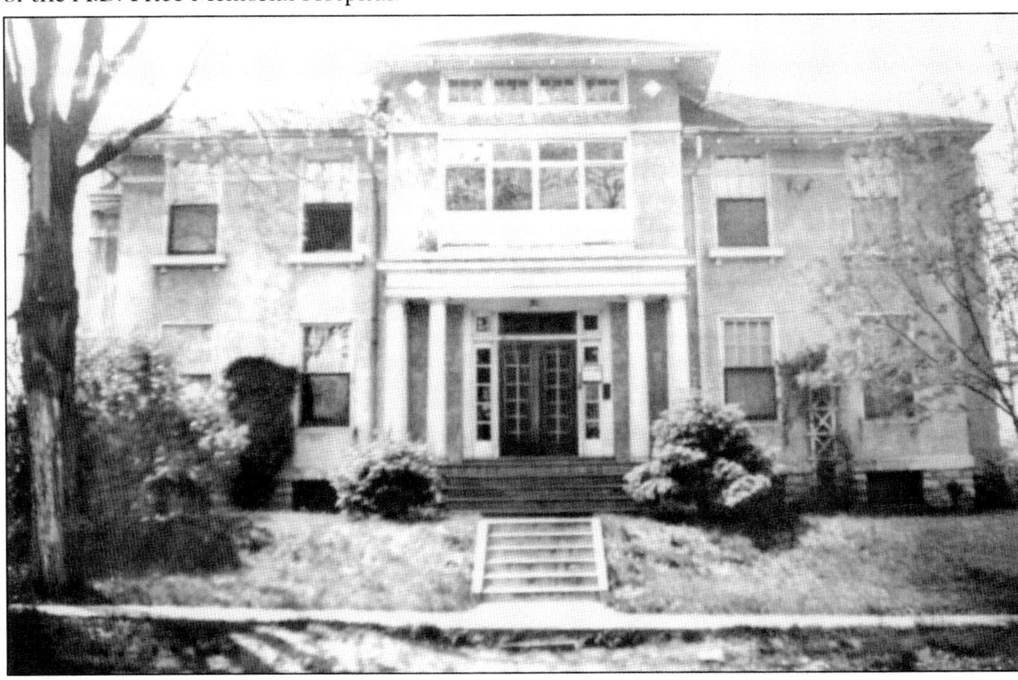

The A.D. Price Memorial Hospital was built in 1915 and dedicated in remembrance of the contribution of Dr. Ansel Daniel Price. A quote from the *Harrodsburg Herald* says of Price that he is "one of the most universally loved men who ever lived in our community and a widely known physician in central Kentucky." This 20-bed hospital served for 34 years, until a larger one was needed and built in 1949.

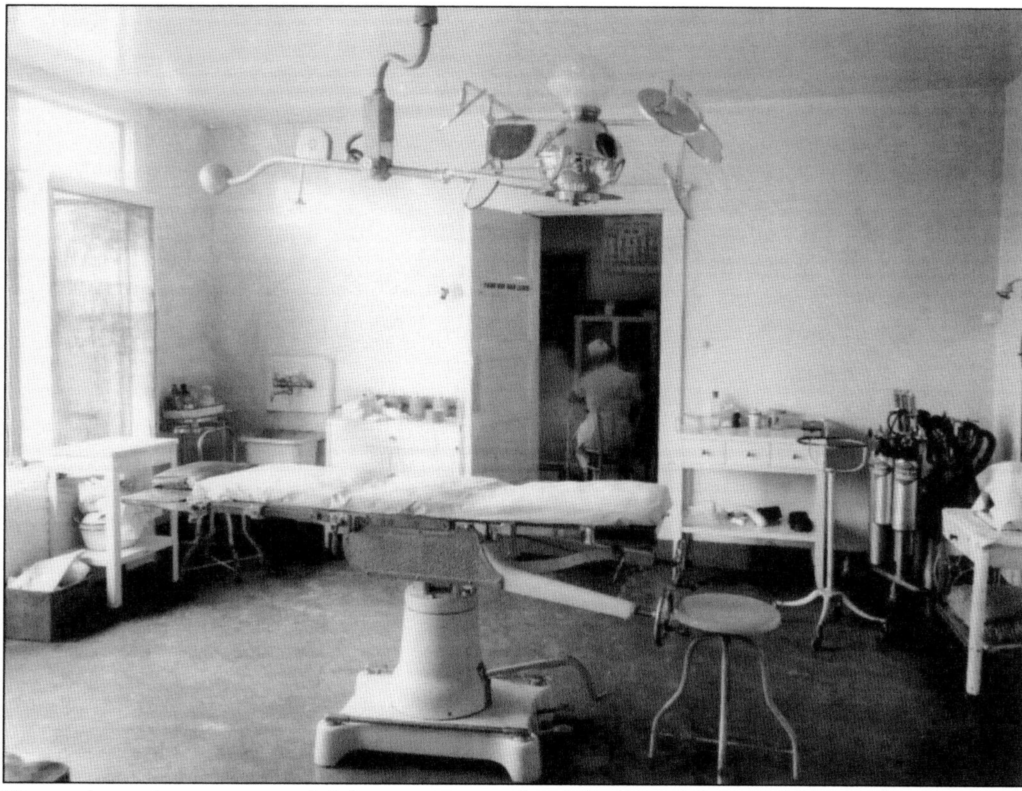

Pictured are the surgery and delivery room at the A.D. Price Memorial Hospital in 1949, just prior to its closing. In spite of its primitive appearance compared to modern standards, it served the community well, with over 2,000 successful deliveries recorded. Rooms could accommodate four to six patients each and had no air-conditioning or television.

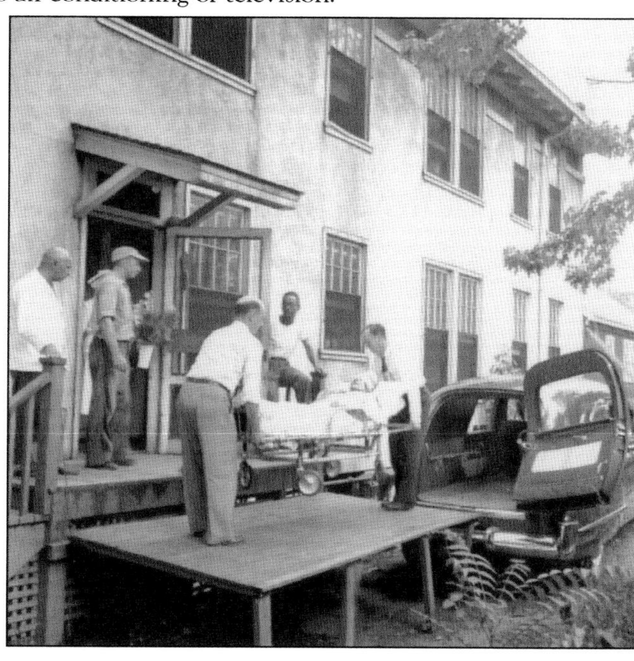

This photograph shows a patient being transported either to or from the hospital. Emergency vehicles were scarce, and funeral home hearses were commonly used as transport. These men appear to be using a homemade platform to get the patient from the building to the vehicle.

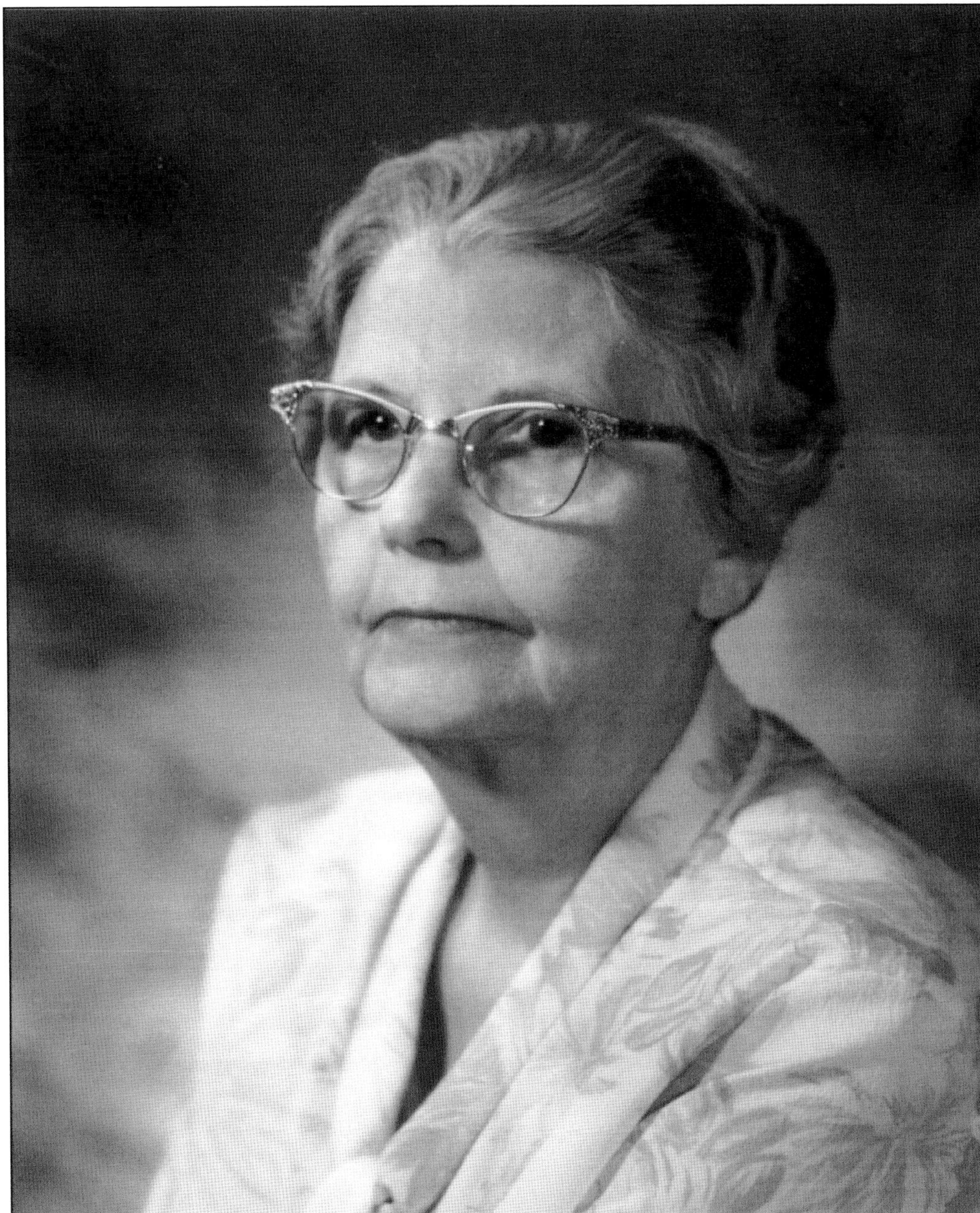

Anna Elliott Bohon was a registered nurse who came to Harrodsburg in 1926 as the superintendent of the A.D. Price Memorial Hospital. At that time, the hospital had one nurse and no patients. By the end of the year, there were four nurses and a growing patient load. In 1939, Bohon was elected to the hospital's board of directors, and from 1940 to 1963, she served as its president. Under her presidency, the hospital secured foundation grants and bought the land for the James B. Haggin Memorial Hospital, which was dedicated in 1949. She was an organizer of the Mercer County Health Department and founder of the Mercer County Cancer Drive. In 1964, a new annex to Haggin Hospital was dedicated in her honor. She was a true community leader and in 1962 was named Woman of the Year by the Harrodsburg Woman's Club. She died in 1993 at age 100.

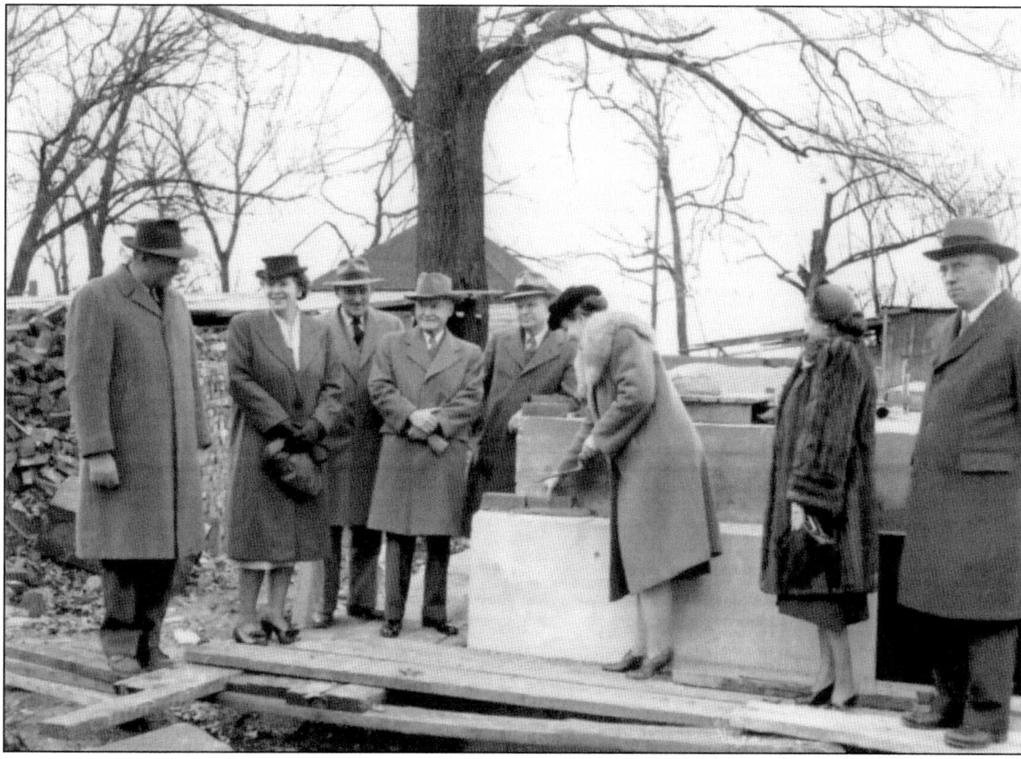

This 1948 photograph shows the ceremonious laying of the first bricks for the Mercer General Hospital on Linden Avenue. Among those present were Maurice Watts (far left), Dr. Condit VanArsdall (fourth from left), and Anna Bohn (laying brick). The hospital was renamed the James B. Haggin Memorial hospital in 1956 after a donation from the Haggin family. It is Harrodsburg's third hospital building and is located on the site of the famous Graham Springs Spa. Many trees grew on the site at that time (as seen below), but they have since been cut down for hospital expansion.

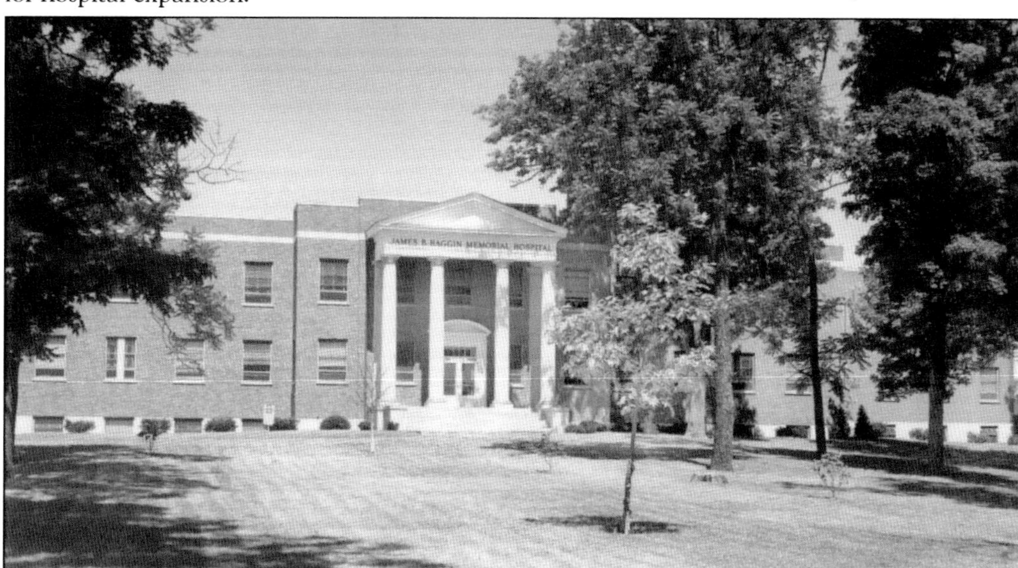

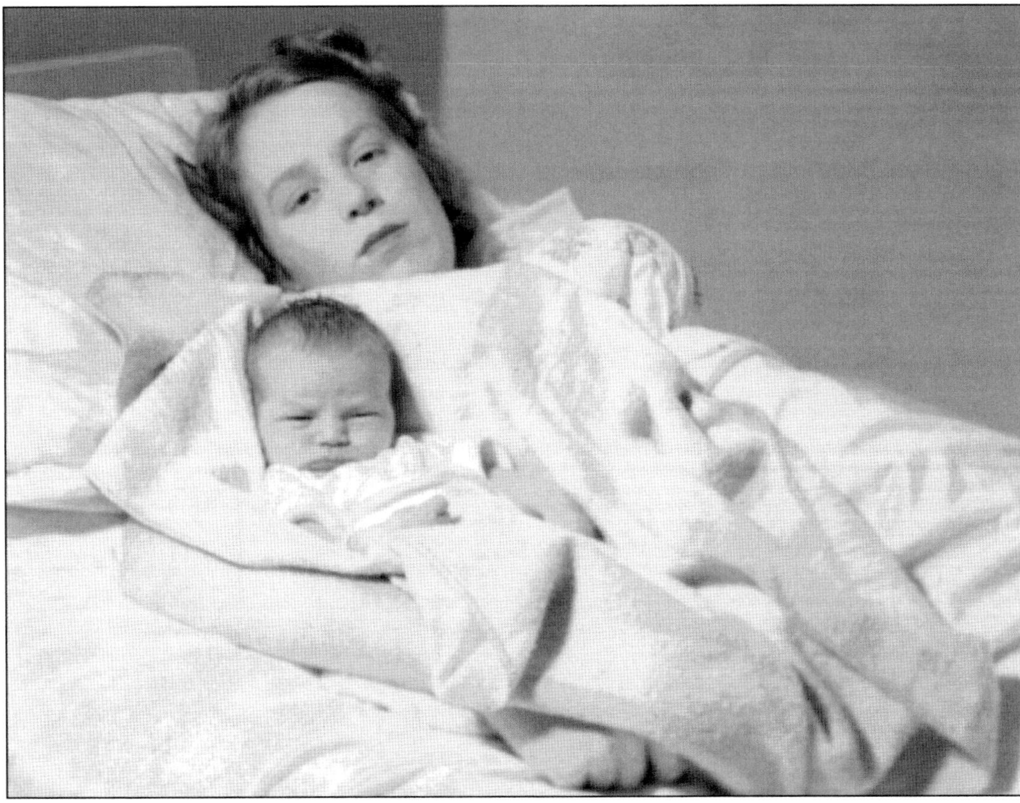

On August 15, 1949, the first baby was born at the newly opened Mercer General Hospital. Pictured are Harrodsburg resident and mother Juanita Yeast and her baby, Claudia Day Yeast Dunning.

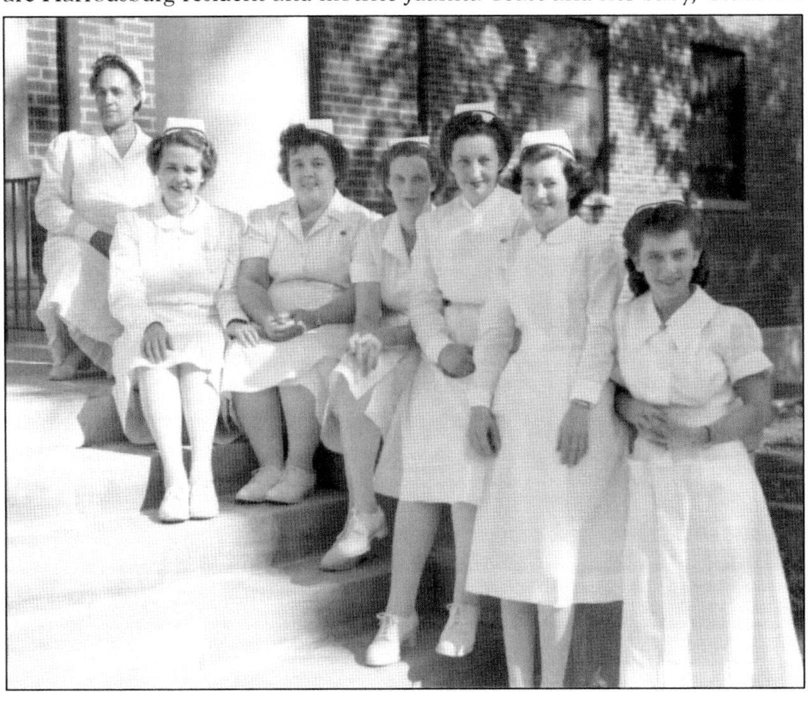

The staff nurses pose on the steps of the new Mercer General Hospital in 1949. They are, from left to right, Mary Utley, Mrs. Wampler, Lyda Todd Cornelius, Louise Stopher, Linnie Merriman, Darcie Millard, and Nellie Watts.

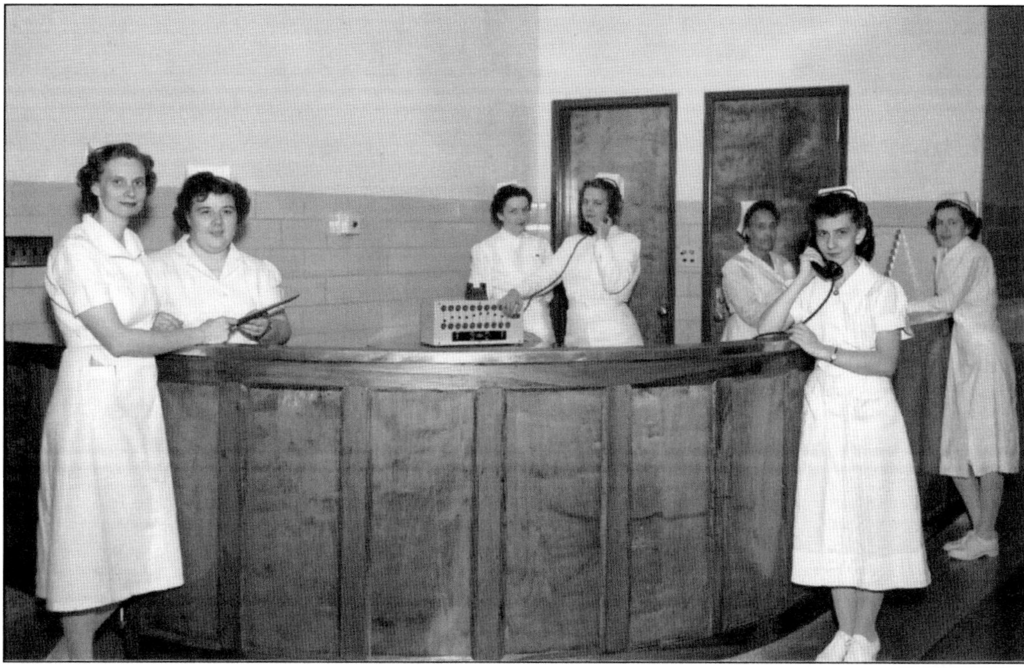

This 1949 photograph shows a group of nurses posing for the camera at the nurses' station in the new Mercer General Hospital. They are, from left to right, Louise Stopher, Lyda Cornelius, Linnie Merriman, unidentified, Mary Utley, Nellie Watts, and Darcie Millard.

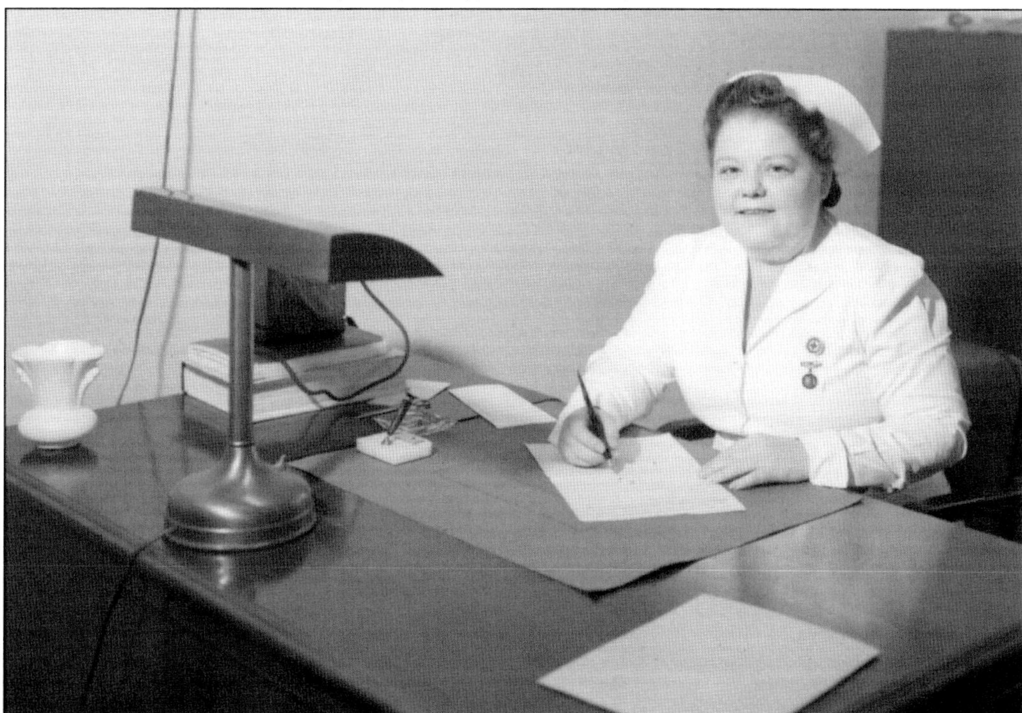

Deloris Wilson, director of nurses, is shown at her desk in 1949 at the new Mercer General Hospital, later renamed Haggin Memorial Hospital.

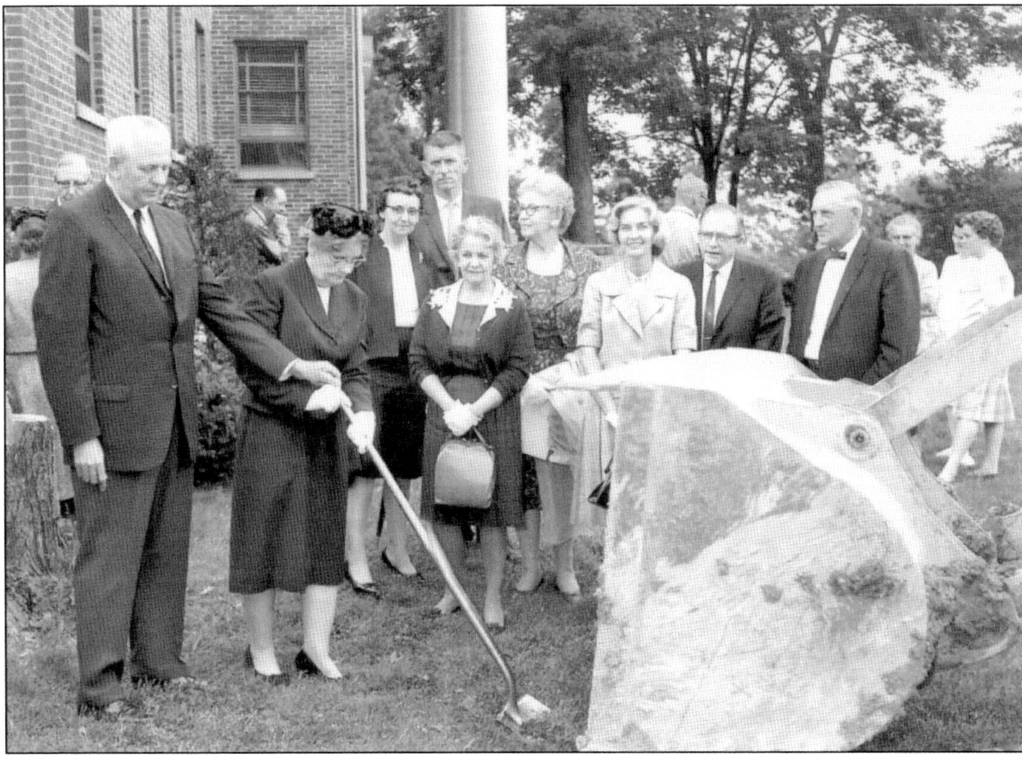

Pictured is the 1964 ground-breaking ceremony for the new Anna Elliott Bohon wing at the Haggin Memorial Hospital. Bohon is shown with the shovel, and assisting her is hospital board chairman Maurice Watts. The ceremony was attended by local civic leaders and residents who were proud to be able to honor Bohon for her years of service to Harrodsburg.

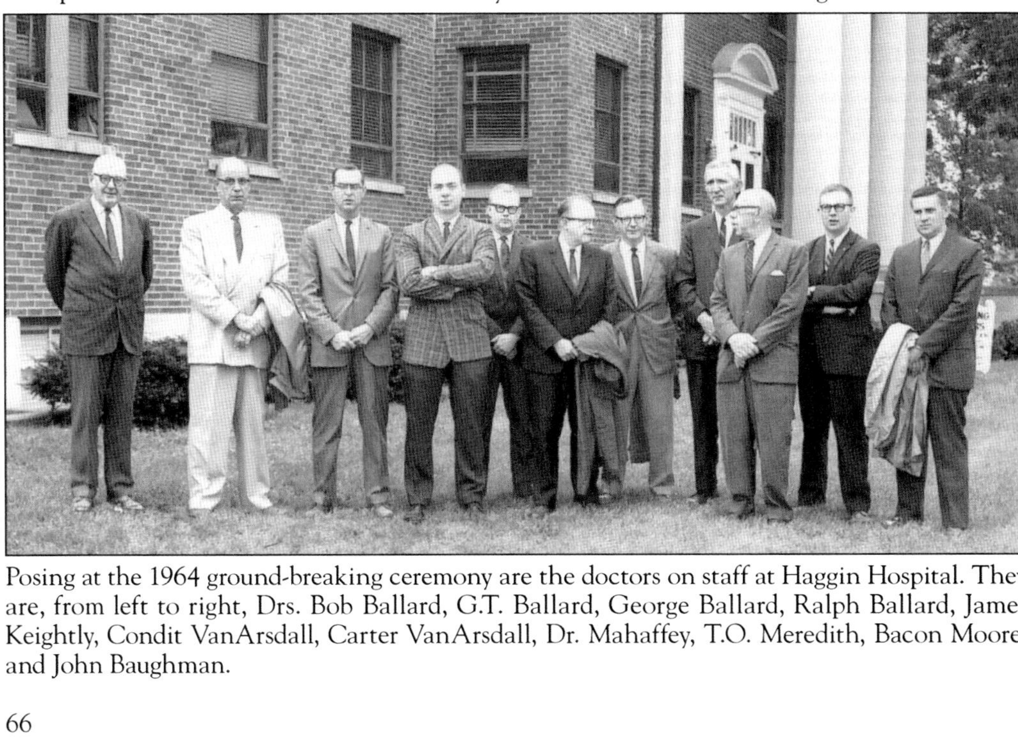

Posing at the 1964 ground-breaking ceremony are the doctors on staff at Haggin Hospital. They are, from left to right, Drs. Bob Ballard, G.T. Ballard, George Ballard, Ralph Ballard, James Keightly, Condit VanArsdall, Carter VanArsdall, Dr. Mahaffey, T.O. Meredith, Bacon Moore, and John Baughman.

Four

Fairs and Parades

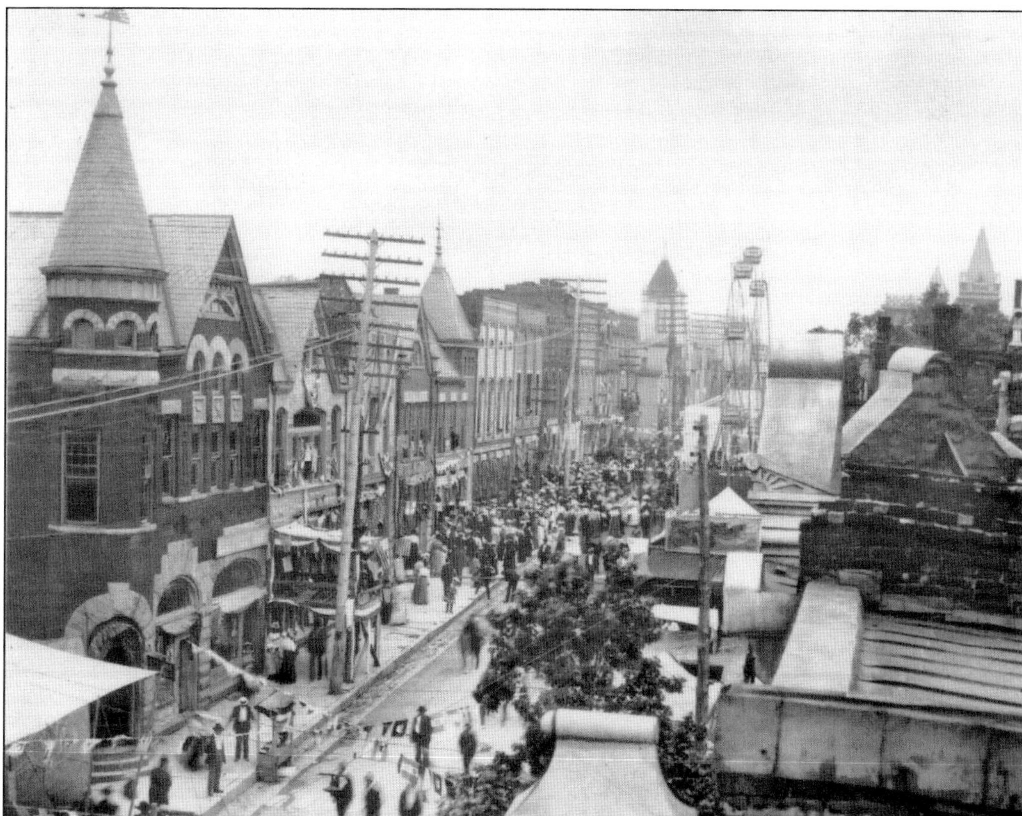

The turn of the century was a time of merriment in the streets. Street fairs and carnivals traveled from town to town during the summer months, literally setting up on Main Street. In Harrodsburg, South Main Street was blocked off for from Poplar Street to the junction with Beaumont and Moreland Avenues. Also around this time, traveling circuses would arrive at the train depot, parade through town to attract attention, and set up in any nearby vacant lot.

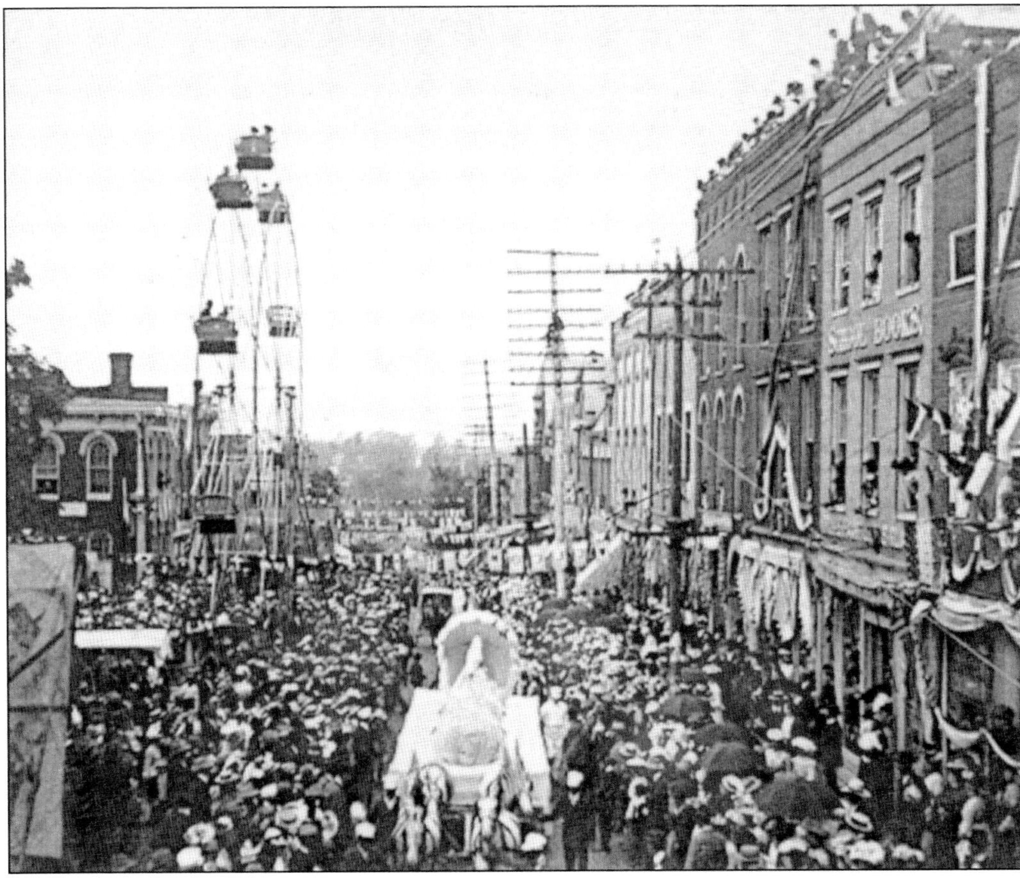

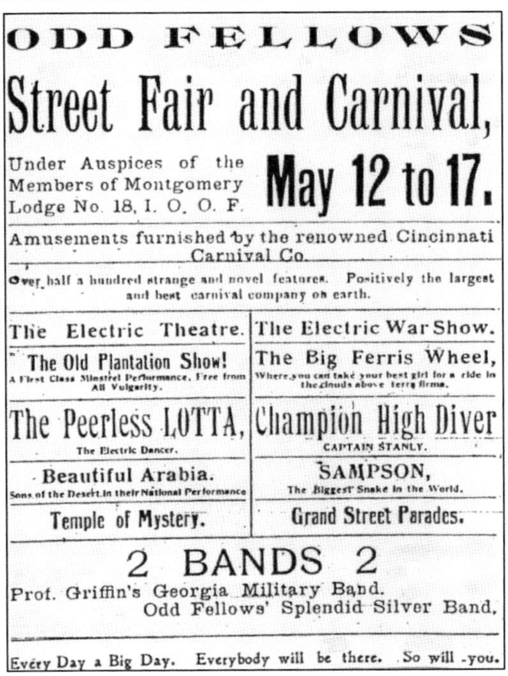

ODD FELLOWS

Street Fair and Carnival,

Under Auspices of the Members of Montgomery Lodge No. 18, I. O. O. F.

May 12 to 17.

Amusements furnished by the renowned Cincinnati Carnival Co.

Over half a hundred strange and novel features. Positively the largest and best carnival company on earth.

The Electric Theatre.	The Electric War Show.
The Old Plantation Show! A First Class Minstrel Performance, Free from All Vulgarity.	The Big Ferris Wheel, Where you can take your best girl for a ride in the clouds above terra firma.
The Peerless LOTTA, The Electric Dancer.	Champion High Diver CAPTAIN STANLY.
Beautiful Arabia. Sons of the Desert in their National Performance	SAMPSON, The Biggest Snake in the World.
Temple of Mystery.	Grand Street Parades.

2 BANDS 2

Prof. Griffin's Georgia Military Band.
Odd Fellows' Splendid Silver Band.

Every Day a Big Day. Everybody will be there. So will you.

In the above photograph, a parade can barely make its way through the solid mass of people on South Main Street. A premium or prize was offered to the person who brought the most people to town in one wagon. The *Harrodsburg Herald* reported in an article, "Carter Rose won for having 132 in his wagon. R.E. Cunningham brought 155, but broke a wagon wheel and was unable to reach Main Street. W.J. Debaun was on his way from Perryville with 513 in his rig, but lost a bolt at Salt River bridge and could get no further." The left picture is a copy of the fair advertisement in the newspaper, listing exotic attractions such as, "Sampson, the biggest snake in the world," "Lotta, the electric dancer," and the "Temple of Mystery." No wonder the streets were packed!

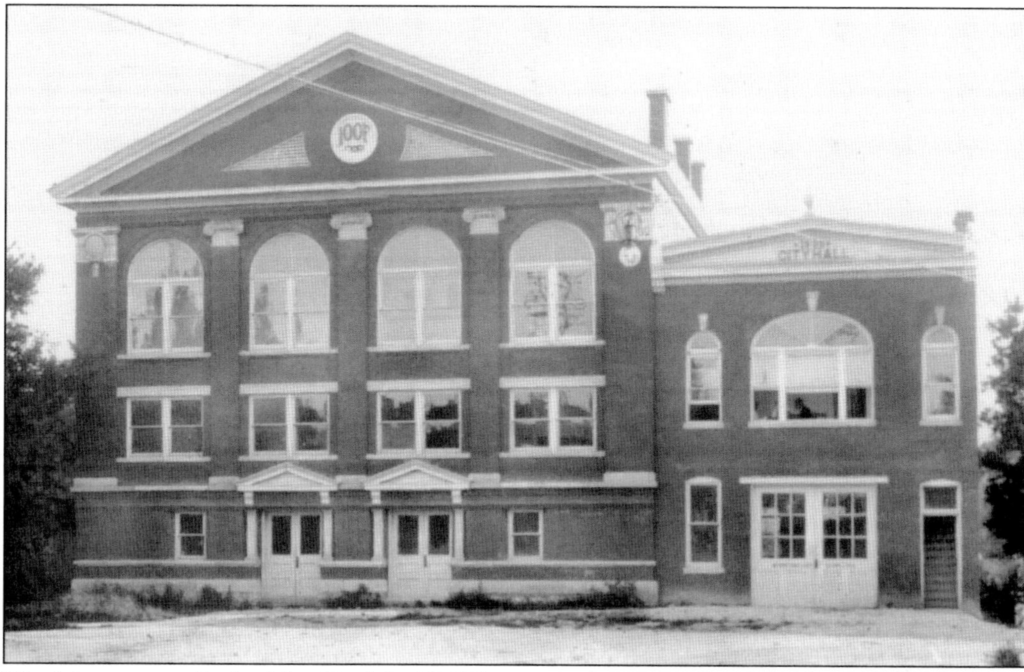

The Montgomery Lodge No. 18 of the IOOF sponsored many of the street fairs. The lodge room was in the opera house at the top of South Main Street, pictured above. Inside the circle at the top of the building is the IOOF emblem, a three-link chain representing Friendship, Love, and Truth. One explanation as to the meaning of the name *odd fellows* says they were odd because it was unusual to find people who followed noble values in the 19th century. The photograph below shows members of the Odd Fellows Lodge gathered on Main Street. Two are identified: Charles Corn and D.M. Hutton (with the ribbon on his lapel) stand together at the center.

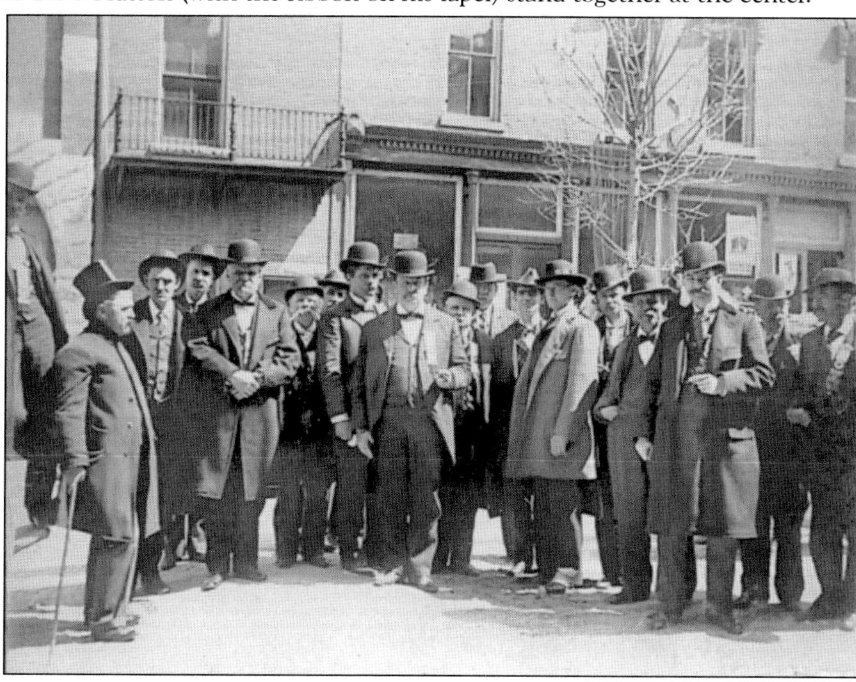

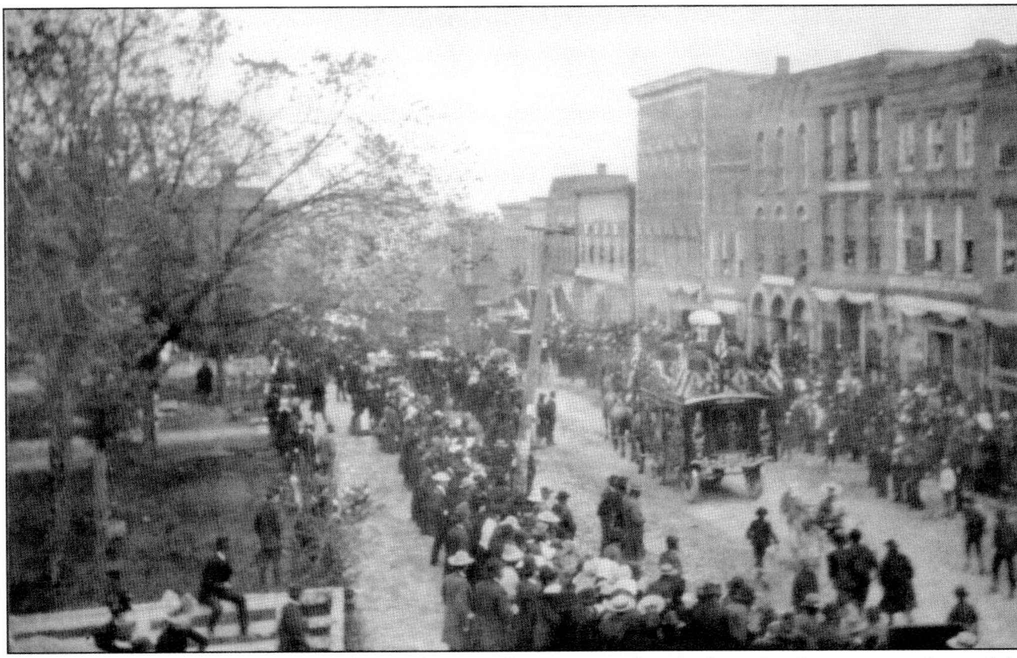

The exact date of this photograph is unknown, but it was taken before the devastating fires of the 1890s, which destroyed much of the Main Street area of Harrodsburg. A circus has arrived by train and is making its way from the Harrodsburg depot to Main Street and on to the staging area.

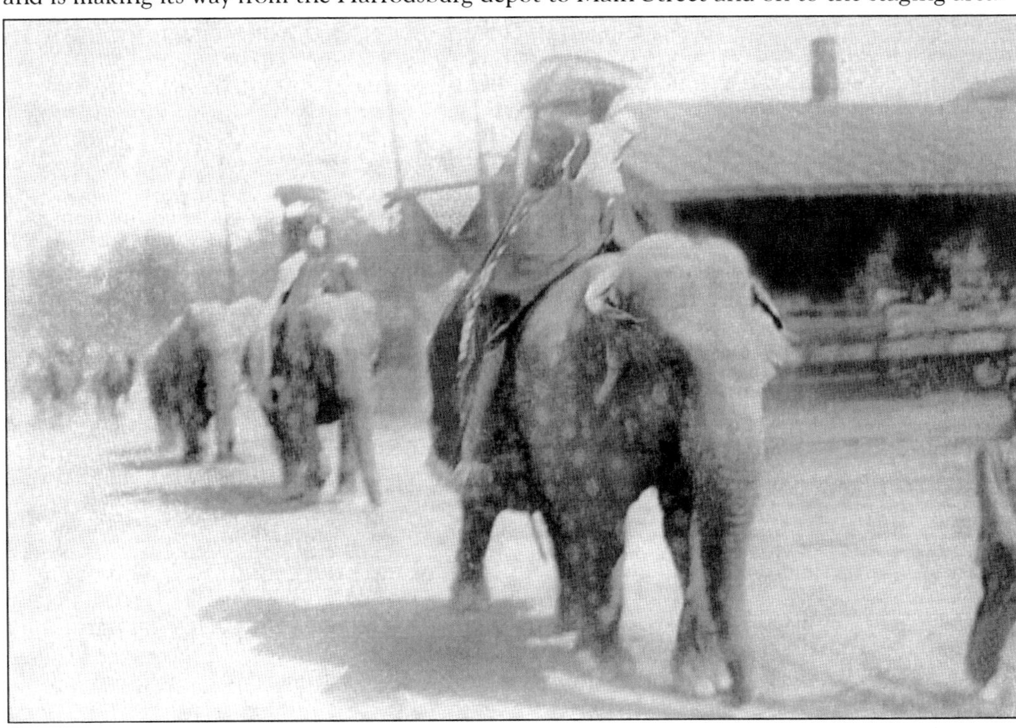

Here, a parade of elephants moves up Marimon Avenue past the Harrodsburg depot. At the rear of the line of elephants are what looks like several camels. These circuses moved by rail throughout the area and would stay for three to four days at a time. (H.C. Wood.)

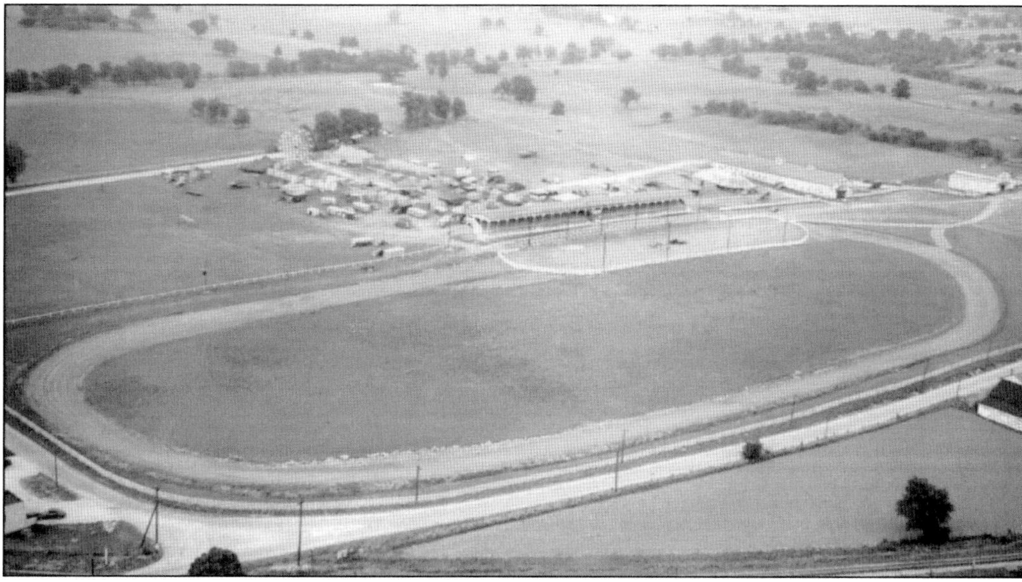

The Blue Grass Fair and Horse Show, located at the city limits on Cornishville Street, opened in 1947 and closed in 1951. Owned by local horseman and business owner Glave Sims, the property, as seen in the above photograph, had a 5,000-seat grandstand, a quarter-mile track, two barns that could stable 225 horses when full, an 11-room house for family, and surrounding acreage. The first show in June 1947 was a four-day extravaganza featuring a parade, a concert by the Lawrenceburg High School Band prior to the horse show, and 10 classes announced by George Swinboard of Lexington, who would become a successful blood stock auctioneer. There was a carnival with 66 "clean and entertaining concessions." Glave Sims won the blue ribbon, competing at his own show in the roadster class. The bottom photograph shows the entry gate to the property.

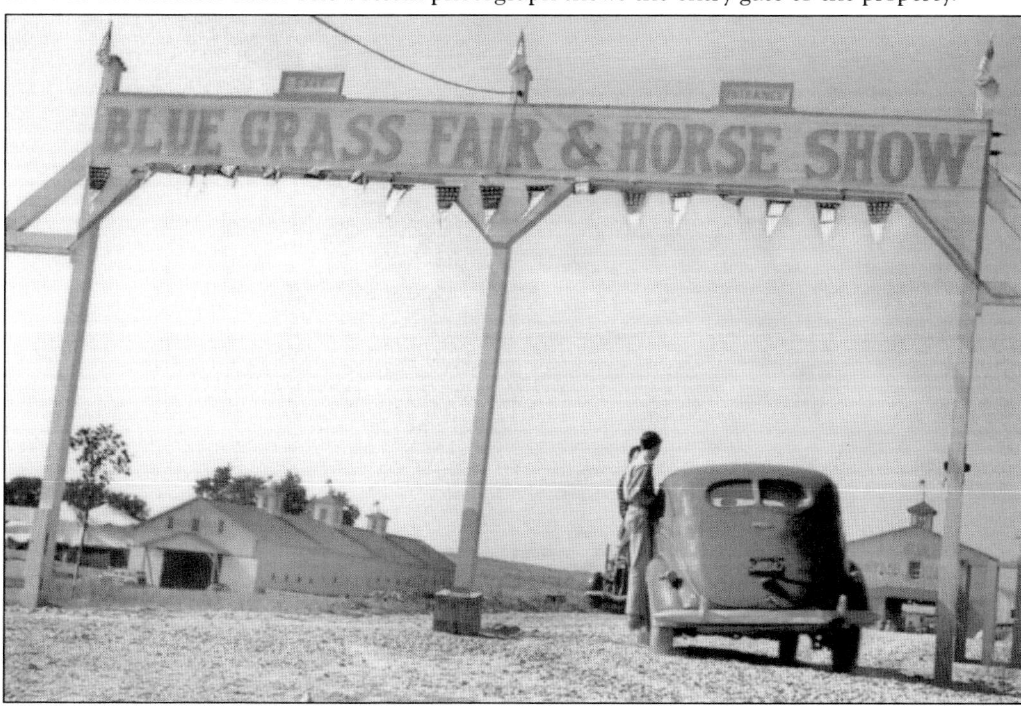

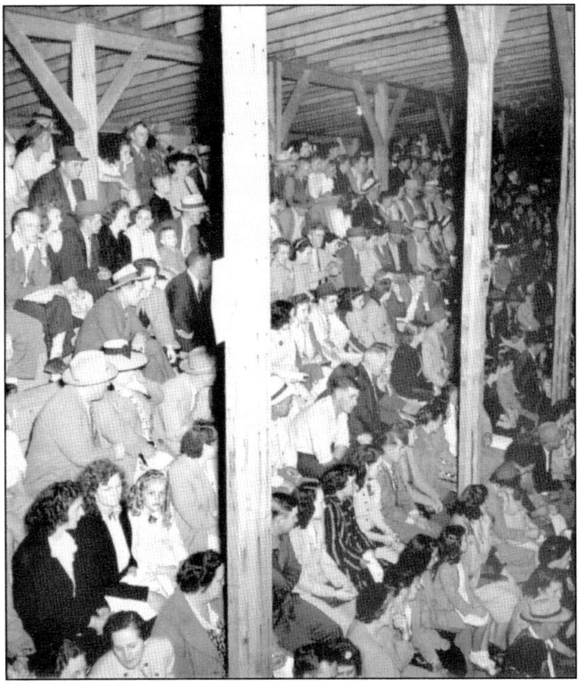

The Blue Grass Fair Grounds hosted yearly horse shows in June (as not to compete with the Mercer County Fair and Horse Show in July), one-day plug horse derbies, mule races, and many other events. The Blue Grass Auto Racing Association, organized in Harrodsburg, used the track to host interstate championships for midget automobile racing. The races featured "big-name drivers from surrounding states." The *Cross Roads Jamboree*, a two-hour radio show, was broadcast there in 1947. In addition to horse activities, there were foxhound, coonhound, and bird dog shows. The picture to the left shows the shoulder-to-shoulder crowd at a 1949 fair. The photograph below shows Anna Armstrong and her mother, Kathleen, on the carousel in 1949.

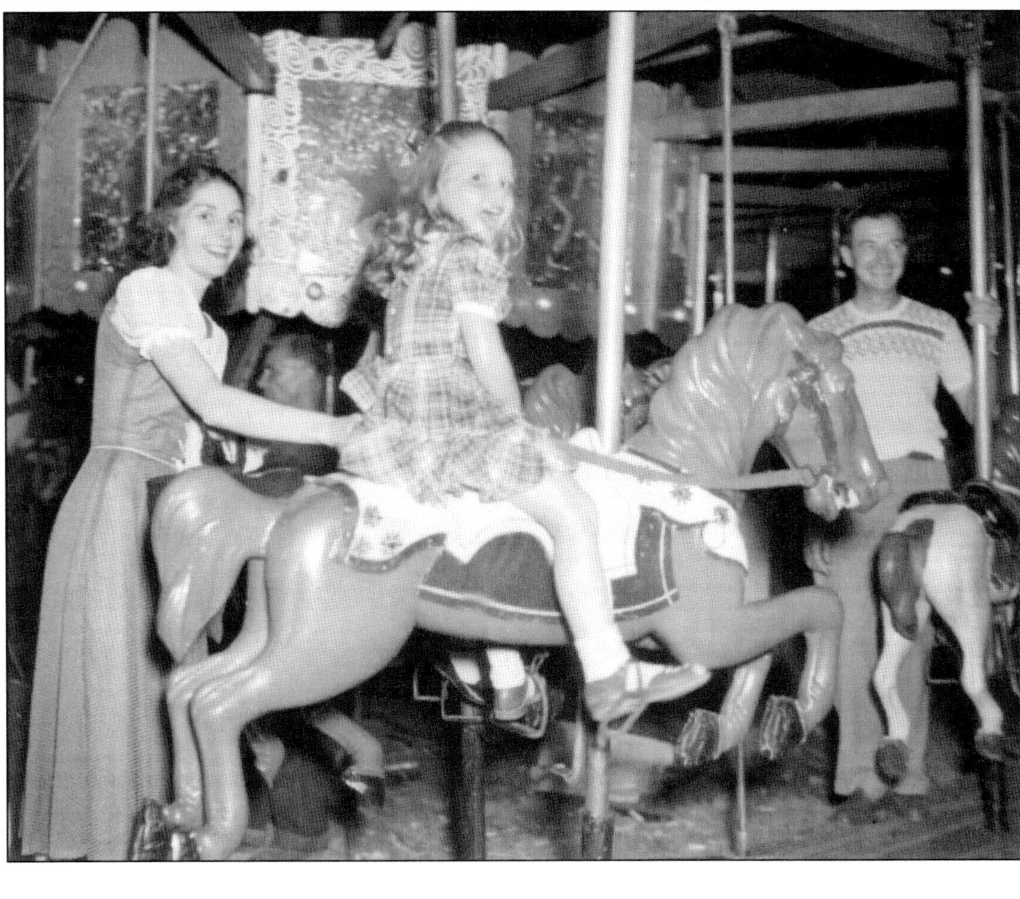

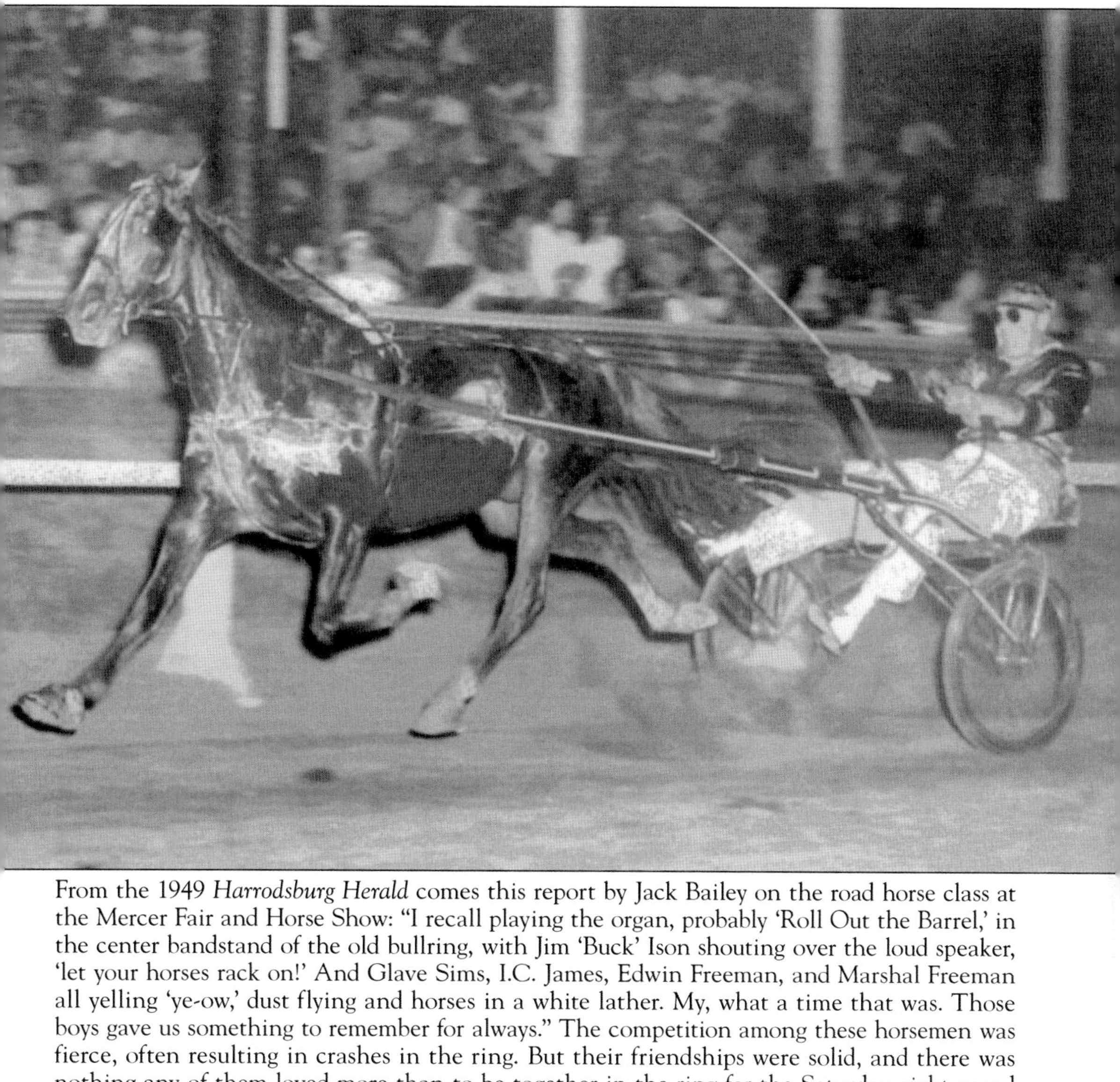

From the 1949 *Harrodsburg Herald* comes this report by Jack Bailey on the road horse class at the Mercer Fair and Horse Show: "I recall playing the organ, probably 'Roll Out the Barrel,' in the center bandstand of the old bullring, with Jim 'Buck' Ison shouting over the loud speaker, 'let your horses rack on!' And Glave Sims, I.C. James, Edwin Freeman, and Marshal Freeman all yelling 'ye-ow,' dust flying and horses in a white lather. My, what a time that was. Those boys gave us something to remember for always." The competition among these horsemen was fierce, often resulting in crashes in the ring. But their friendships were solid, and there was nothing any of them loved more than to be together in the ring for the Saturday-night grand championship class. Glave Sims not only drove road horses, but he also bred and trained them at his Blue Grass Farms, which was part of the fairground property.

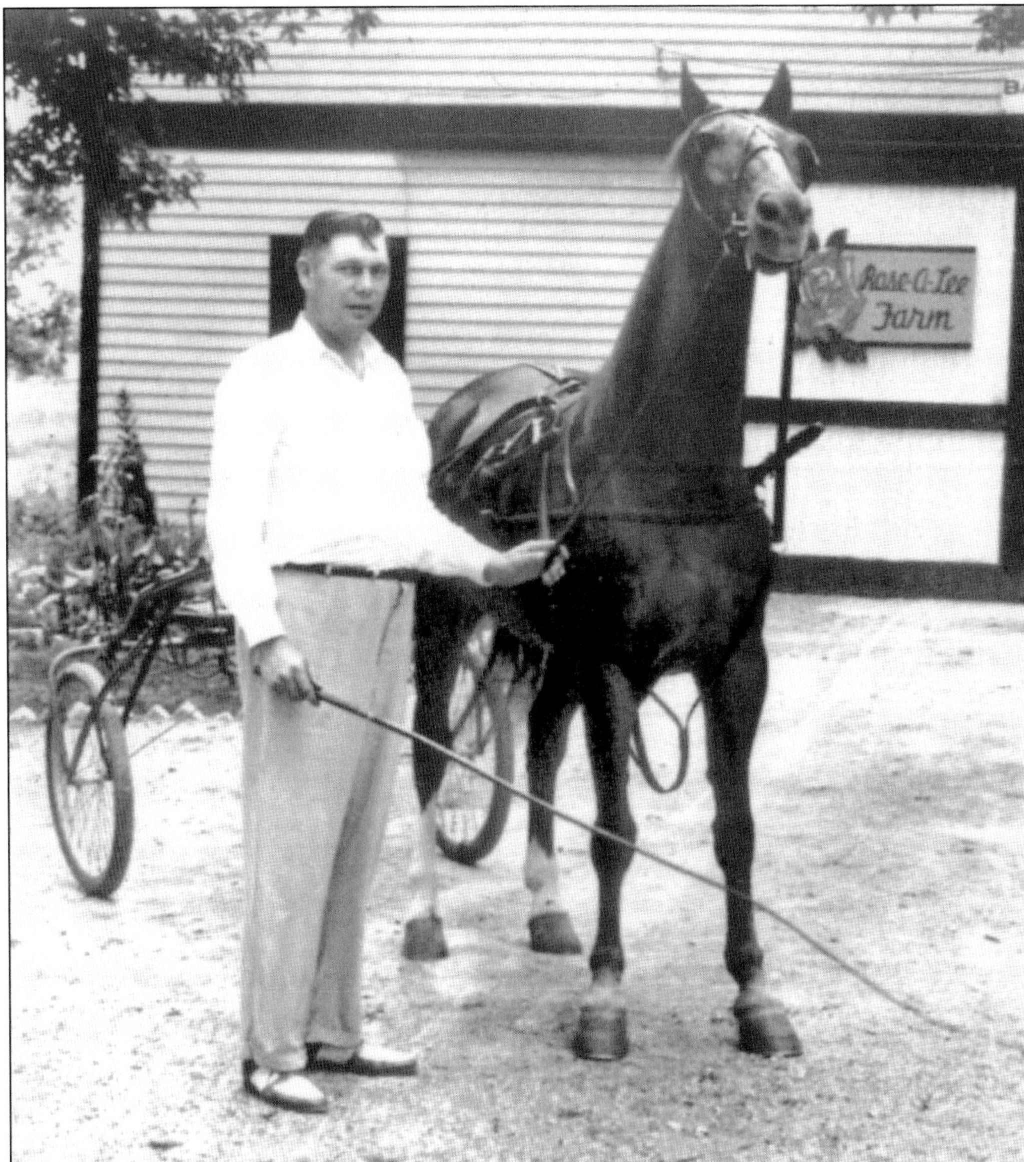

Glave Sims is pictured with his good roadster horse, Guy Baine, who won many blue ribbons in Kentucky and surrounding states. Glave Sims, Dean Pugh, and horses from the Sims stables, including Guy Baine, went to Georgia for shooting of the 1951 film, *I'd Climb the Highest Mountain*. They supplied horses, doubled for the stars in dangerous scenes, and served as technical advisors. This 20th Century Fox movie starred Susan Hayward, William Lundigan, and Rory Calhoun. Guy Baine died in 1954 at age 14. Because of failing health, Glave Sims sold the Blue Grass Fair Grounds property at absolute auction in 1951, thus ending the five-year run for the horse show. The grandstand and a barn were demolished, and the acreage was divided for the Blue Grass Farms Fair Grounds subdivision. The family home and one barn remain in use today.

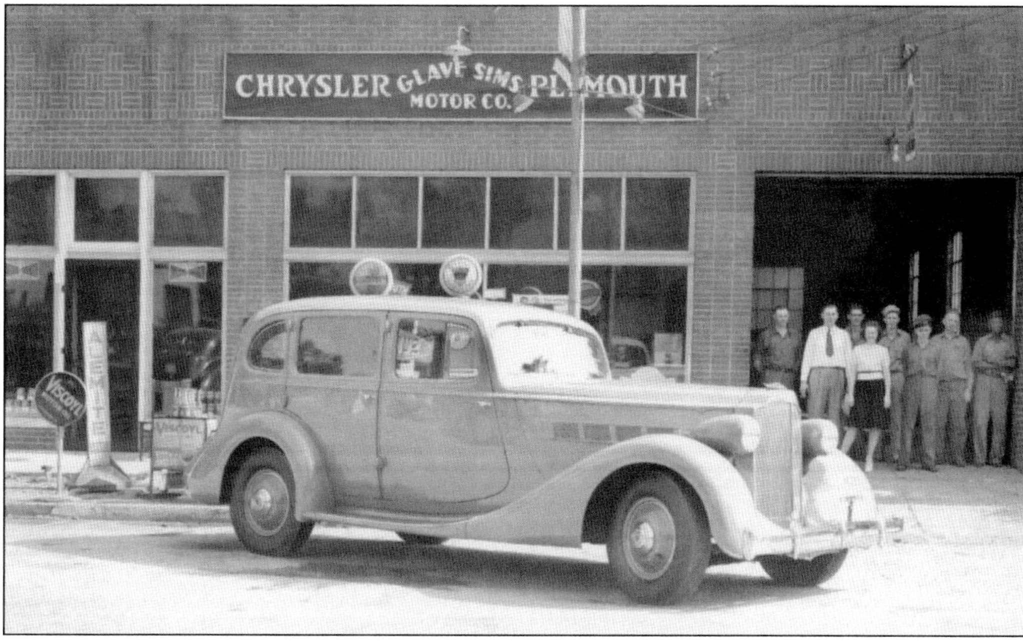

In addition to his love of horses, Glave Sims was a local businessman who worked hard and played hard in his short life of 48 years. In the 1930s and 1940s, he operated Glave Sims Motor Company on West Lexington Street. In 1943, he sold it and bought the Coyle Funeral Home on East Lexington Street and renamed it Glave Sims Funeral Home, where he died of a heart attack in 1958. During the 1940s and 1950s, he owned a realty company and was an auctioneer. Locals often referred to him as "the man who gets the high dollar" and "the man with the silver-tongued voice." Sims (in the white shirt) and his employees at the dealership pose for an advertising picture in the photograph above. The picture below shows the funeral home and its ambulance and hearse.

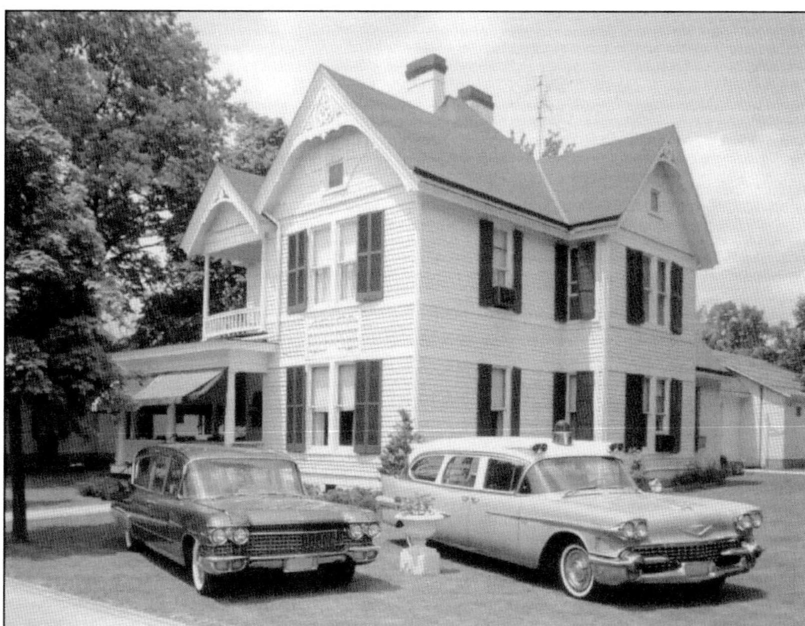

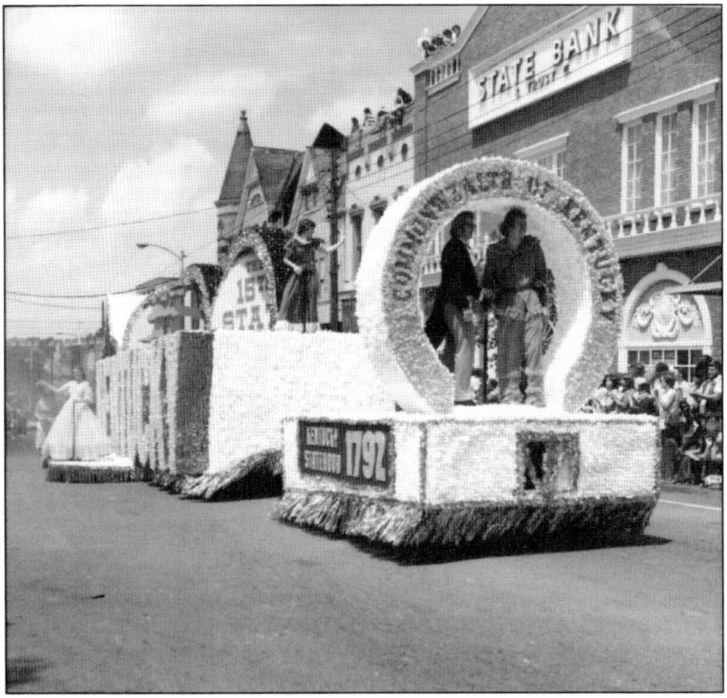

Harrodsburg has hosted many parades through the years, but the one on June 16, 1974, for Harrodsburg's Bicentennial Celebration was a first-class one. This photograph shows the large and professionally made Commonwealth of Kentucky float on its way up Main Street.

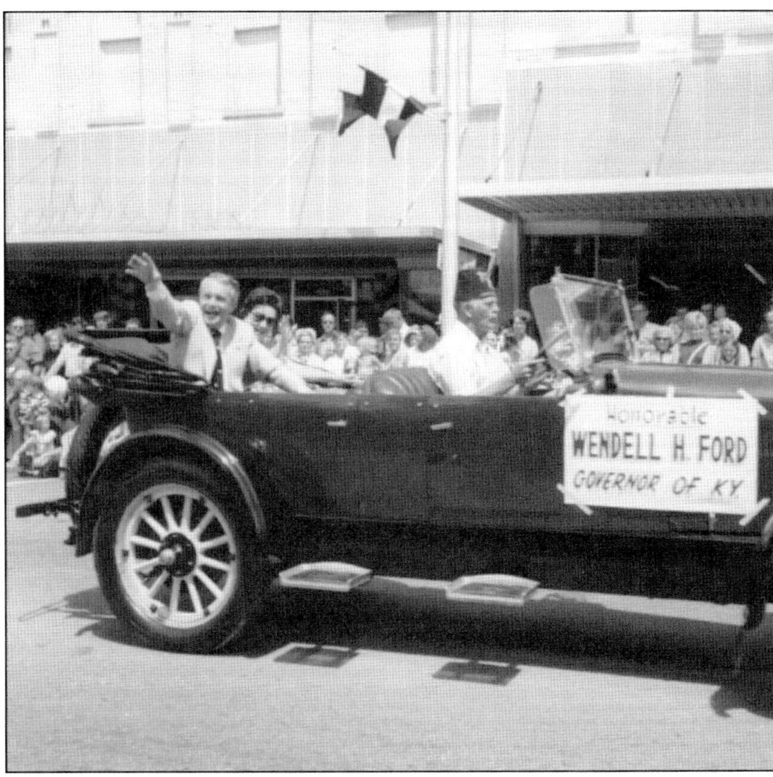

Kentucky governor Wendell Ford appears in a vintage car on his way to Fort Harrod, where the ceremonies for the 200th anniversary of the founding of Harrodsburg were held.

Five

Businesses

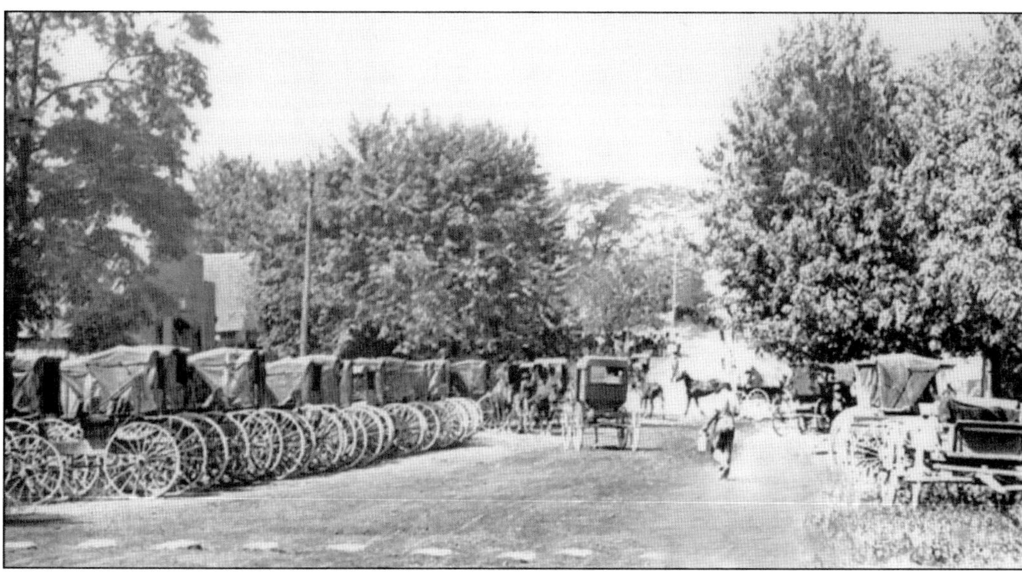

This late-1800s view of Broadway Street between Main and Chiles Streets shows a long row of buggies in front of Givens Livery. At the turn of the century, Broadway Street was often referred to as Market Street because market days occurred there three days a week. Farmers would bring in their produce to sell to the townspeople. Whether this is a market day or not, it looks like business is booming.

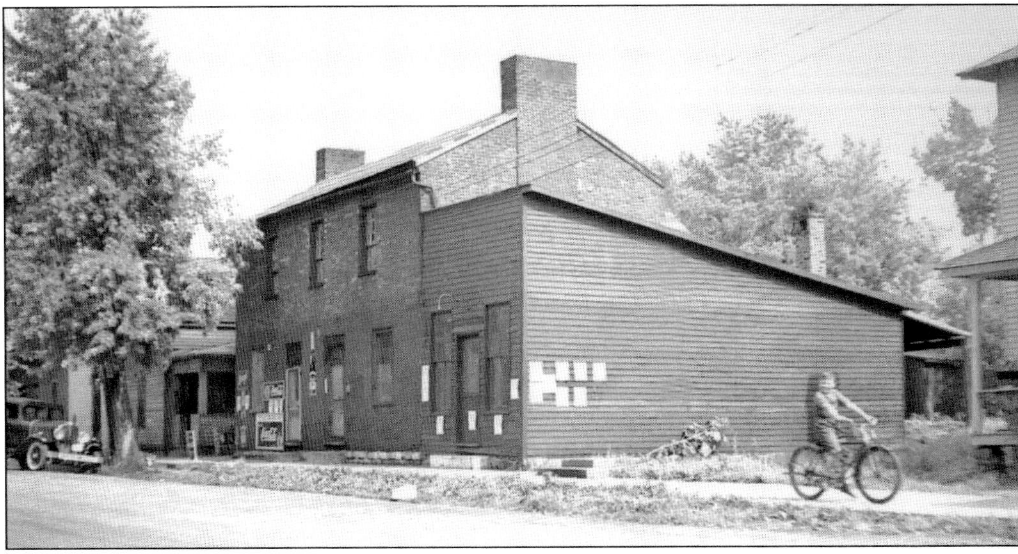

This south-side block of Broadway Street between Main and Chiles Streets (above) was once the location of several longtime landmarks. This 1930s photograph shows the two-story brick building that was Doneghi's Tavern in the mid-1800s. According to a newspaper report, the Irish "turnpikers" who were building a section of road nearby entertained in a "vigorous style" on Saturday nights, often staging fights among themselves, as was the tradition among many early construction gangs. The building was razed in 1938. The Broadway Cafe (below) was a longstanding landmark in the black community, noted as early as 1908 on the Sanborn insurance map as a lunchroom. It was a happening place in the 1950s. According to recollections of Jack Bailey, on hot summer Saturday nights, the jukebox blared while the folks inside jitterbugged relentlessly. The café was razed in 1962.

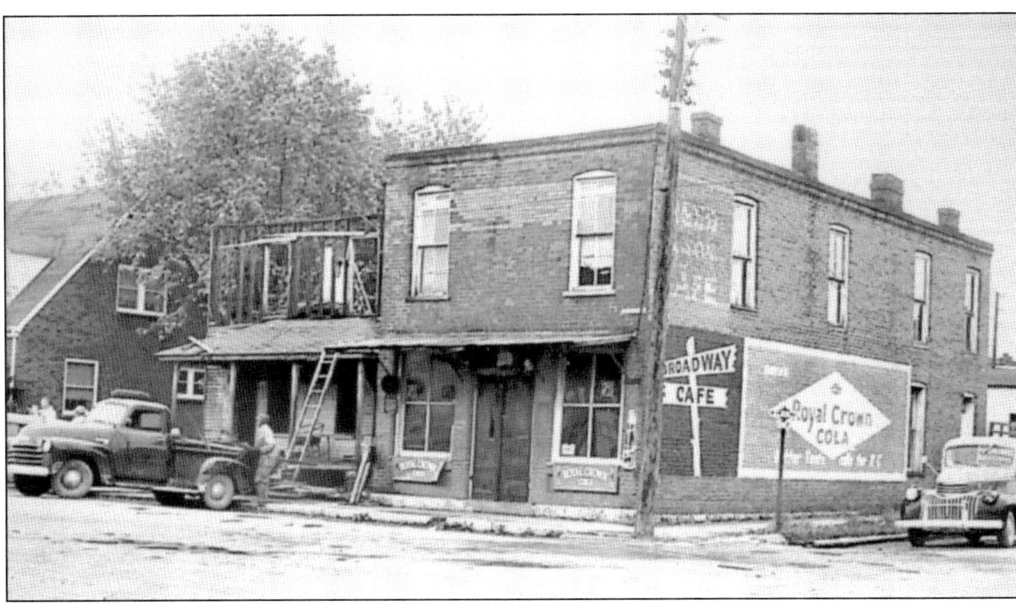

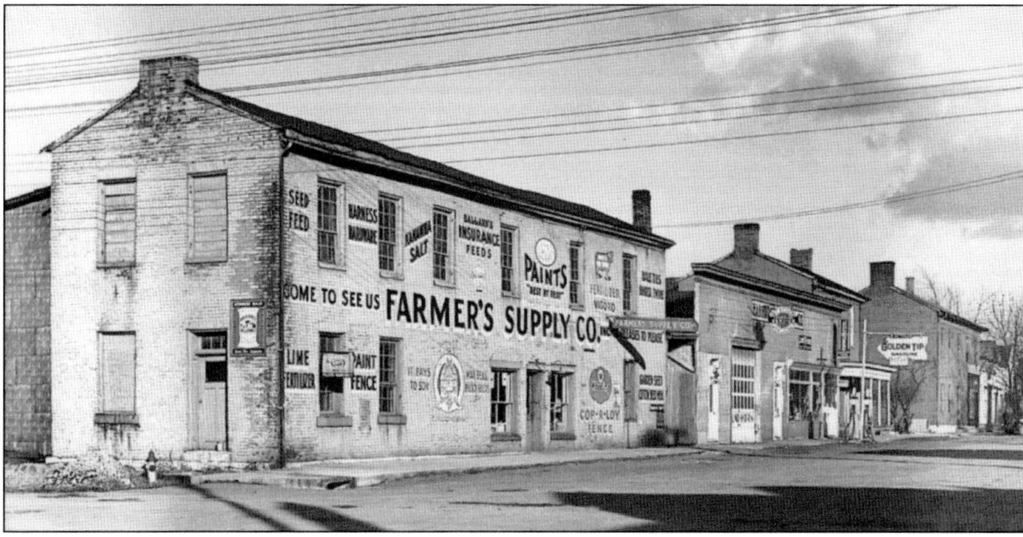

From the late 1800s to the early 1900s, this north-side block of Broadway Street between Main and Chiles Streets was a busy, commercial area. A 1908 Sanborn insurance map shows a steam laundry, a livery and farm implement store, a boardinghouse, and a grocery. The Farmer's Supply Company building was originally Dallas Chinn's Steam Laundry, but by 1914, that business had been replaced by a second livery stable. Both liveries went out of business—most likely during the 1920s—when the horse and buggy gave way to the automobile. The Farmer's Supply building continued as a seed-grinding and farm supply business until it was bought by the city in 1967 and torn down to make way for the new site of the police and fire departments. The image below shows the Harrodsburg Motor Company, which replaced Givens Livery Stable.

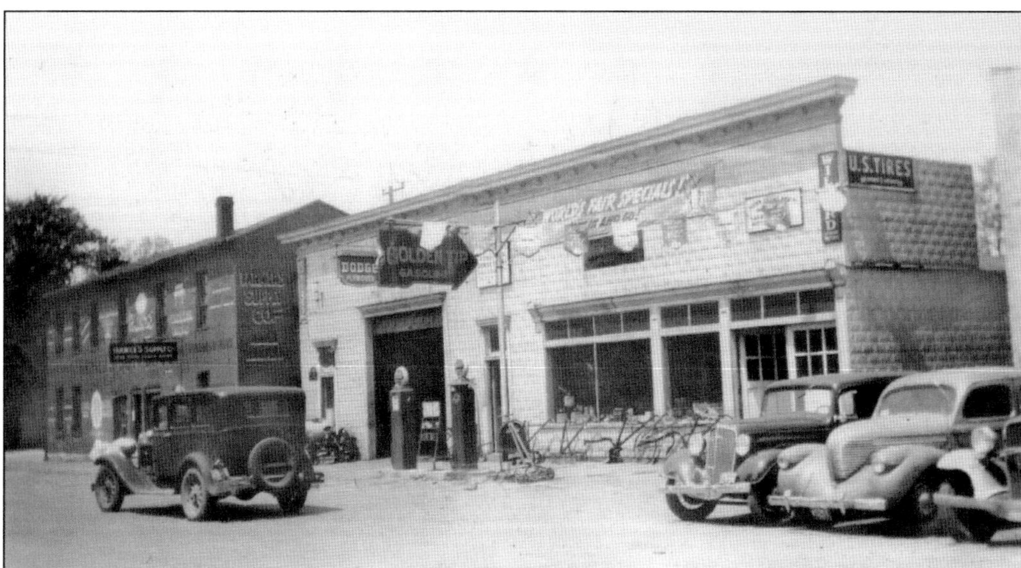

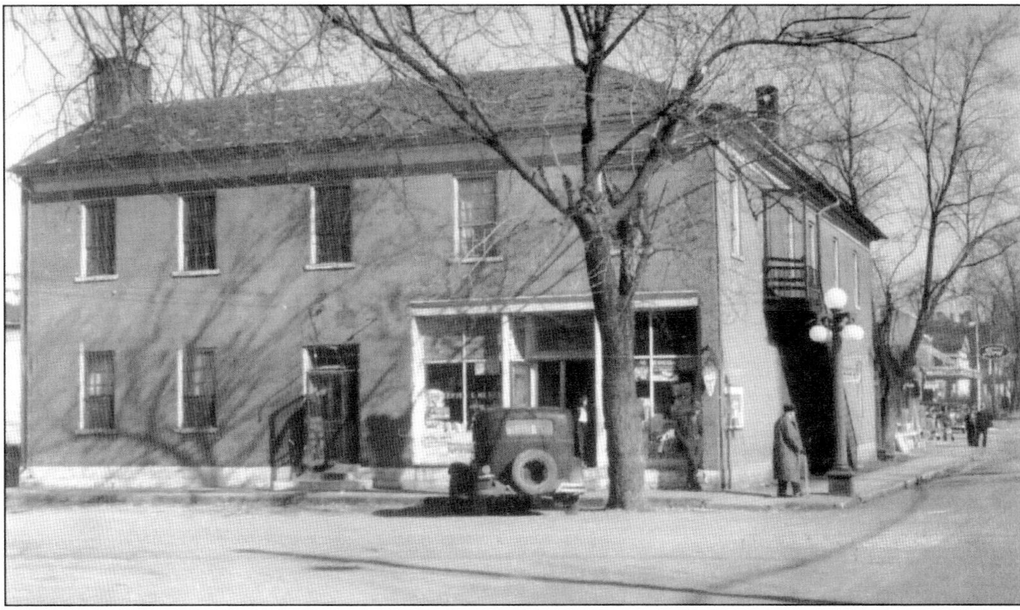

Above is a 1930s view of the building that has been a landmark on Broadway Street since it was built by Benjamin Passmore around 1843. It has passed through many hands, and during its 168 years, it has been a hotel, stagecoach stop, boardinghouse, grocery, and is now the offices of the *Harrodsburg Herald* newspaper. When it was the Mercer House, an advertisement read, "The bar is furnished with pure liquors and the best will be sold by the barrel if desired." The photograph below shows the pressroom just after the building became the new home for the *Harrodsburg Herald* in 1953. The machine in this picture is a linotype, which can set an entire line of type on a single metal slug; it was operated by a keyboard similar to that of a typewriter.

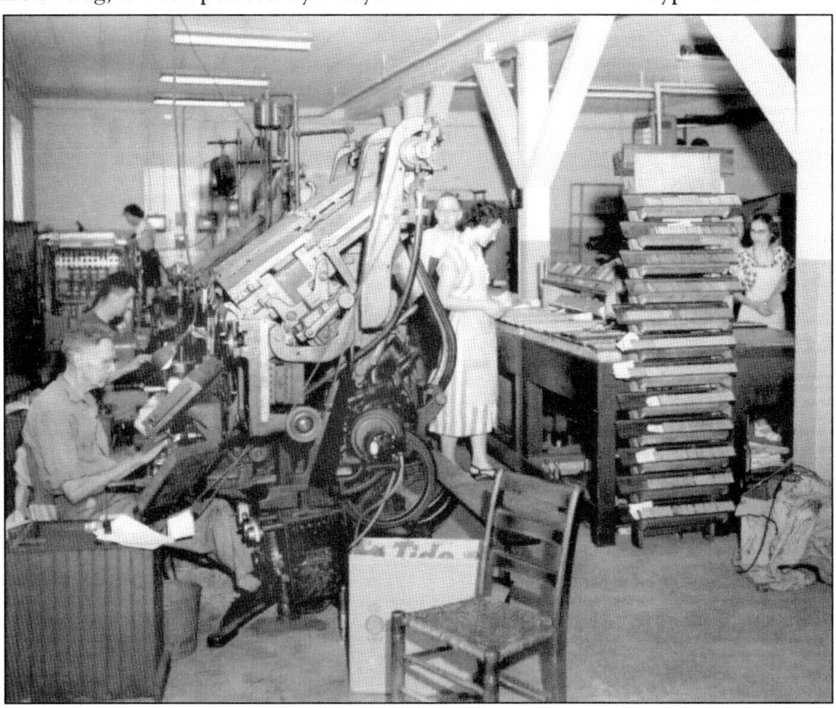

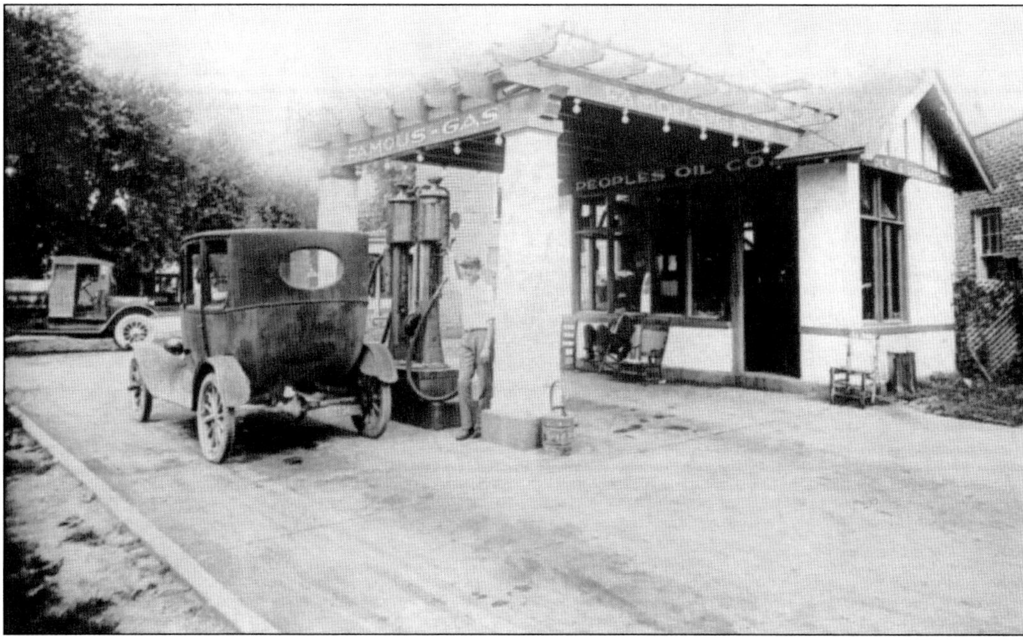

Another fixture at the corner of Broadway and Main Streets was a uniquely styled building for Harrodsburg that housed the town's first service station. An article dated November 16, 1920, reads, "The wayfarer need not lack for gasoline as the city gets its first service station in addition to the established garages. The building is new and erected by the company of Consumers Service Stations, Inc. Rock Island, Illinois and is a bungalow type. Mr. Charles Davis, a Mercer County man who was a local farmer, was in charge of the station." The photograph above shows the original station. Below is a remodeled station with trucks bearing the logo of People's Aetna Oil Co.

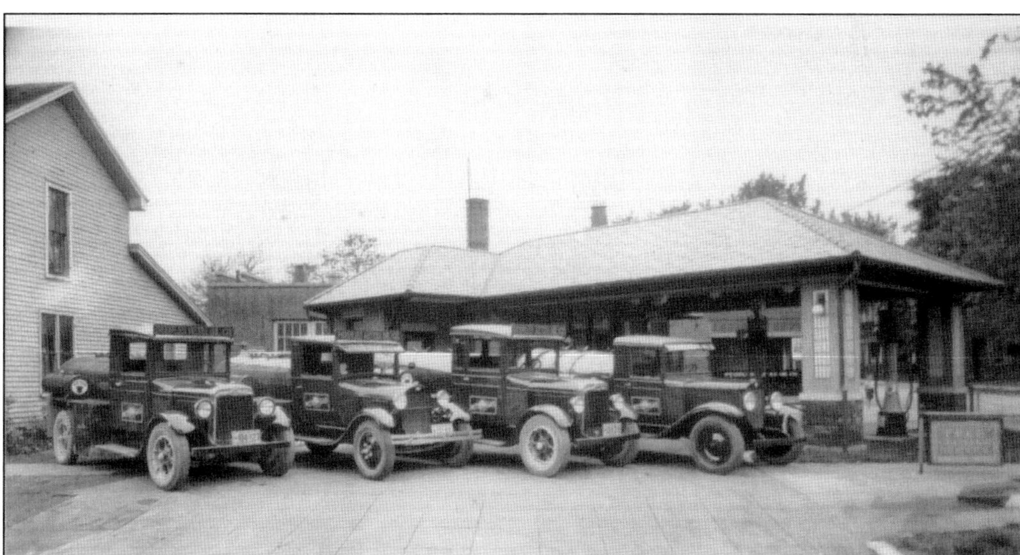

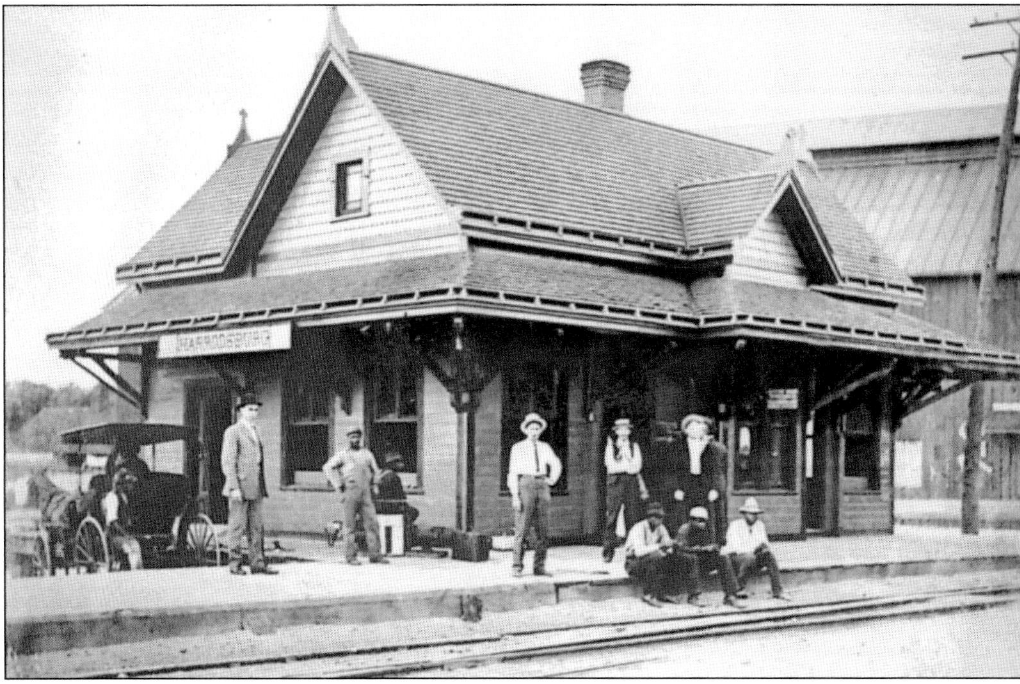

This photograph from the early 1900s shows passengers waiting at the Harrodsburg depot located on Marimon Avenue south of Office Street. Sometime in the early 1900s, the old Southwestern depot on the corner of Office and Greenville Streets (site of the Bus Station restaurant now) was abandoned and this new depot built. By the 1970s, passenger service was no longer profitable, and this building was torn down when it ended.

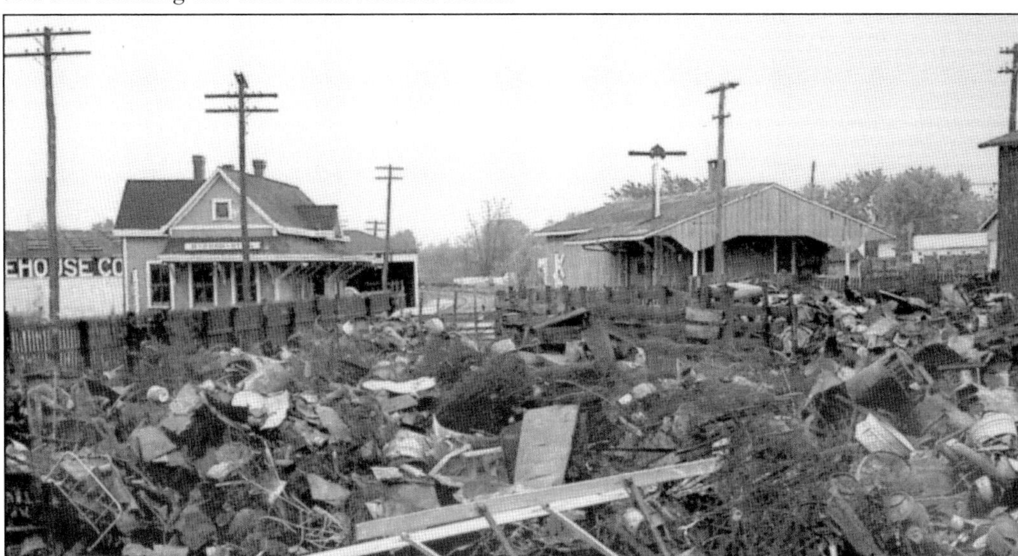

A 1940s view of the Marimon Avenue area shows both the Harrodsburg passenger depot (left) and the freight depot (right). Harrodsburg's rail service started in 1888 when the Louisville Southern line from Lawrenceburg to Harrodsburg began operation. A machine shop, roundhouse, and rail yard with a cattle pen was maintained there. By 1973, Harrodsburg's rail services had ended, and the freight building was being used by a feed and grain business.

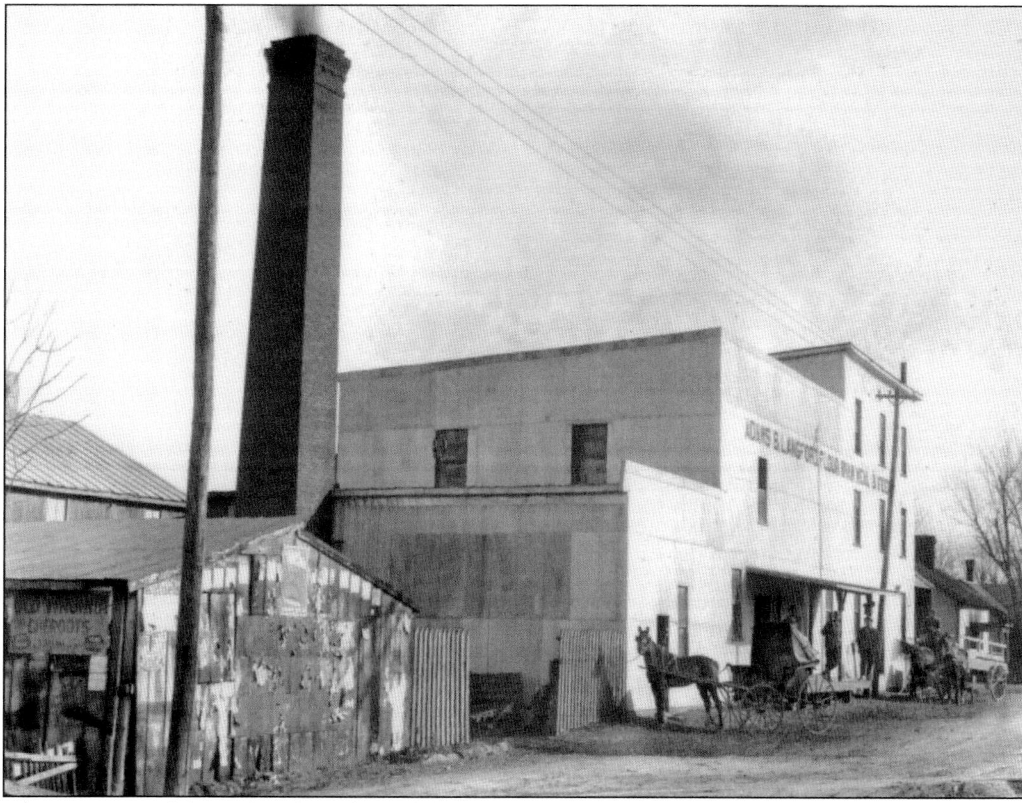

The presence of the railroad tracks and depot in the Marimon Avenue and Office Street area has attracted businesses such as coal yards, brickyards, flour mills, and grain elevators—all benefiting from the close proximity to shipping. In the late 1800s, J.D. Marimon had a flour mill here. By 1908, it was known as the City Roller Mill, and by 1914, it was Adams and Langford, as shown in the photograph above. In the early 1920s, the Sandusky brothers took over its operation. The picture below shows D.T. Cogar's grain elevator and coal yard in the early 1900s. Both Marimon Avenue and Cogar Streets were named for owners of area businesses.

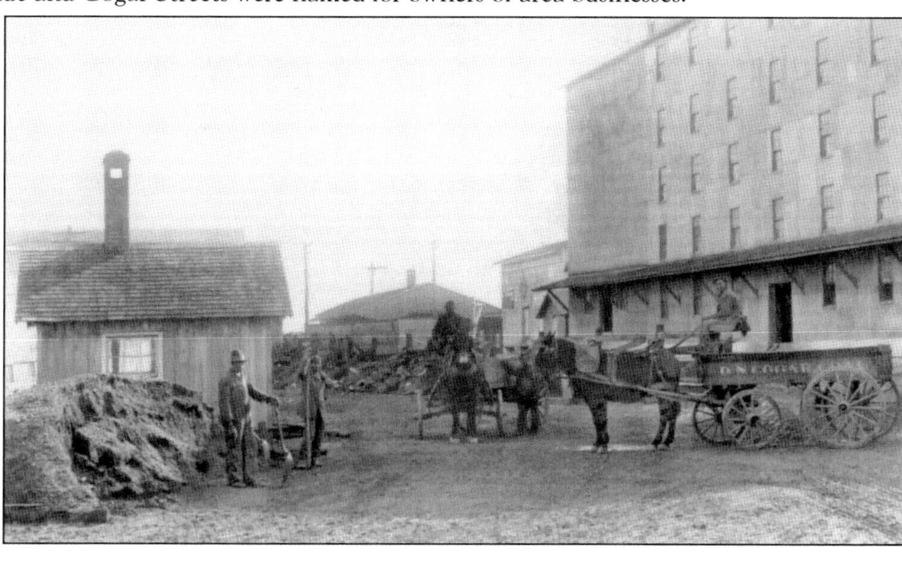

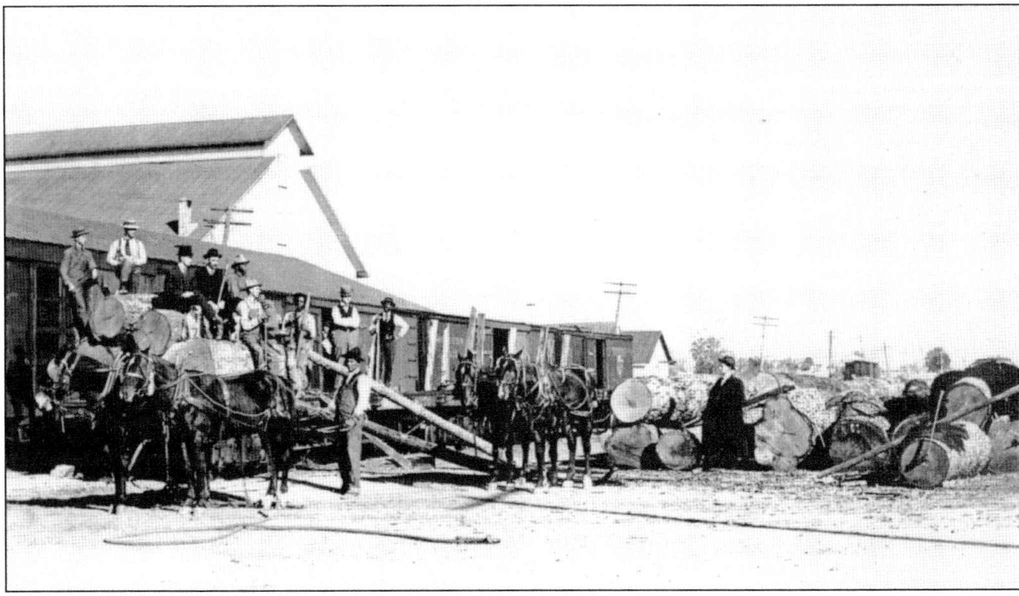

The photograph above is a late-1800s view of the Harrodsburg depot area showing a train waiting for cargo to be loaded. Jack Davenport, the owner of Davenport's Transfer Lines, is standing next to the horses with his hands in his pockets. He has acquired a supply of logs cut in the surrounding area and brought them for shipment. The sizes of the logs indicates a lot of old-growth forest was still left in the county. Below is another photograph of Jack Davenport, with his crew traveling through Harrodsburg with cargo headed for the depot for shipping. But there appears to be only one massive log on the wagon, and the crew is sitting atop it. Logs of this size have long since disappeared from the county.

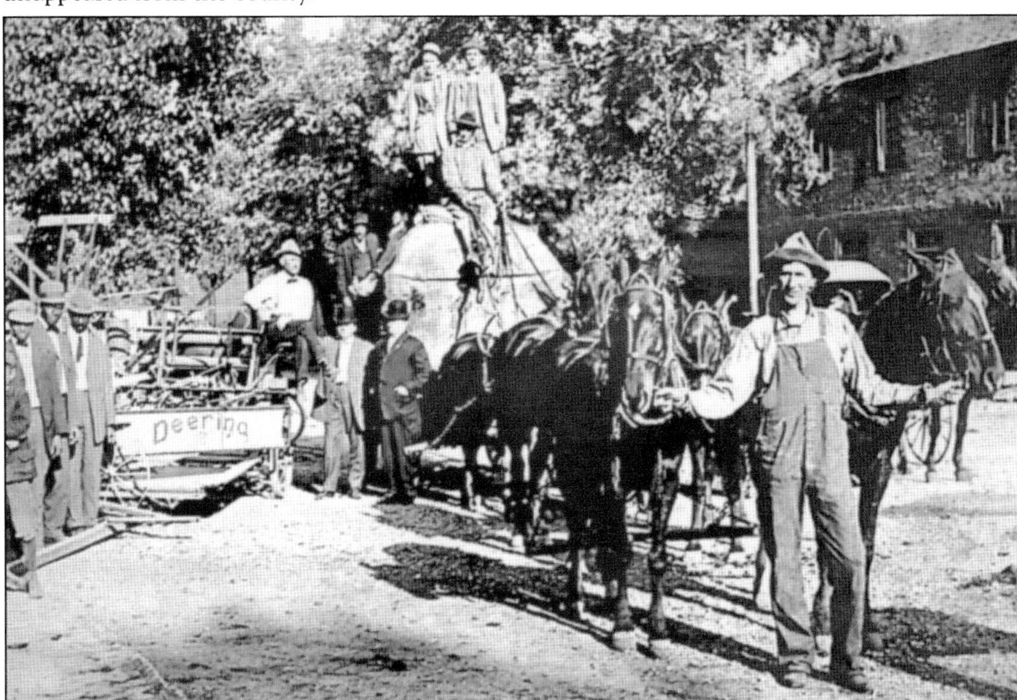

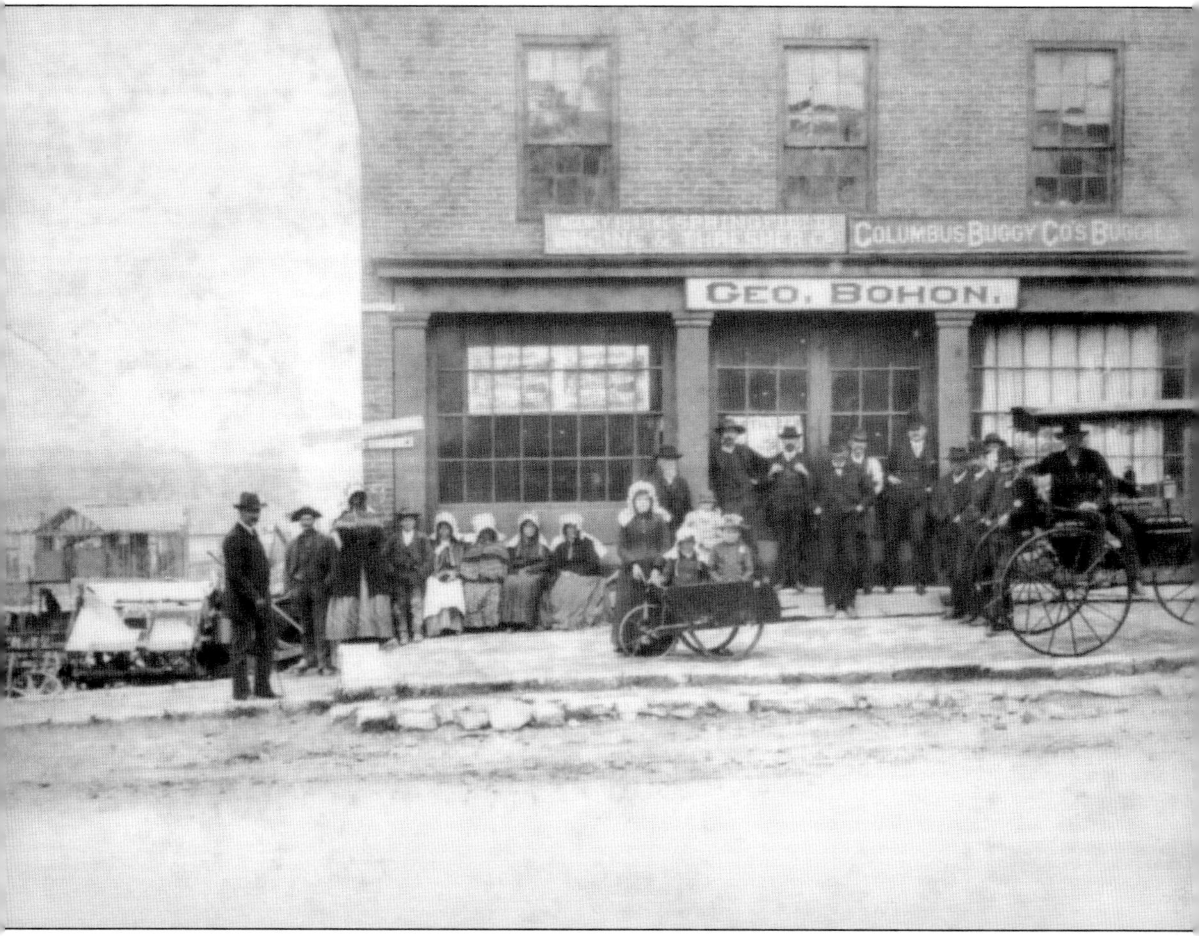

The 1886 Sanborn insurance map shows the George T. Bohon Carriage Factory on the corner of Main and East Office Streets, suggesting the manufacturing of Bluegrass Buggies was begun there. George Bohon had varied business interests before starting as a dealer in buggies, wagons, and agricultural implements. A description of the business on a sale flyer reads, "The most reliable house in Central Kentucky for any kind of farming implements is that of George Bohon. If you want a farm wagon, buggy, carriage, engine, sawmill, or thresher, he can supply you with the best make. Too many goods—they must go! Hemp and manila twine for everybody!" The business closed in the early 1920s, and the building was demolished to make way for the Harrodsburg Christian Church.

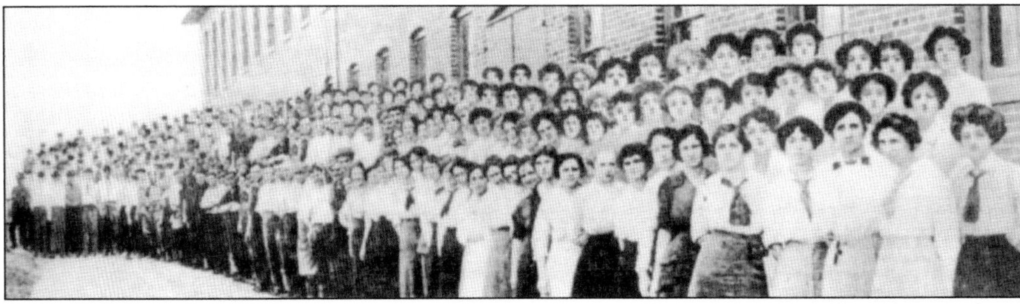

This photograph, taken from one of Bohon's catalogs, shows what are "part of our factory force, most of them being Kentuckians, and they are upright, honorable citizens and are a credit to any community. They are not floating, careless elements to be found in large cities." Such a large workforce had to have been drawn from the surrounding area. For the period, the D.T. Bohon Company was surely the biggest employer in the county. Its economic benefit would have been considerable, with new employees moving in from out of town and salesmen coming through. The company's closing must have increased the impact of the Depression on the local economy.

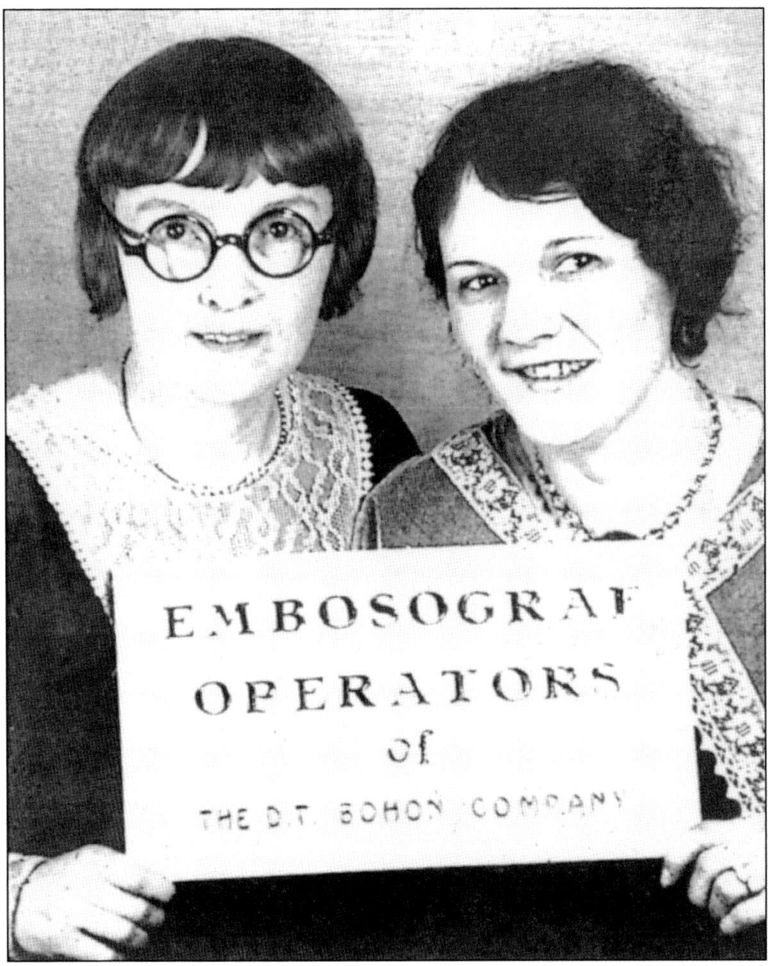

This photograph shows two unidentified women who were embosograf operators, stamping some sort of logo on equipment.

The D.T. Bohon Company had its beginnings when William Bohon came to Harrodsburg in 1856. By 1914, his sons D.T. and Hanly had established Bohon's Bluegrass Buggies and sold them through a mail-order department housed in a building similar to the one pictured on the catalog cover seen here. Bohon's motto said, "Hitch your thoroughbred to the thoroughbred of buggies." In 1923, the large structure was being built on East Office Street. Sometime between 1935 and 1937, the company ceased to exist, possibly because of both a large fire in 1932 and the economic depression that was enveloping the country. The photograph below shows the abandoned building in 1969 before it was razed sometime in the 1970s.

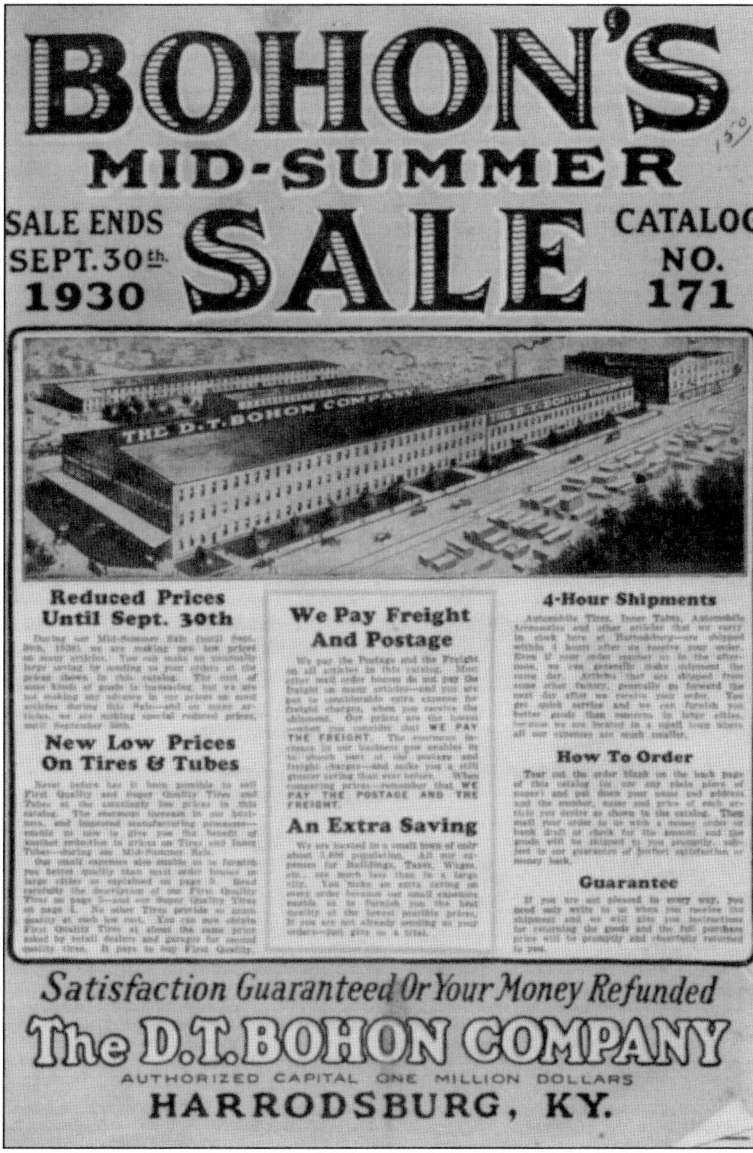

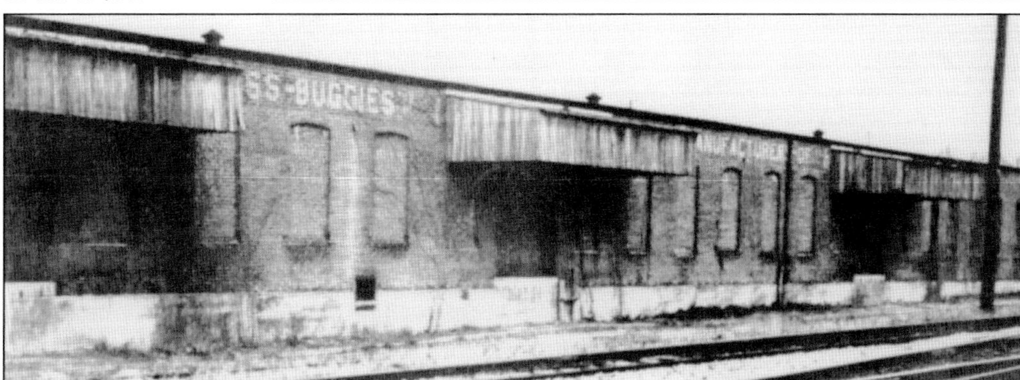

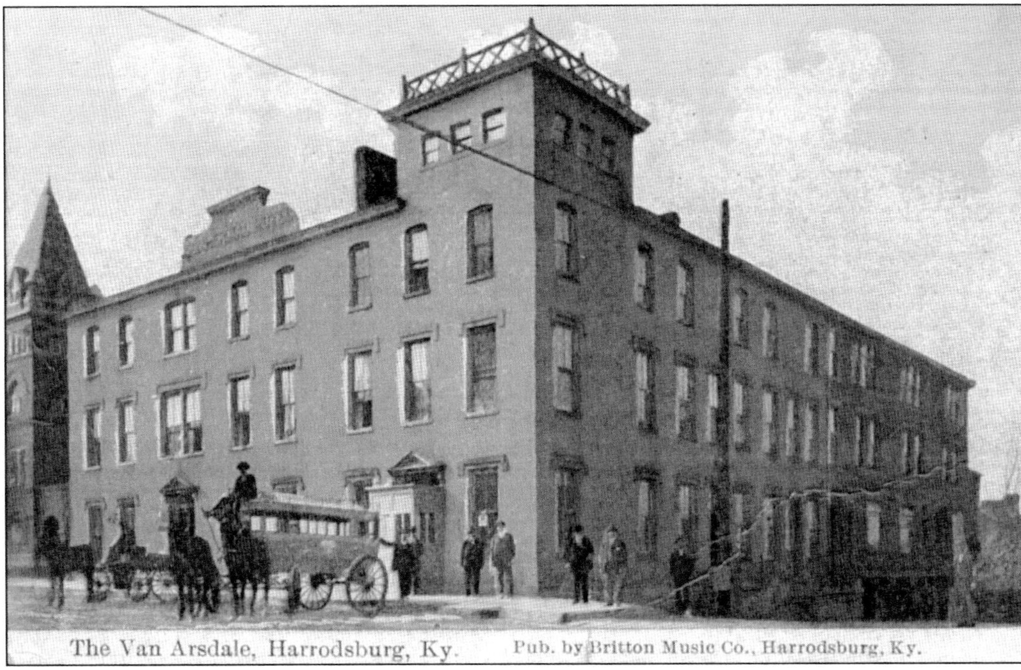

The postcard above is the earliest photograph of the Hotel Harrod, originally known as the Van Arsdale, in operation from 1852 until 1941. Note the horses and buggies unloading at the front entrance. Located on the southwest corner of Main and Office Streets, this hotel was thoroughly modern, with 75 guest rooms and dining areas. The Hotel Harrod was known for its famous food: Kentucky country ham, Southern fried chicken, and Western steaks served year-round. The photograph below is a 1940s picture after the hotel's name was changed to the Avalon Inn; automobiles have replaced horses and buggies along the streets. According to Harrodsburg resident Ann Nooe, "A lot of pretty old ladies lived there [in the hotel], and they sat out in front of the hotel on the sidewalk at night.Many had beautiful white hair that was fixed just right."

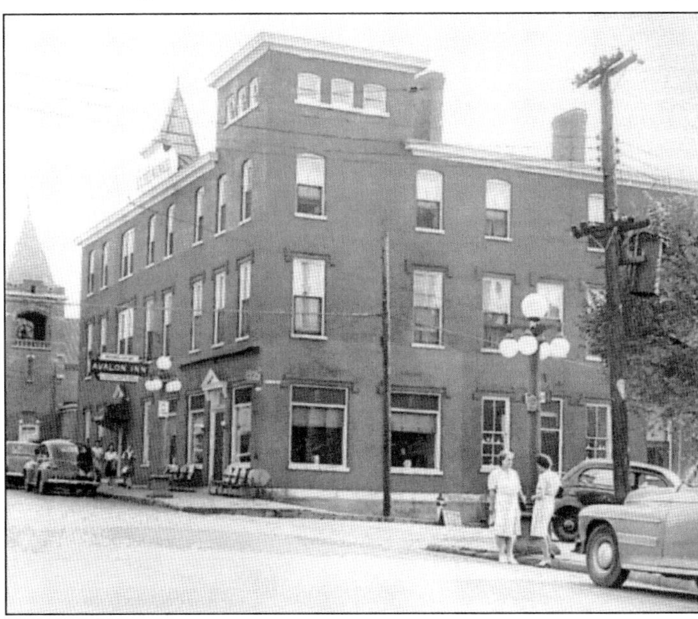

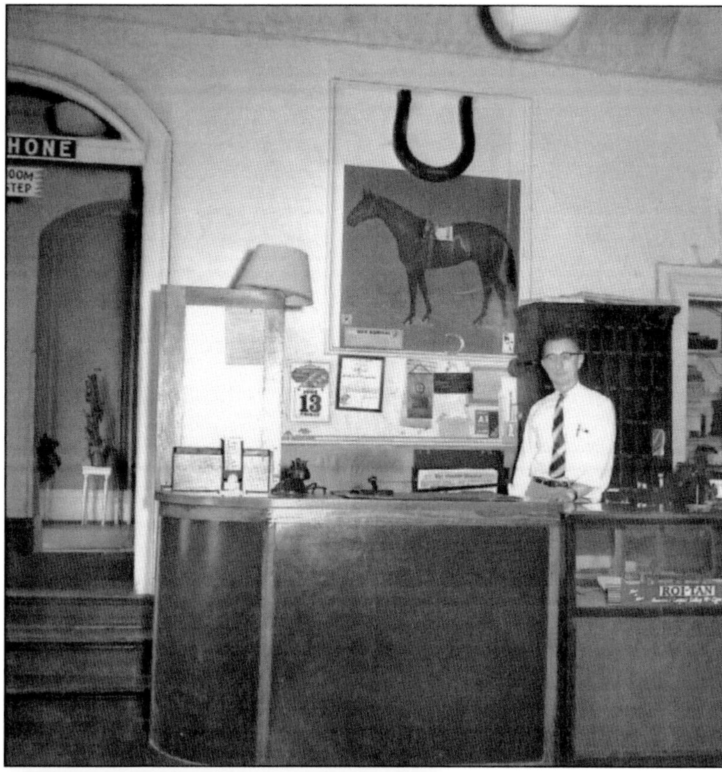

This photograph is of Holly Demaree, who was the desk clerk at the Avalon Inn in the 1950s. Demaree kept the desk area clean and ready for service. In addition to the calendar and certificates hanging on the wall, there is also a painting or photograph of War Admiral (a Triple Crown of Thoroughbred Racing winner) with a gigantic lucky horseshoe above. The desk clerk also sold a fine selection of cigars, postcards, and a variety of souvenirs for patrons.

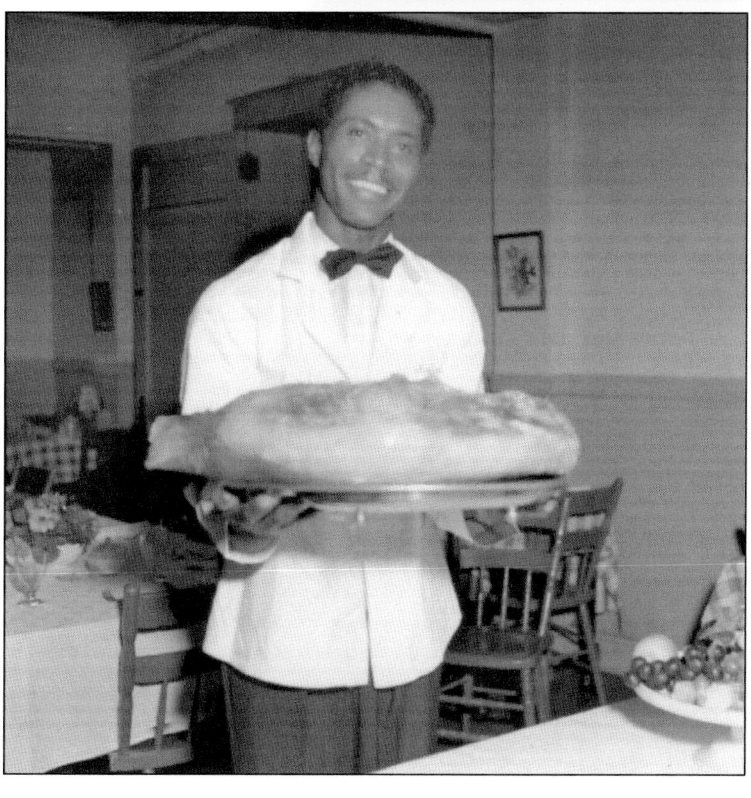

In this photograph, Elija Bryant, from Harrodsburg, is holding a mouthwatering country ham, probably cured on a Mercer County farm. Dressed in his waiter's uniform of black pants, a crisp white shirt, and a black bow tie, Bryant was a longtime employee of the Avalon Inn, and he took pride in his work.

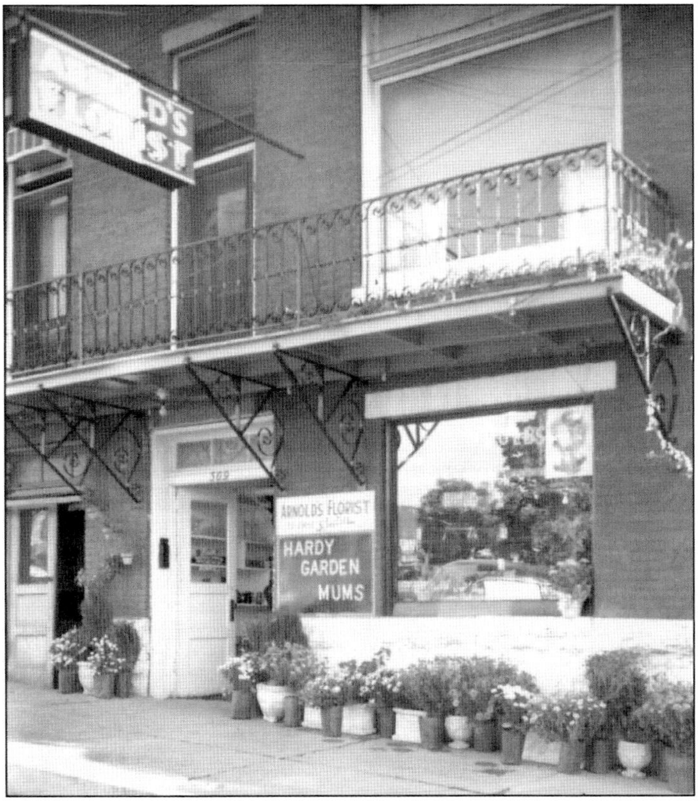

In 1952, Arnold's Florist started business in the basement of the Avalon Inn. Guests at the Avalon could walk out on the balcony and smell the fresh, fragrant aroma of the flowers wafting up from below. The hardy chrysanthemums lining the sidewalk indicate that this photograph was taken in the fall. The photograph below shows the inside of the florist. The cooler is for keeping fresh flowers, and the shelves are lined with artificial flowers and all types of containers. The center display holds knickknacks. Potted plants are placed on top of the cooler in order to keep them warm during the winter months.

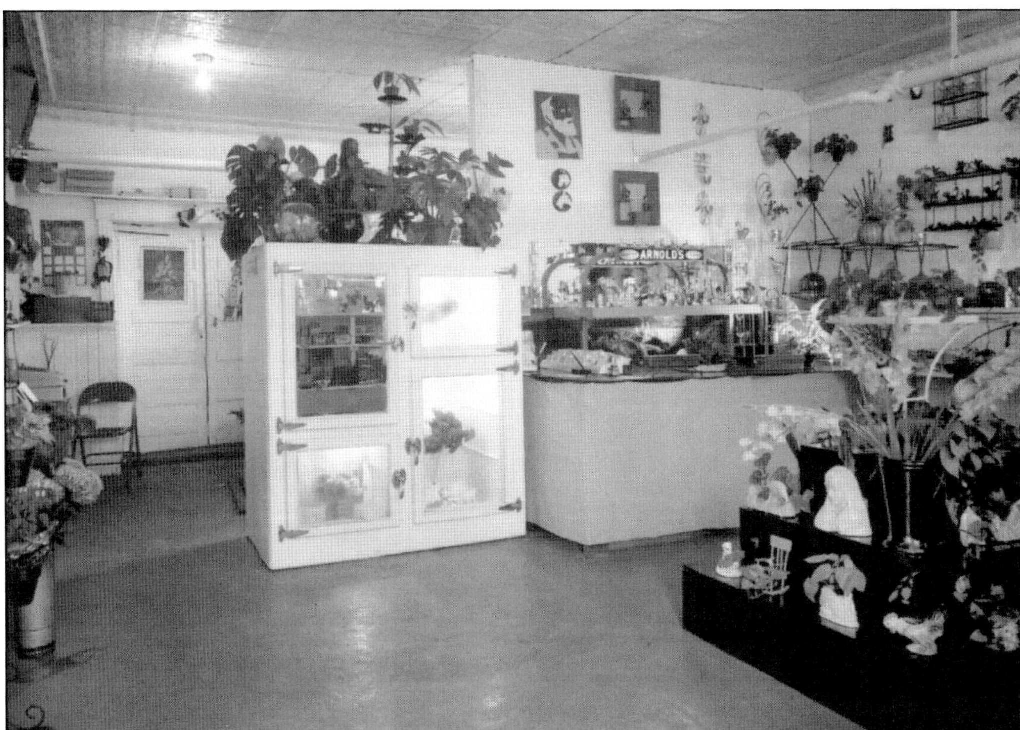

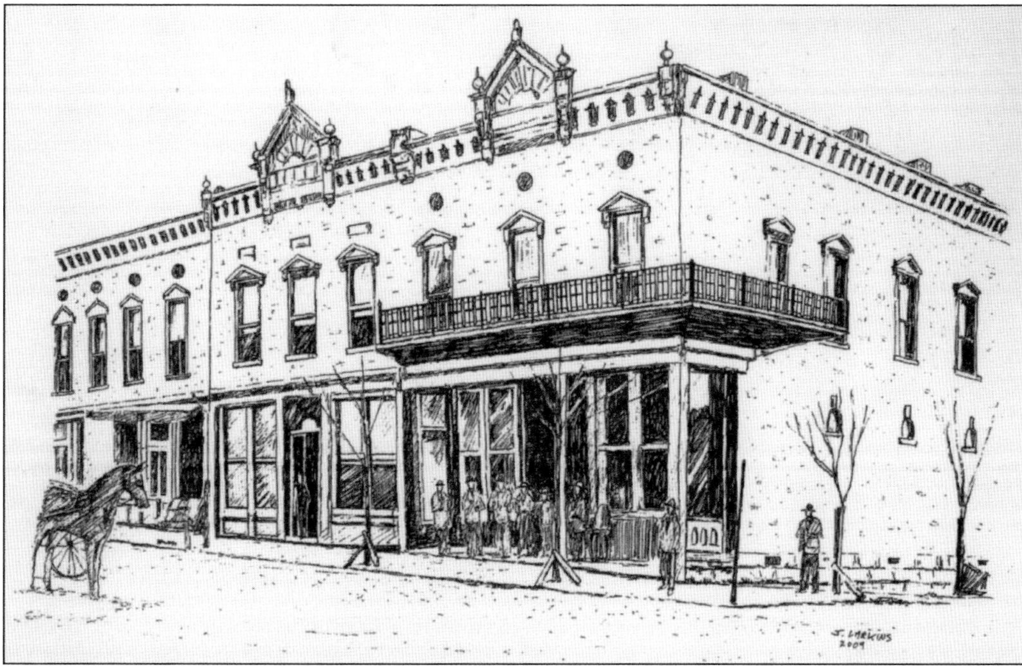

The drawing above by local artist Jackie Larkin is from an original photograph. The building is on the southwest corner of Main and Lexington Streets and was built by P.T. Dedman in 1888. The Democrat Printing Company and the Dedman Grocery and Confectionery shared two buildings, which became known as the Dedman Block. Although some of the ornate cornice and moldings are still present, the balcony was removed during one of the renovations.

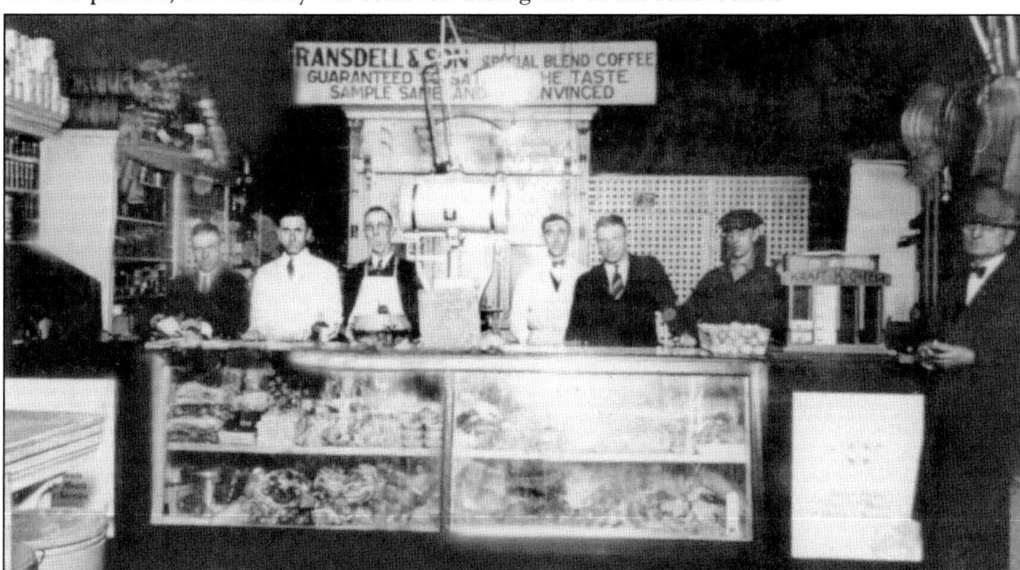

The 1923 photograph shows Ransdell Grocery, located at 102 South Main Street. From the left are Kelley Perkins, Bill Powell, Sky Bonta, Ben Britton, Dave Sweeney, Tom Adkinson, and Minor Ransdell. An early advertisement for Ransdell's states, "Ransdell & Son are now agents for A. Engelhard & Sons Company COFFEES. They also carry the well-known brands Pendennis and Grandma's Cup. Buy more, and stock up."

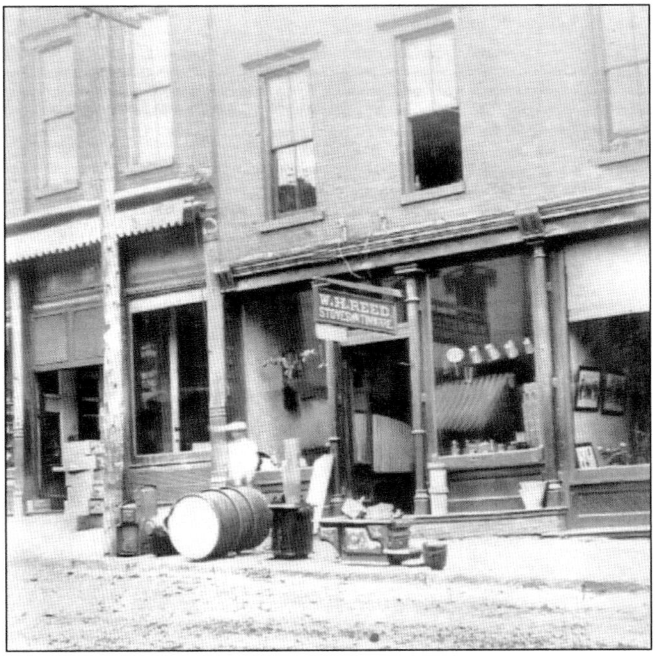

The left photograph is a late-1800s view of W.H. Reed's stove and tinware store on Main Street. This structure burned in 1891, but was rebuilt and became the home of the *Harrodsburg Herald* from 1929 to 1953. In the 1951 picture below, moving day has arrived, and the scene of the heavy presses and printing equipment being manhandled onto the truck is providing some entertainment for the onlookers. Owner Jane Hutton shared the dreams of her father, D.M. Hutton, of making the newspaper an instrument for positive change and the betterment of the community. (Left, courtesy of the private collection of Ron Reed)

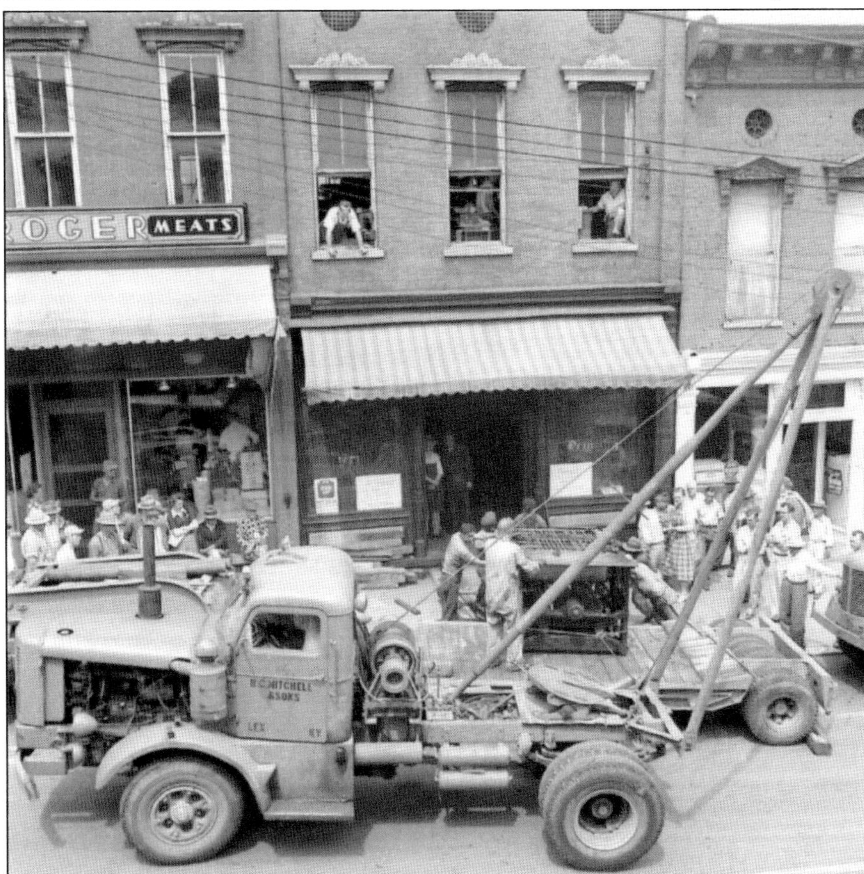

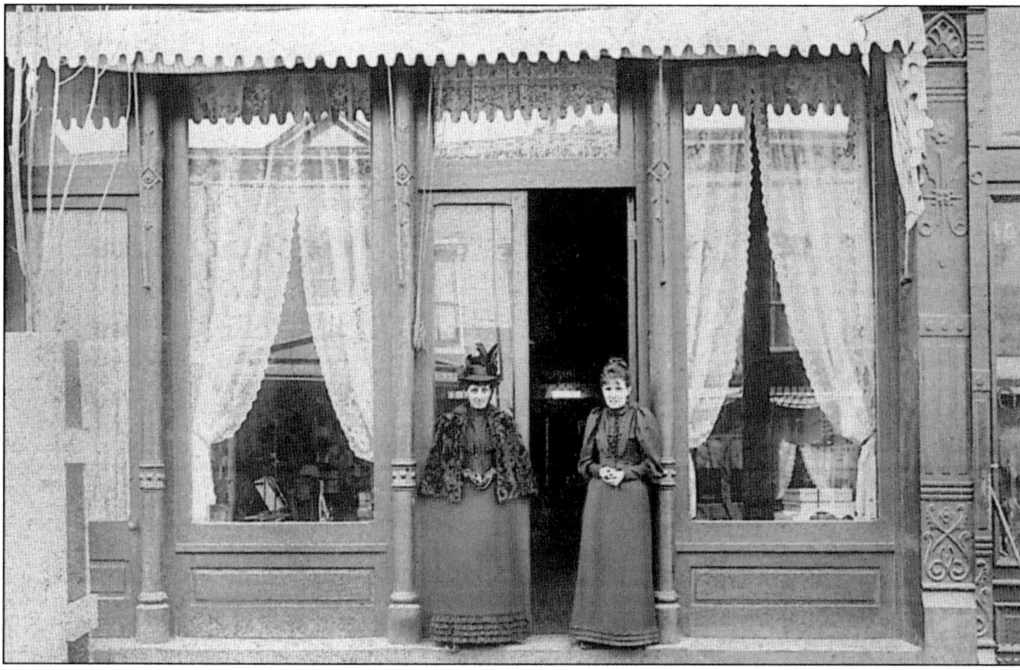

The storefront above was a millinery from 1896 to 1901. In 1920, Green's Barber Shop opened and operated there until 1939. The photograph below shows the six chairs with the barbers ready to work. Everyone had his hair cut there. In a interview in 1991, Fred Taylor recalled, "I started out in 1927 and worked on the laundry truck, and my salary was $8 a week, but I was training for barber, and I couldn't go to barber school because it was segregated, and Mr. Green could not get me in, so he got me a transcript to stay through the University of Kentucky—that's the way I got to be a barber in 1927."

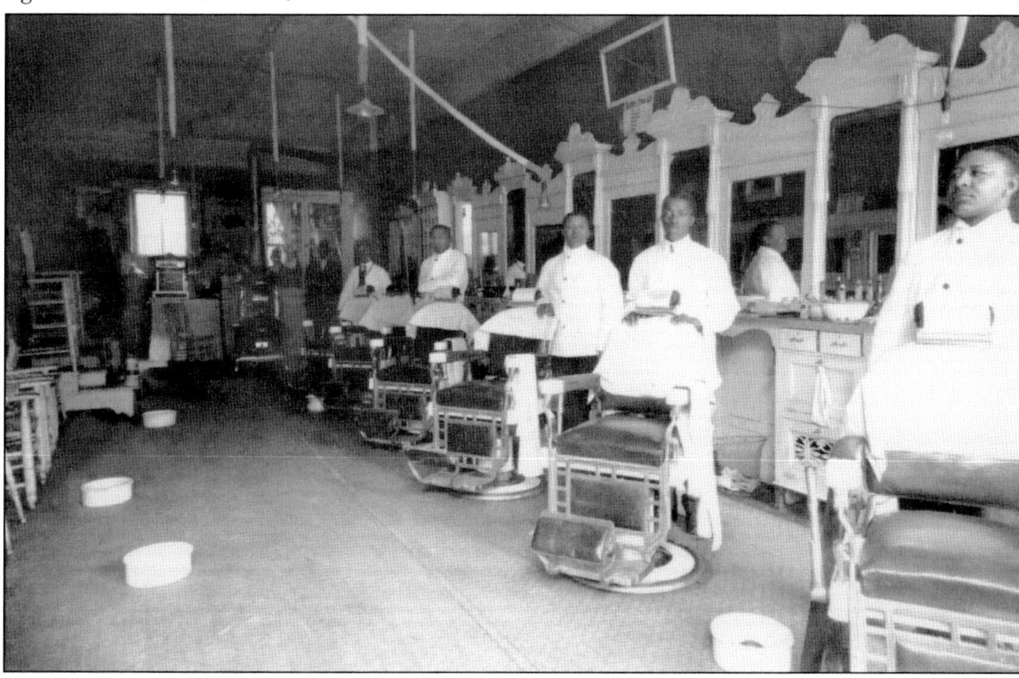

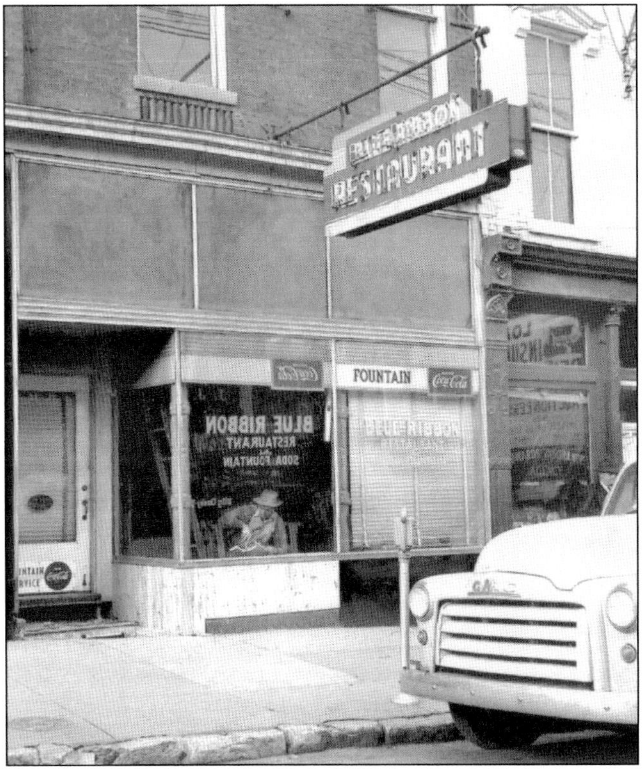

The left photograph from the early 1900s shows the Blue Ribbon Restaurant, one of the favorite hangouts for residents of Harrodsburg. According to proprietor William Pruitt's grandson, he was always impressed by the large size of the freezers in the restaurant. In a 1990 interview, Harrodsburg resident Ann Cherry said, "the Blue Ribbon had many ice cream tables and chairs with a marble fountain and mirrors." Although the Blue Ribbon was located in several different stores along Main Street at various times, this picture was taken at 124 South Main Street. The authors cannot explain the mirror image on the two front windows. The photograph below is William Pruitt, the former proprietor of the Blue Ribbon, which he co-owned with his brother, Ernest Pruitt.

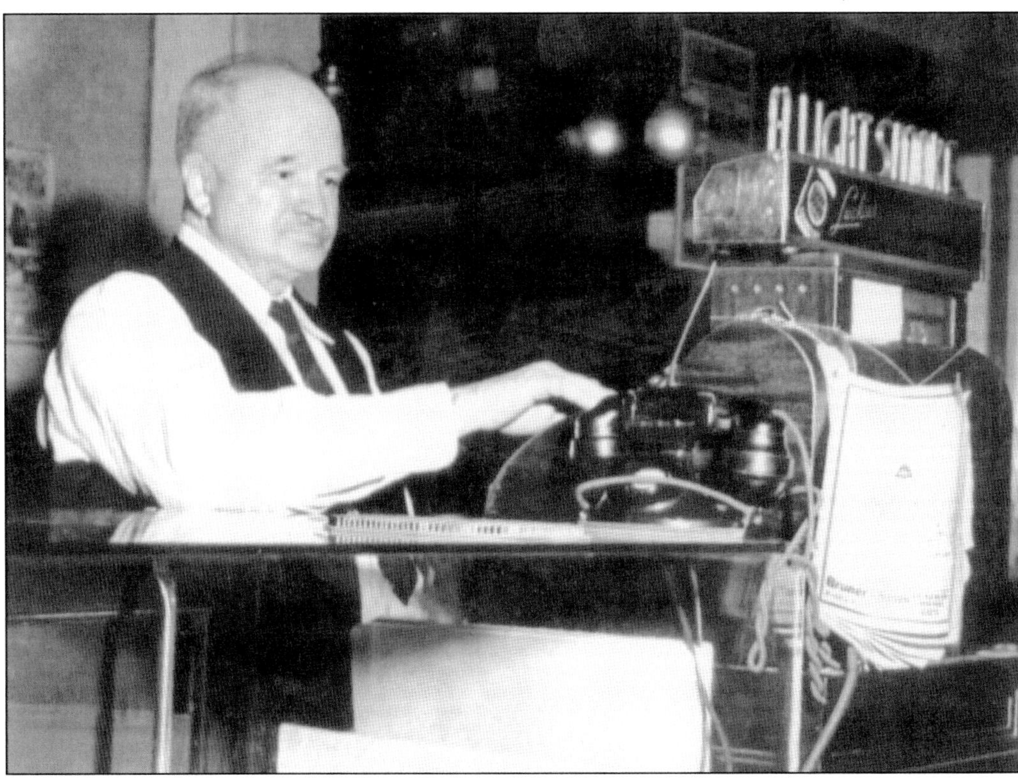

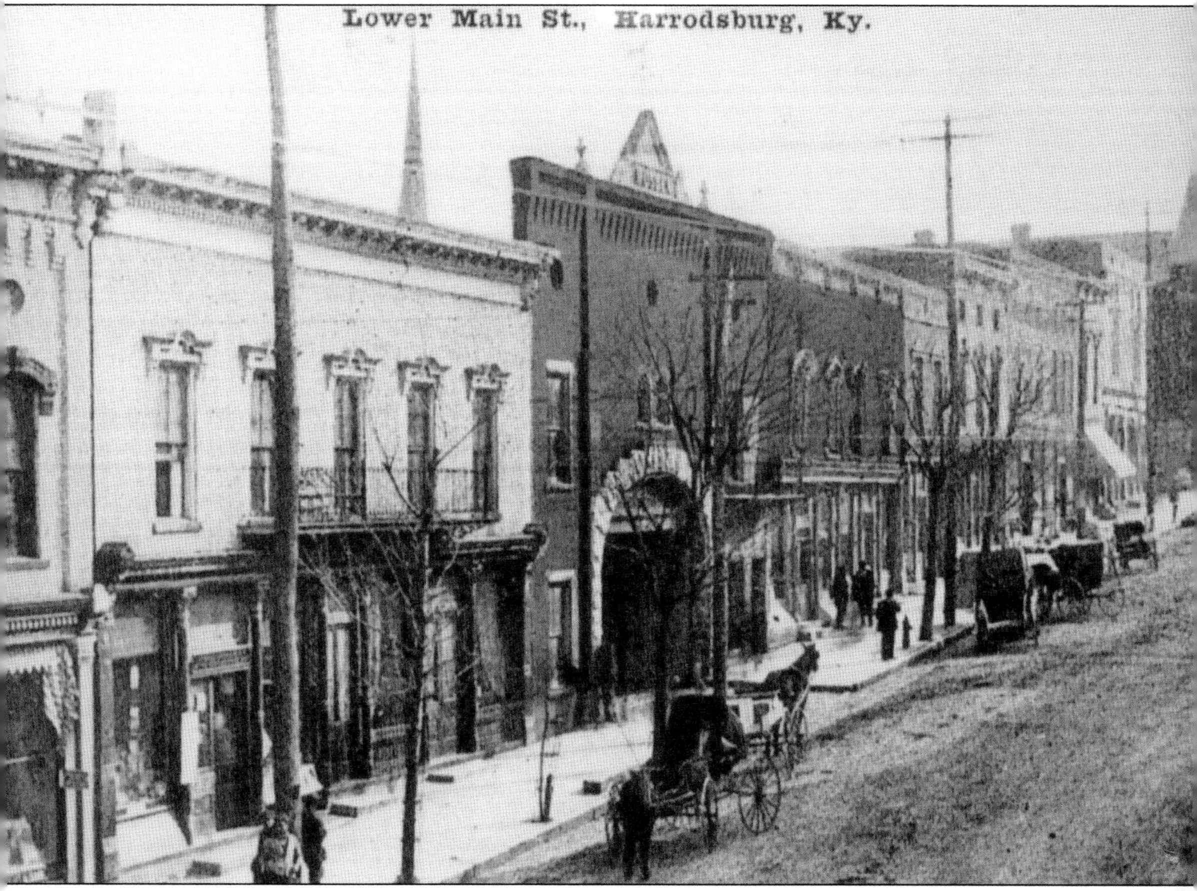

This photograph taken for a postcard from the late 1800s shows what Main Street was like then: handsome brick buildings with cast iron ornamentation, colorful awnings to shield goods displayed in the windows from the sun, fancy iron balconies on many structures, trees planted at intervals along the sidewalk, and a dirt street free of trash. These are all signs of a thriving business district at the turn of the century. The Arcade Livery Stable sits in the middle of the block and was the grandest such business in town—brick with a stone archway for its entrance. Anything that was needed could be had by just shopping the three blocks of Main Street, including groceries, medicine, clothes, jewelry, hats, shoes, hardware, and livestock supplies. A person could eat and drink and play billiards in any number of places. And neighbors could visit and exchange the latest gossip.

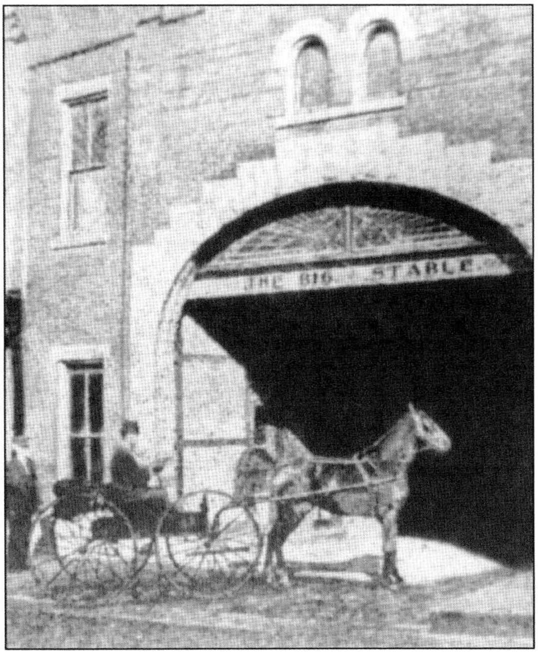

The Arcade Livery, or Big Stable as it was also called, is pictured at left at the turn of the century. The *Harrodsburg Democrat* of 1890 says, "Erected by R.E. Coleman in 1884, this well-equipped brick livery style is double-decked with inclined driveway. The stable extends from Main to Greenville Streets, is large and roomy and equipped with cribs, mows, stalls, water works, electric lights, and ladies parlor." Another article written in 1885 called the Arcade "the largest, most commodious, and the best equipped stable in Kentucky. Its stock consists of drummers' wagons, buggies, road carts, omnibuses, landaus, phaetons, and surries. Together with the best of horses. Prices are as low as the lowest." The photograph below, taken by local businessman and photography hobbyist William H. Reed, is labeled, "Mr. Willis Slaughter, March 1896." The Arcade stable is seen in the background.

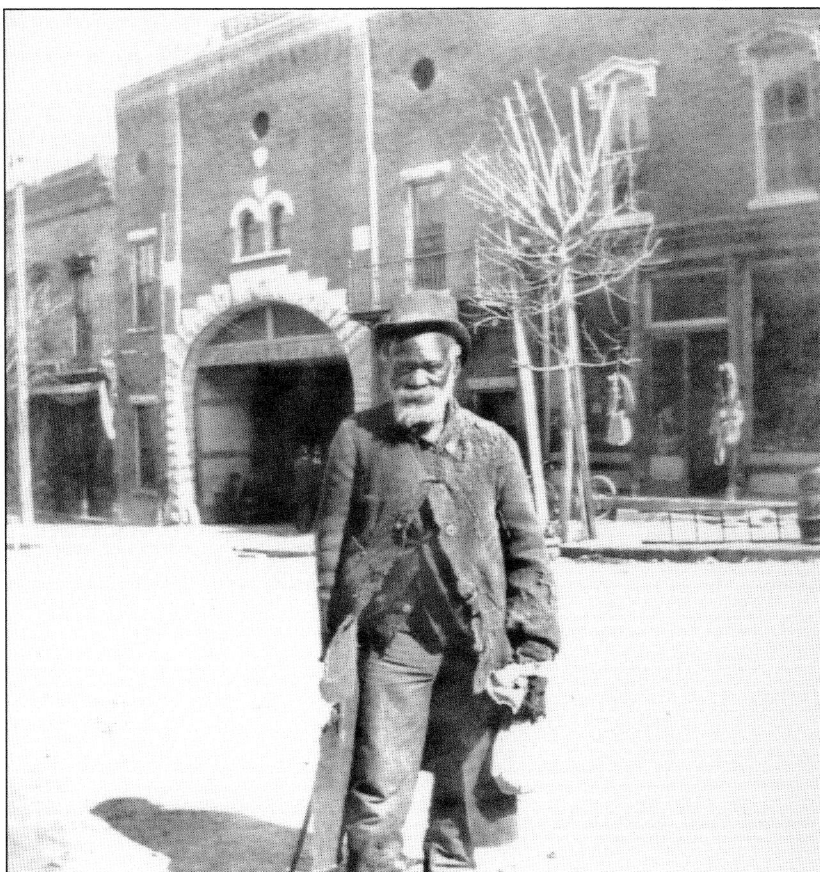

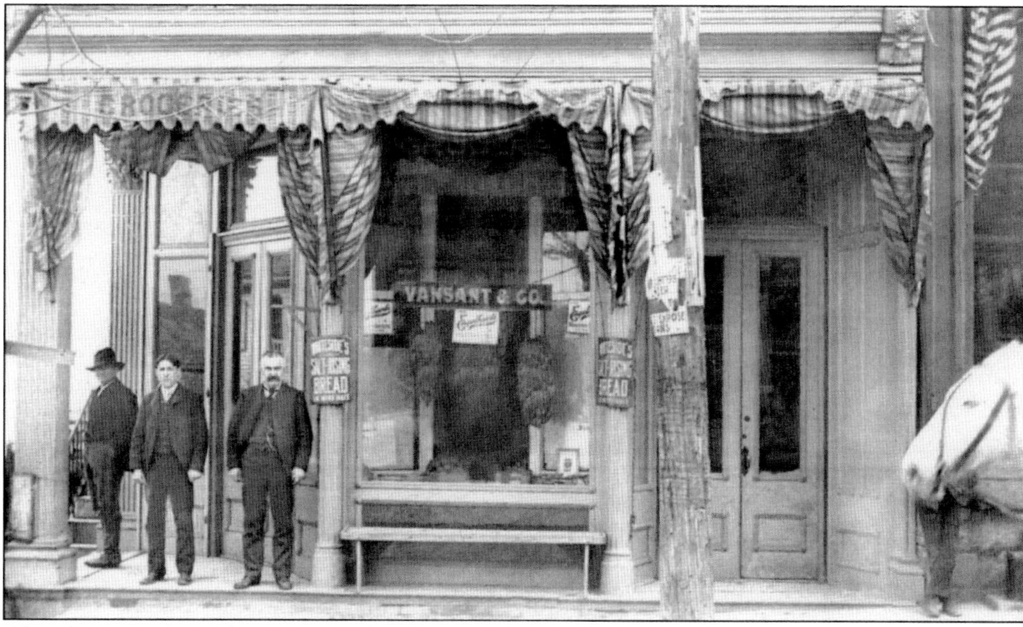

This photograph is of Vansant and Company, one of several grocers on Main Street around 1900. This handsome building, built around 1886, is on the corner of Lexington and Main Streets, and the business looks new and prosperous. Bananas hang in the window, salt-rising bread is advertised, tomatoes are priced at 10¢ a can, and flour is $2.40 for 100 pounds.

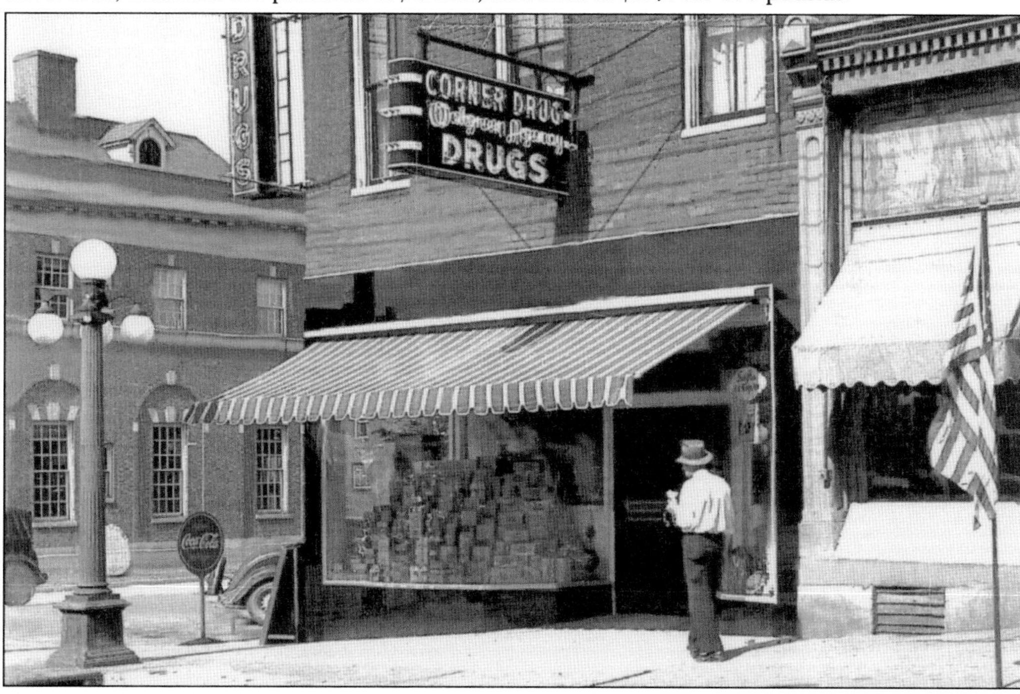

This corner building housed a drugstore for 80 years, having as many as six differently owned businesses there throughout that period. This photograph of the Corner Drugstore is from the 1940s. It was truly a versatile store, selling paint and household goods, filling prescriptions, and providing a fountain and luncheonette.

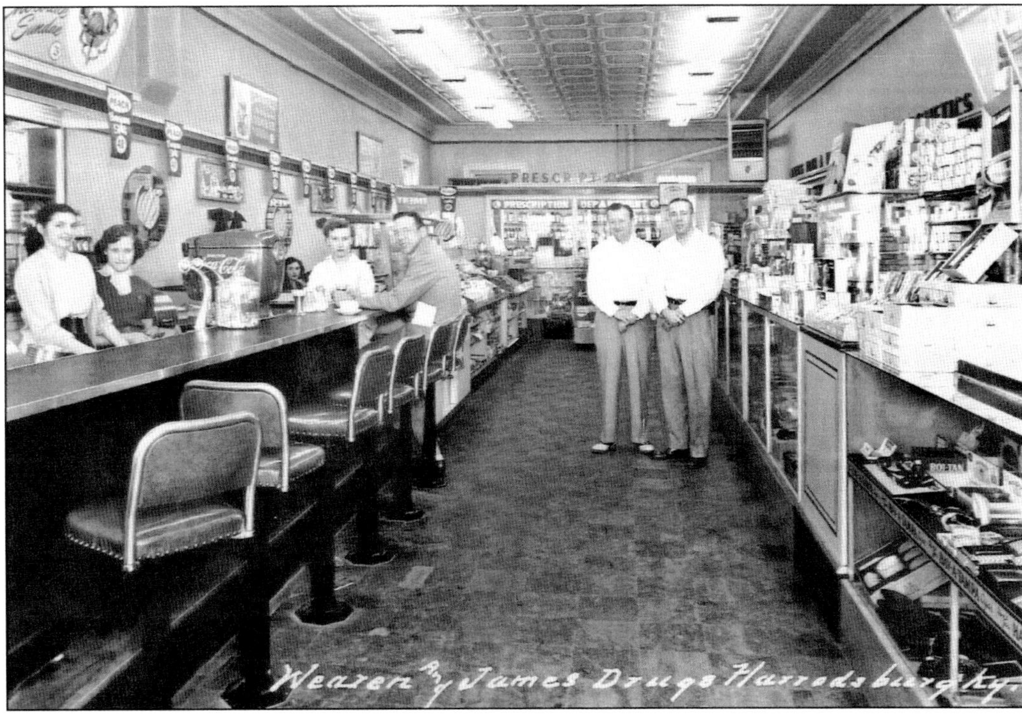

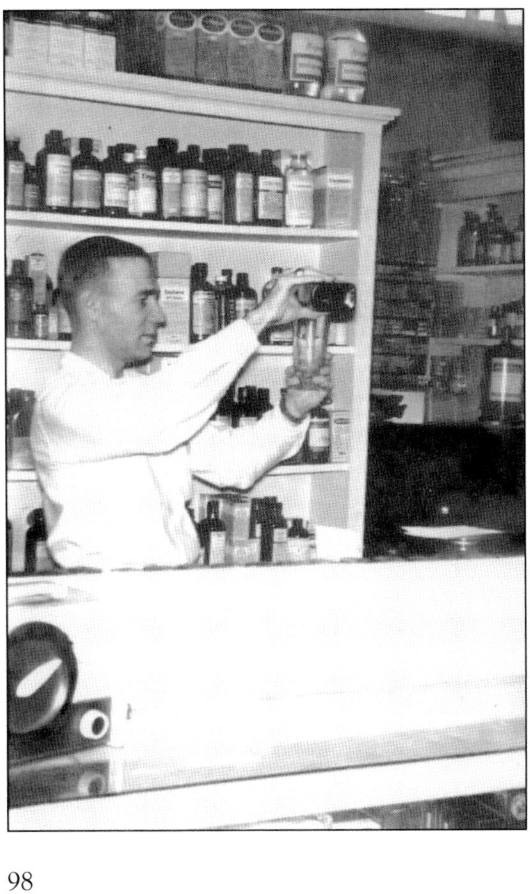

Johnny James (left) and George Wearen are shown standing inside their new Wearen and James Drugstore just after its grand opening in 1950. The store was a Walgreen agency and represented the latest in merchandising concepts, including air-conditioning (the first business in town to have this), store-length fluorescent lighting, and self-service aisles; it also had one of the best-equipped fountain luncheonettes in Harrodsburg. The left photograph shows George Wearen, the registered pharmacist, filling a prescription. From earlier days when James was a customer at the corner pharmacy, he decided he liked the drugstore business; in becoming a partner, he realized that dream in the very same store. The business closed in 1985 and was the last drugstore to be located there.

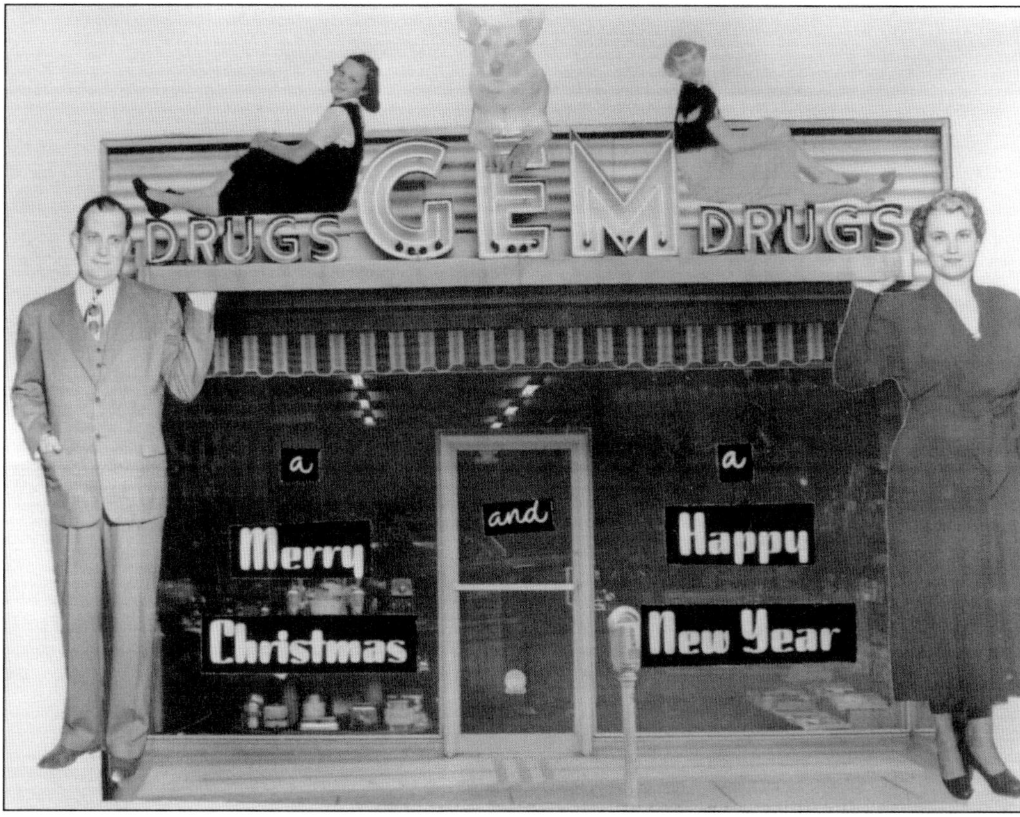

A photograph of the Gem Drugstore has been turned into a holiday greeting card featuring owners Larry and Ruth Rice, daughters Carol and Shirley, and the family dog. Homemade pie was a favorite at this store, which was a fixture on Main Street for close to 50 years. Larry Rice's interest in photography prompted him to add a camera and photographic supply department in the 1950s when the store was remodeled.

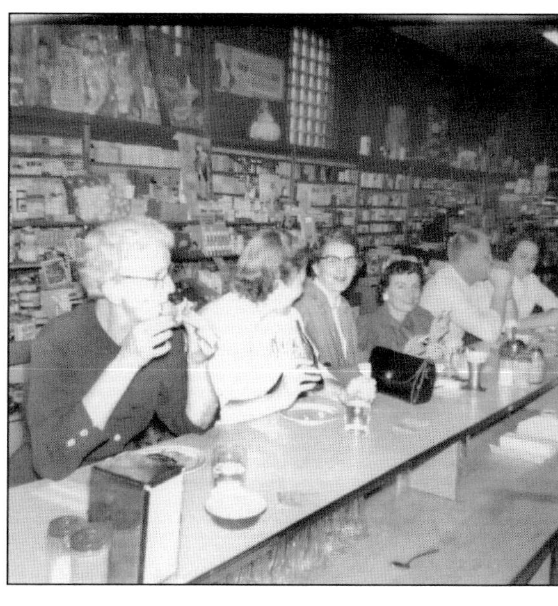

In 1958, this soda fountain at the Gem Drugstore was a gathering place for all ages. Coffee klatches started their days early here. Lunchtime brought in employees on lunch breaks and shoppers—yes, people actually shopped on Main Street then—for sandwiches, pie, and ice cream. After school, students rushed in to grab a stool, gossip, and have a treat.

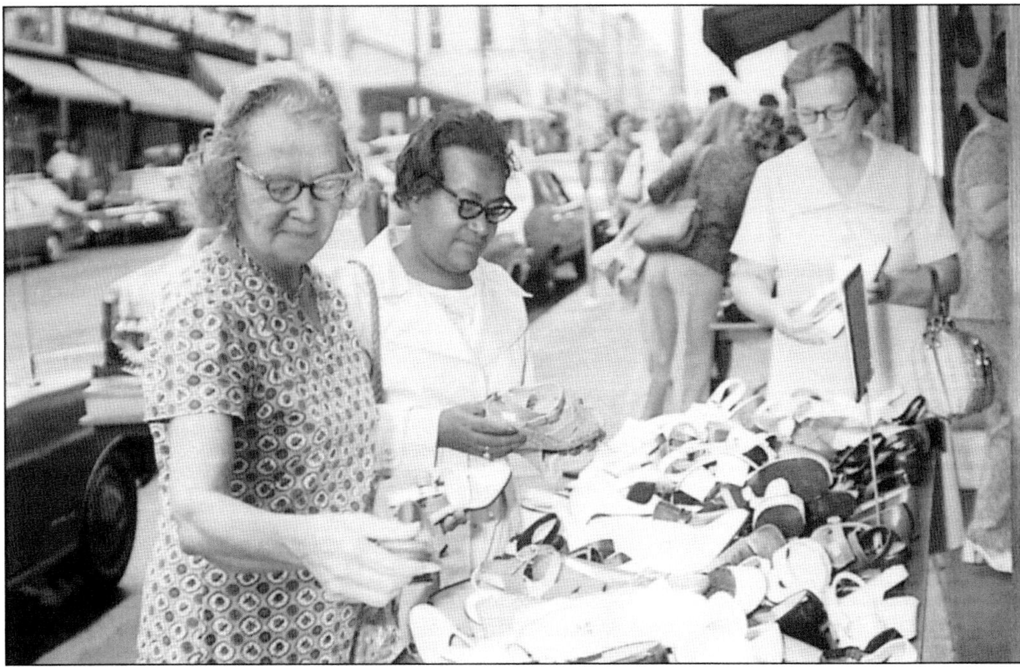

This 1977 photograph was probably taken on a Saturday during sidewalk days. Store owners would set up tables outside their shops to display an assortment of merchandise and bargain prices for this promotional effort. This was popular during the 1960s and 1970s, before malls changed people's shopping habits forever.

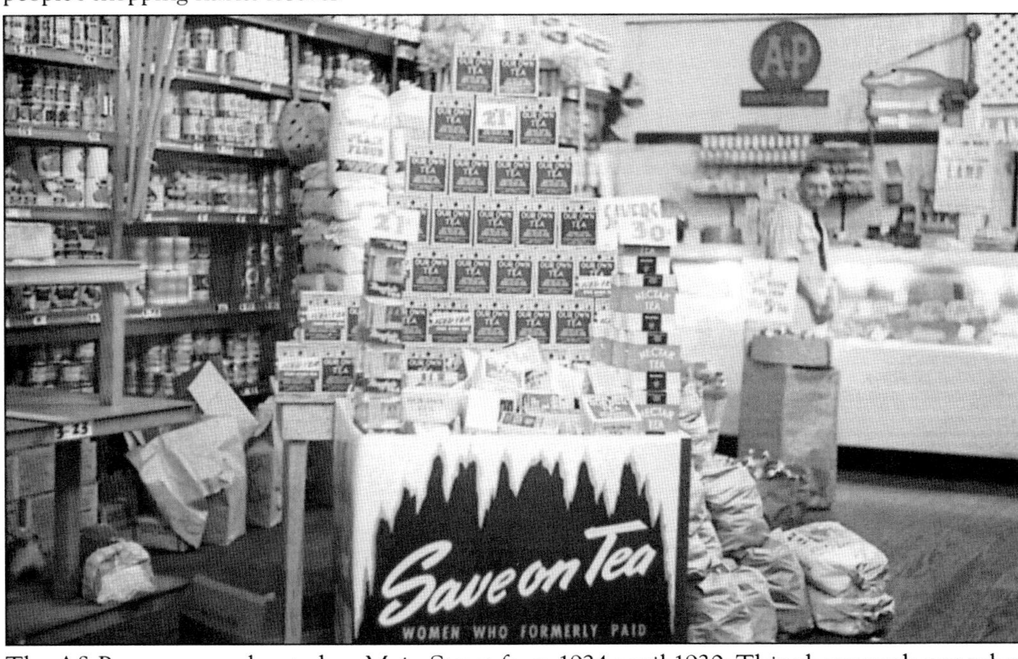

The A&P grocery was located on Main Street from 1924 until 1930. This photograph was taken sometime during the late 1920s. The store was one-room deep, meaning there was only a single room in which the merchandise could be displayed. Customers only had a limited choice of brands, and prices were kept low because the overhead was low.

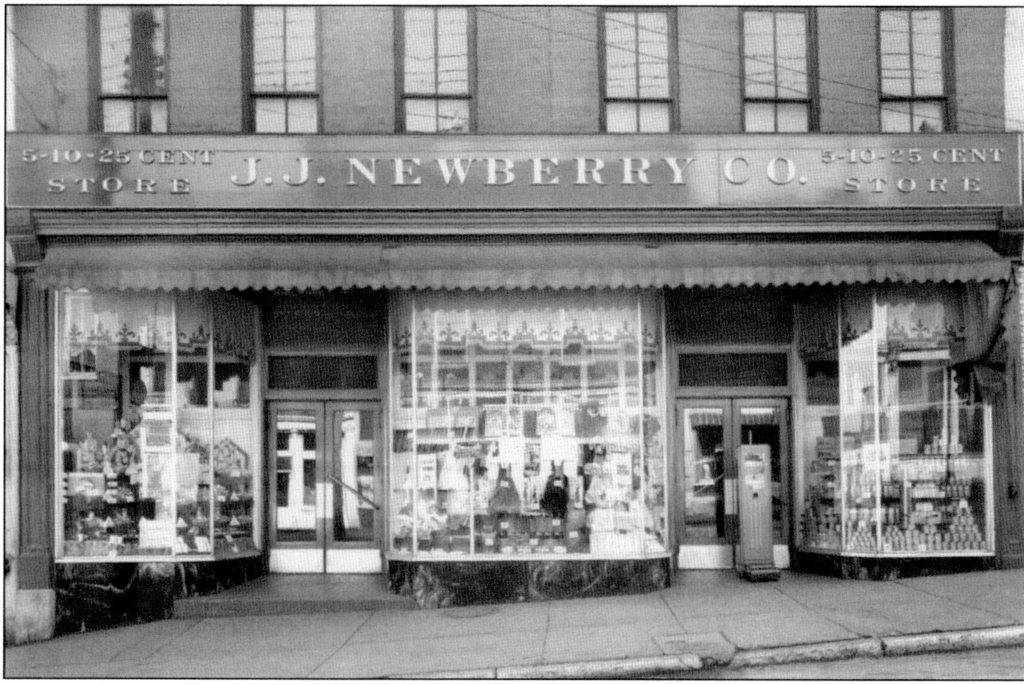

Taken in about 1950, the photograph above shows the J.J. Newberry Co. 5-10-25 Cent Store. The store was owned by Jerry Newby and remained in operation from 1936 until 1975. Three large window fronts were changed often to display new and modern items. Harrodsburg area residents could buy almost anything they needed here; it was *the* place to come. Bobbi Rightmyer remembers "buying my Trixie Belden books there, as well as my first embroidery equipment." In 1976, the store began to decrease inventory until it only carried furniture and appliances. Though still owned by Jerry Newby, it became known as the Discount House. Unfortunately, the store burned in 1989, as seen in the photograph below. Firemen worked hard to save the building while protecting nearby stores. They managed to salvage some furniture and appliances, but the structure was a total loss.

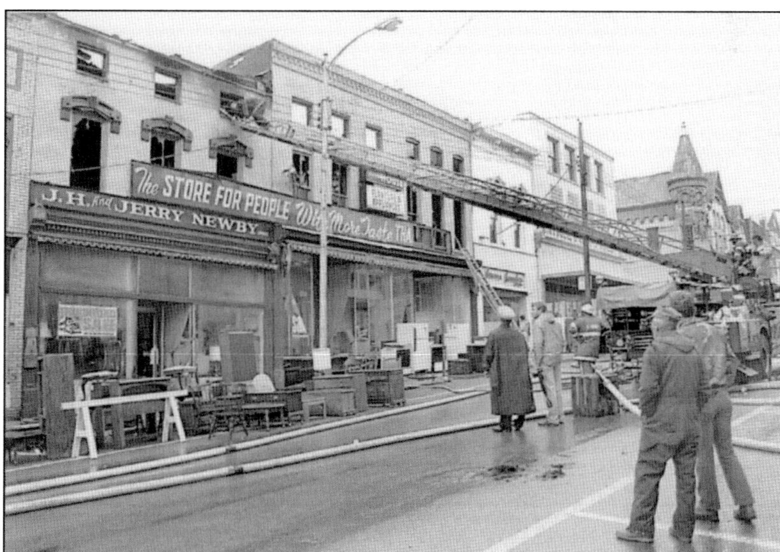

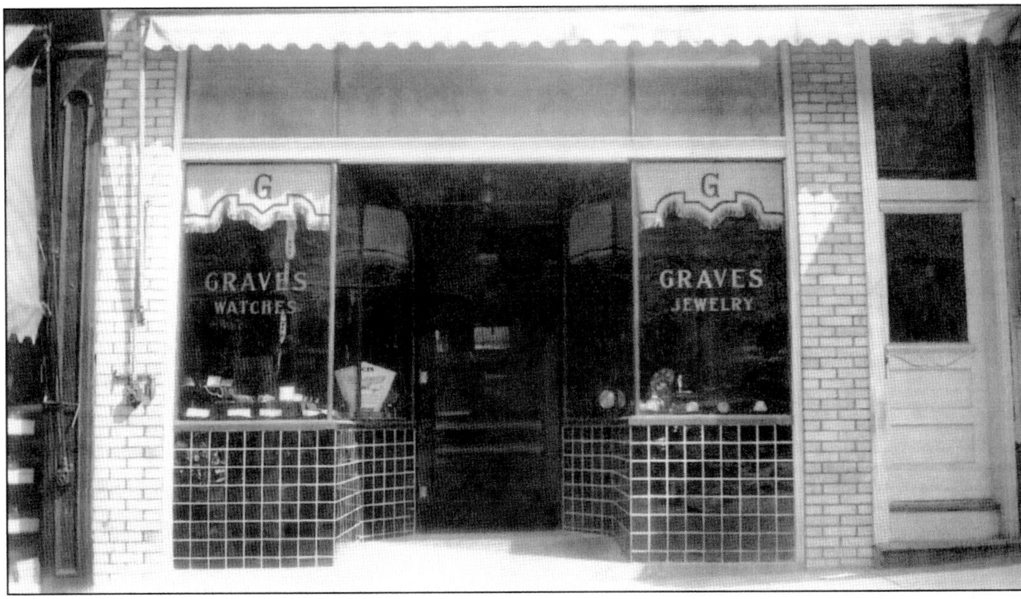

This photograph from the 1920s shows Graves Jewelers, owned and operated by the Graves family from 1904 until 1989. Graves sold not only jewelry but also fine china, crystal, and collectibles. Fires on both sides of the business claimed all the other buildings between Olde Towne Park and the vacant lot at the corner of Main and East Poplar Streets.

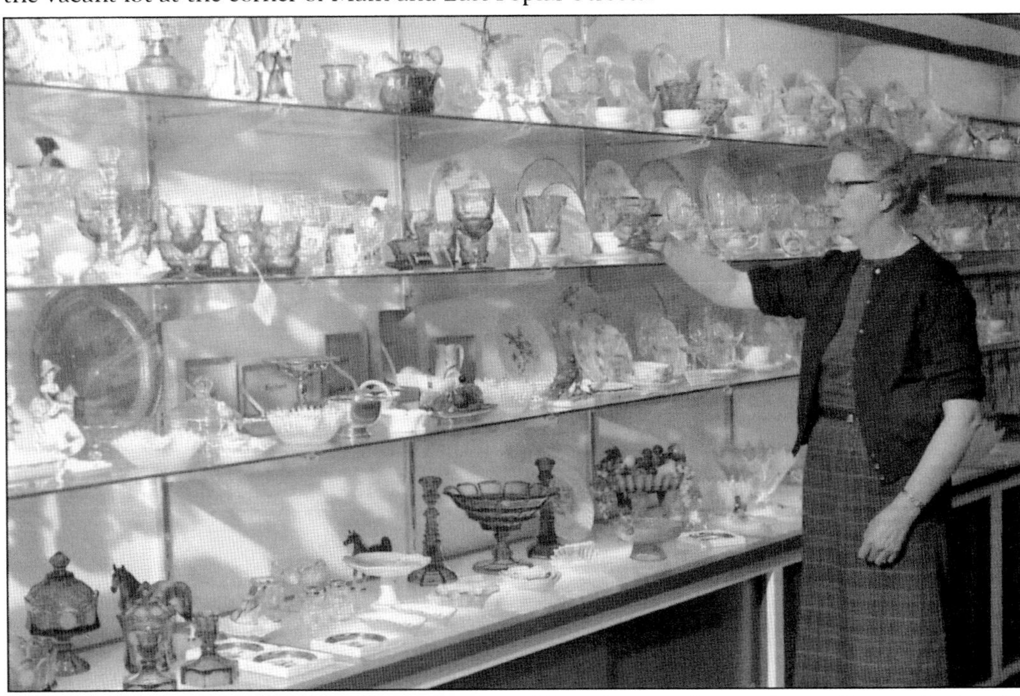

Lucille Graves took great pride in her collection of fine china and crystal as well as in the jewelry she had to offer her many loyal customers. Although several jewelry stores operated on Main Street during the time Graves was in business, Lucille states in an interview from 1990, "There was no rivalry [between jewelry stores]; we always cooperated with any jeweler that has ever been in Harrodsburg."

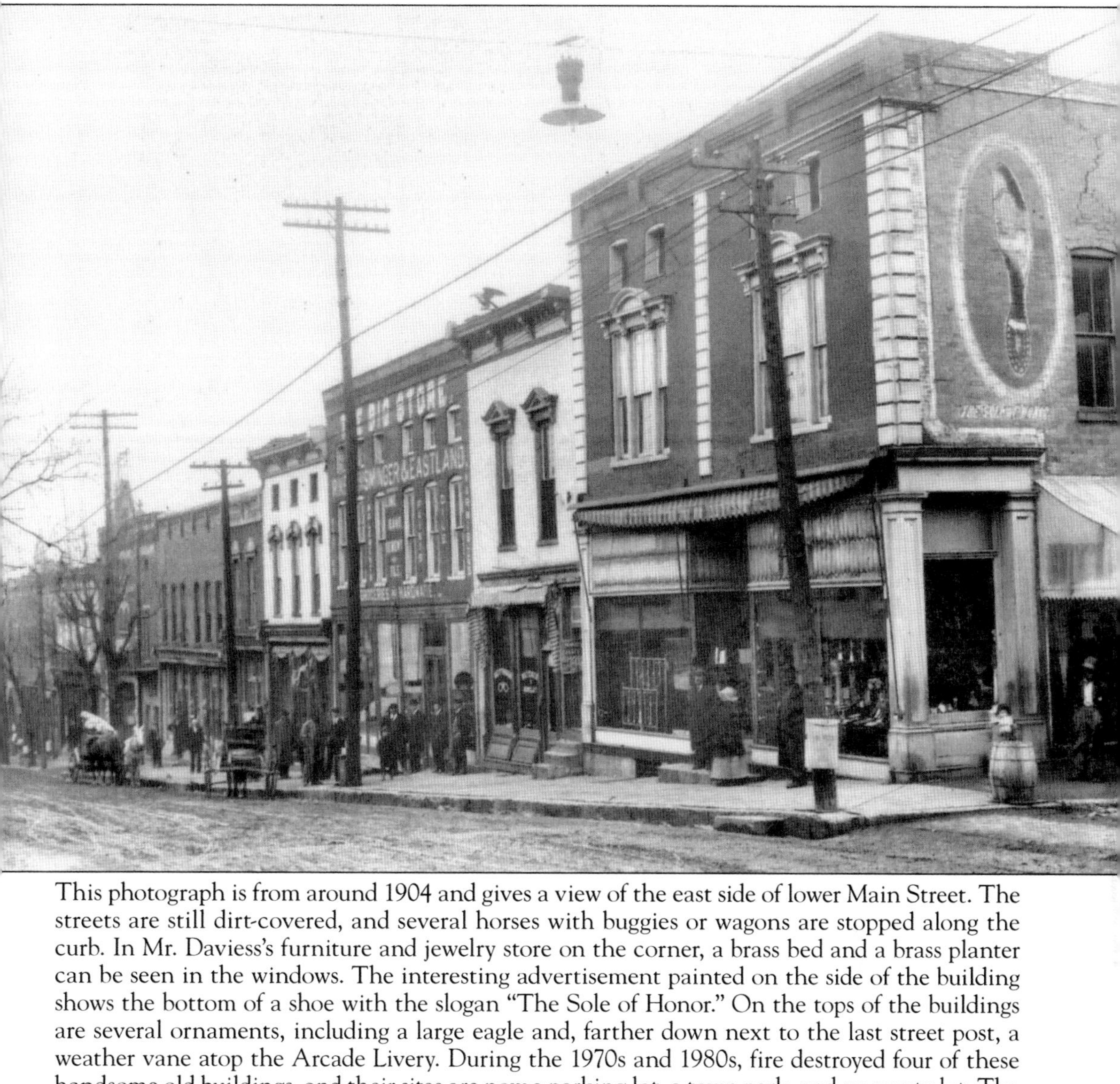

This photograph is from around 1904 and gives a view of the east side of lower Main Street. The streets are still dirt-covered, and several horses with buggies or wagons are stopped along the curb. In Mr. Daviess's furniture and jewelry store on the corner, a brass bed and a brass planter can be seen in the windows. The interesting advertisement painted on the side of the building shows the bottom of a shoe with the slogan "The Sole of Honor." On the tops of the buildings are several ornaments, including a large eagle and, farther down next to the last street post, a weather vane atop the Arcade Livery. During the 1970s and 1980s, fire destroyed four of these handsome old buildings, and their sites are now a parking lot, a town park, and an empty lot. The corner building would become home to Lay & Lawson in the 1950s; the furniture store appears on the next page.

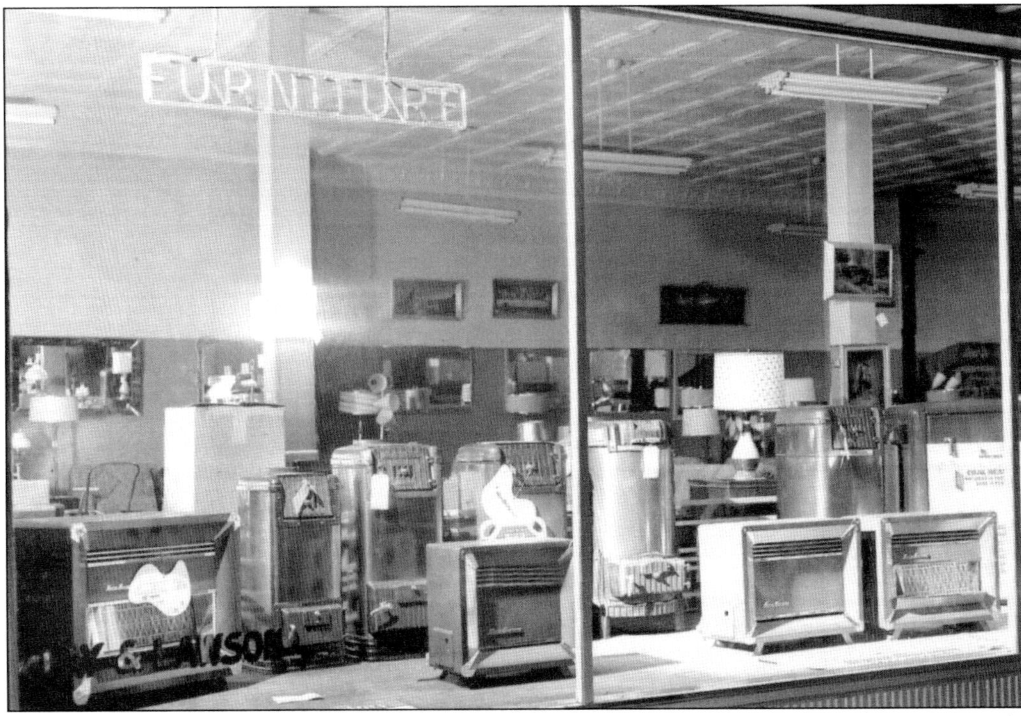

Lay & Lawson Furniture and Appliances appears in this photograph taken in the late 1940s. The window display shows numerous styles of stoves (gas, coal, oil, and wood) and shapes (short, tall, wide, and narrow) for sale. In addition to stoves, Lay & Lawson also sold name-brand washing machines, ranges, refrigerators, mattresses, chairs, and other types of furniture. The building was two stories; appliances and stoves were on the first floor, and the furniture was on the second level. The photograph below shows the Lay & Lawson delivery truck, ready to transport purchases at a moment's notice. The three-digit telephone number on the side of the truck—187—reflects what a young town Harrodsburg still was.

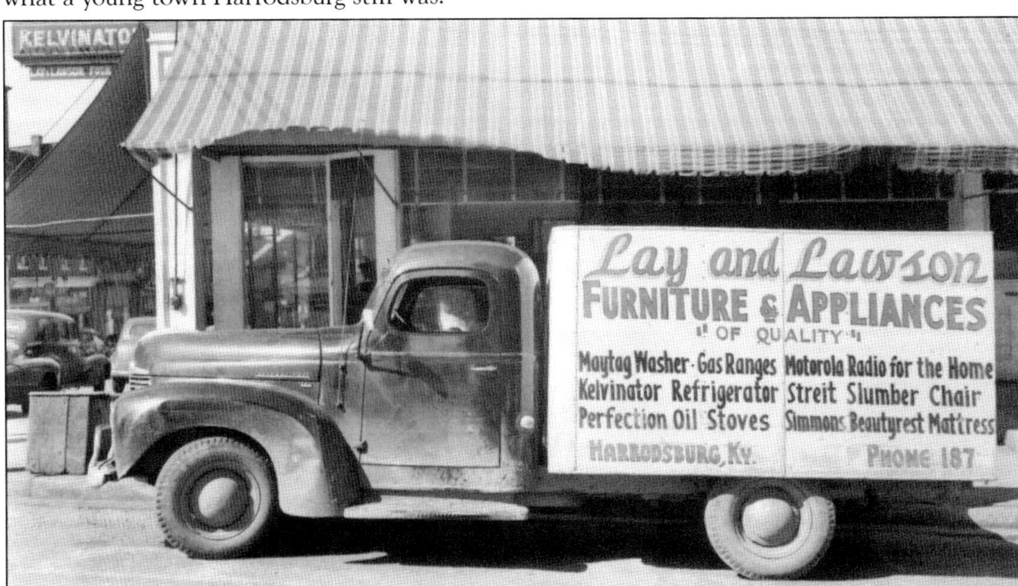

The right photograph shows the Curry and Morgan Drug Company. Selling more than just pharmaceuticals, it operated on Main Street from 1940 until 1967. At Christmastime, larger items such as dresser sets were offered; the sets contained a mirror, brushes, combs, and scissors in a beautiful case. Other items for sale included perfume, soap, and dusting powder as well as fine cigars and tobacco plug-cutters for men. Mr. Morgan's son-in-law Joe Russell used to work in the store and was able to learn the tricks of the trade. In 1958, Russell bought the store and remained on Main Street about 10 years. The image below shows the remodeling of the Russell Drugstore. New floors, wallboards, and rows of shelves and counters were added. This picture appears to have been taken during the grand opening.

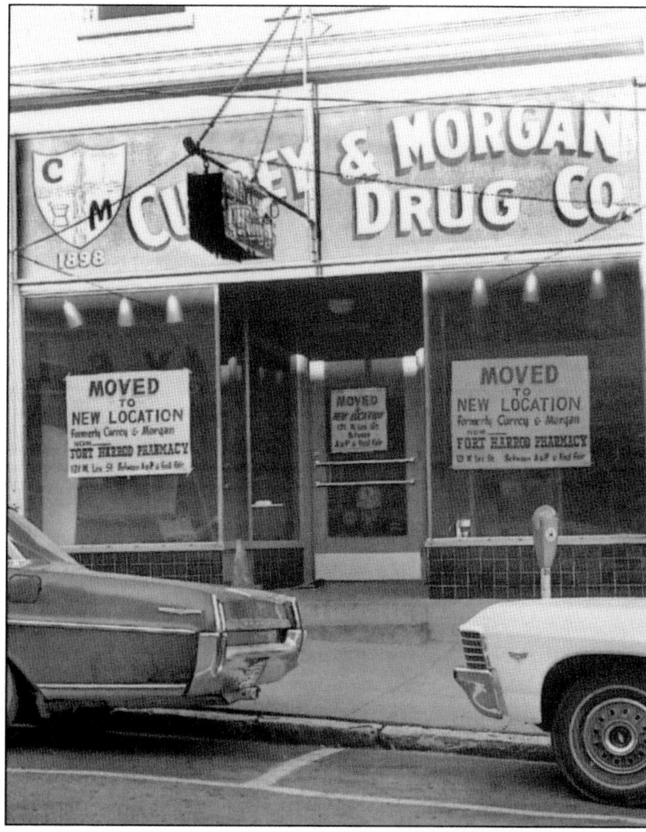

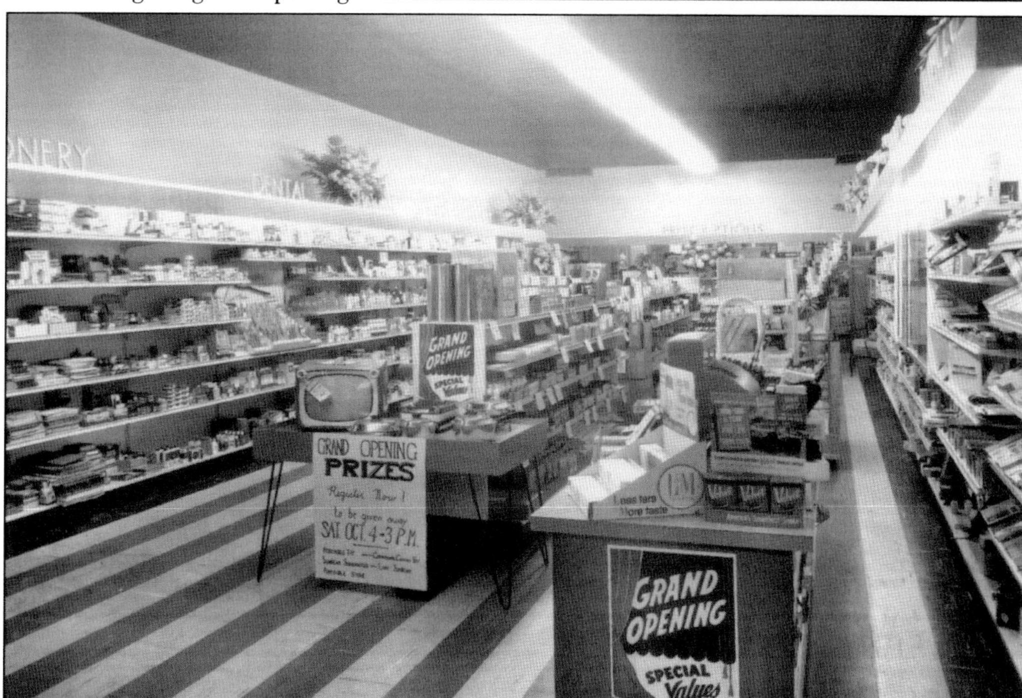

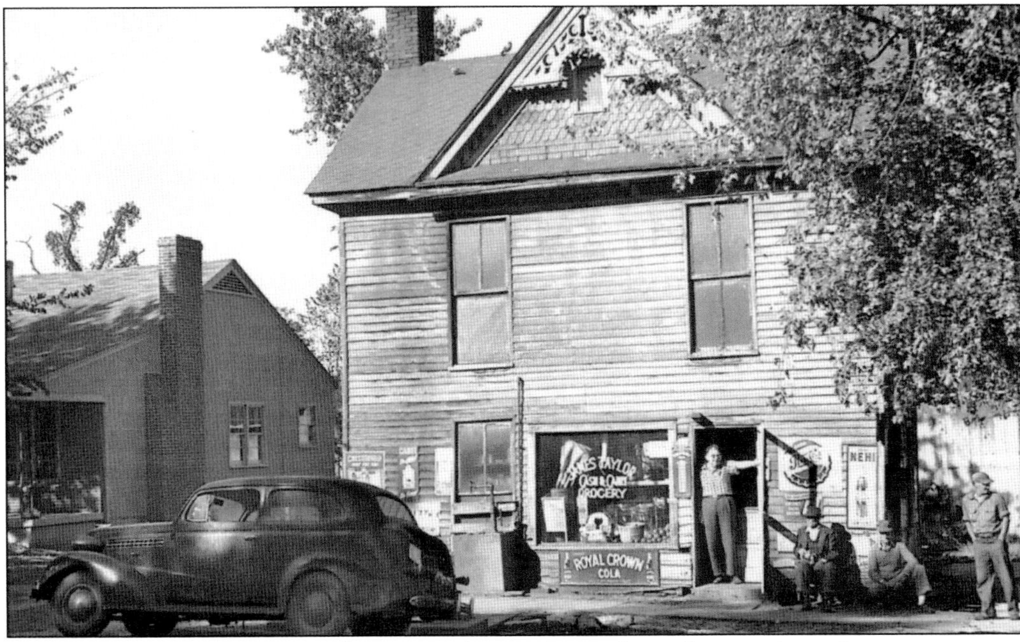

Above is an image of Jimmy Taylor's general store. A popular gathering place, the store remained in business for over 50 years on Chiles Street. When Taylor sold the property in 1969, it was to make room for progress. During the demolition of the building, a log structure dating back as early as 1797 was found under the weatherboarding. In the photograph below, note the exposed logs just before it was razed. In his poem "Jimmy Taylor's Store," Harrodsburg resident Tony Sexton writes, "It's good to live in a town where some things never change. / Like Jimmy Taylor's store . . . It reminds us / the simplicity of life still remains for those who want it. / It's good to know in our world of fast food chains and freeze dried coffee / There is still a store in our town selling taters by the pound."

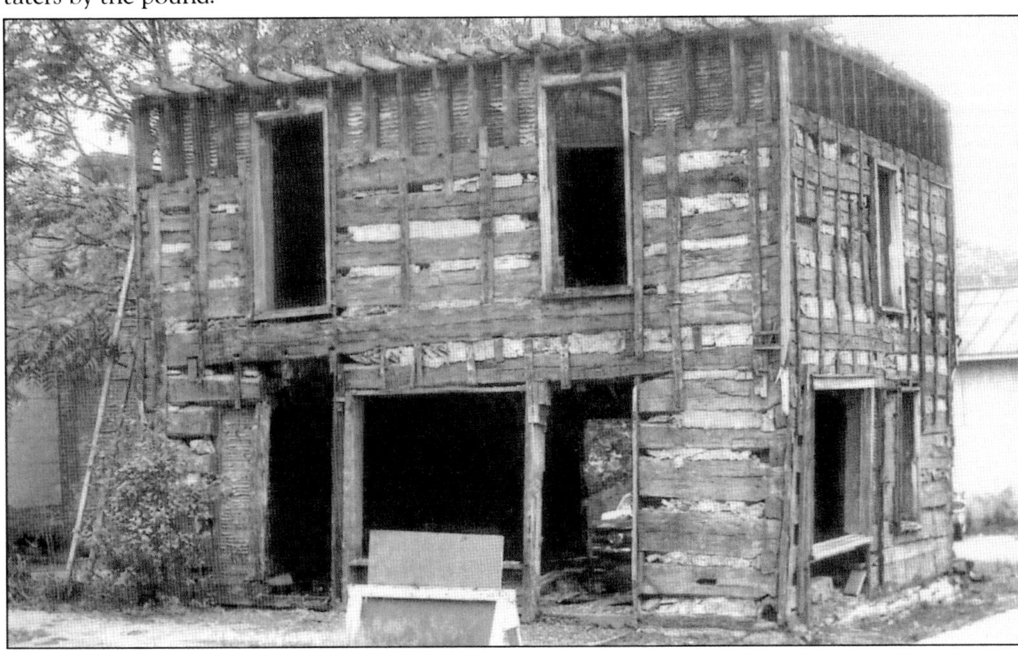

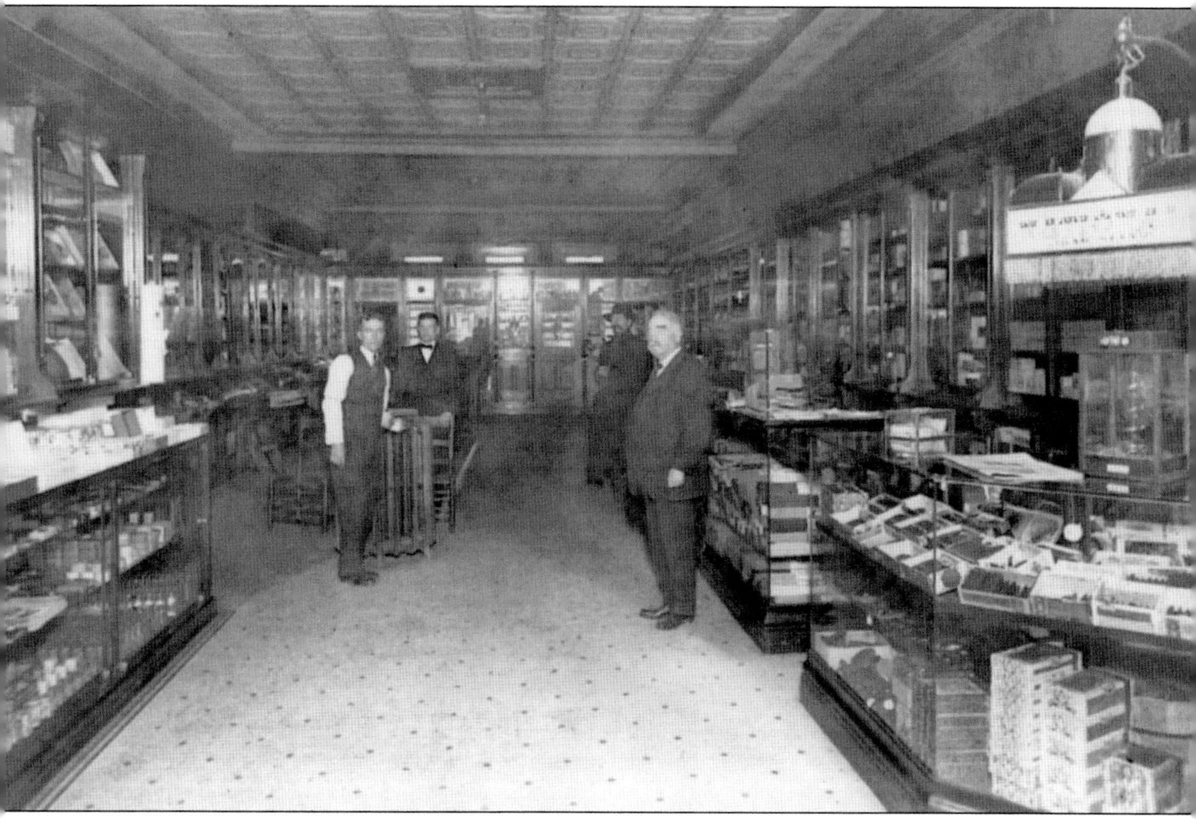

This is the inside of Dedman Drugstore. The man on the right is C.M. Dedman, and the others are unidentified. Glass display cases are on both sides at the front of the business. The soda fountain is near the back on the left side, and solid cherry apothecary drawers line the back wall. The second floor of the building was used to sell paint and wallpaper and included aisles of books, perfumes, comb-and-brush sets, and more.

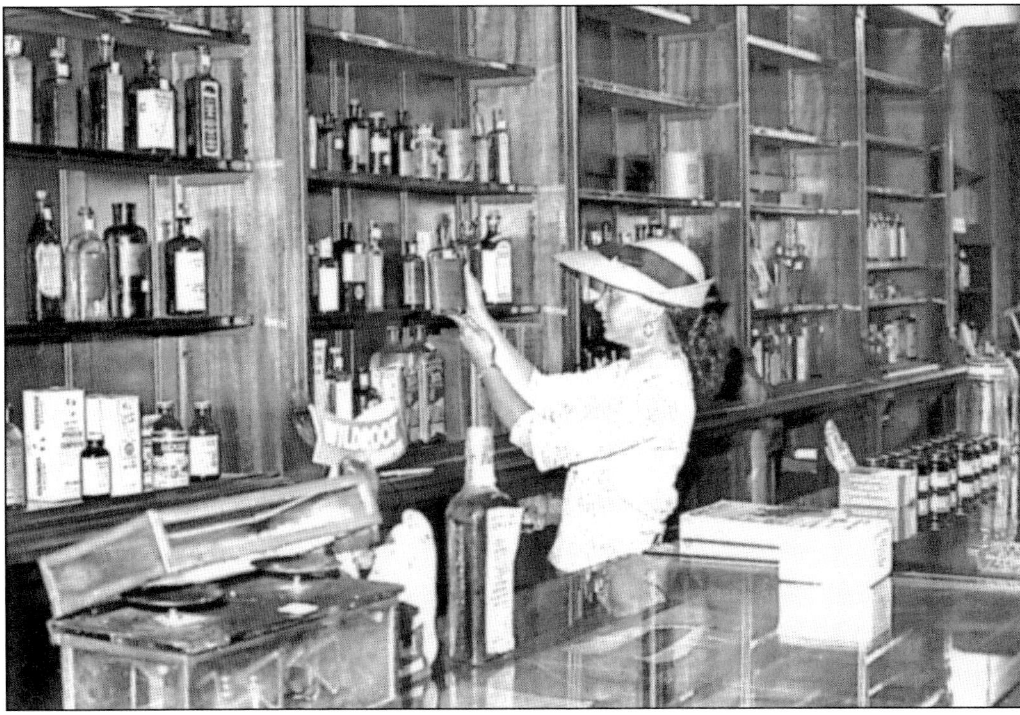

The photograph above, taken in 1983, shows Harriett Ruby arranging antique bottles in the cherry cabinets of the drugstore when it was her antique store. Although Dedman Drugs changed ownership many times after opening in 1868, it remained a pharmacy until 1983. From that time until 2001, the building served as several different antique stores. In 2001, with the help of Ralph Anderson, the James Harrod Trust was able to buy the property and restore it to its turn-of-the-century beauty. The photograph below shows the outside of the restored building where the Kentucky Fudge Company at Dedman Drug Company Store is once again a meeting place for those seeking food and conversation.

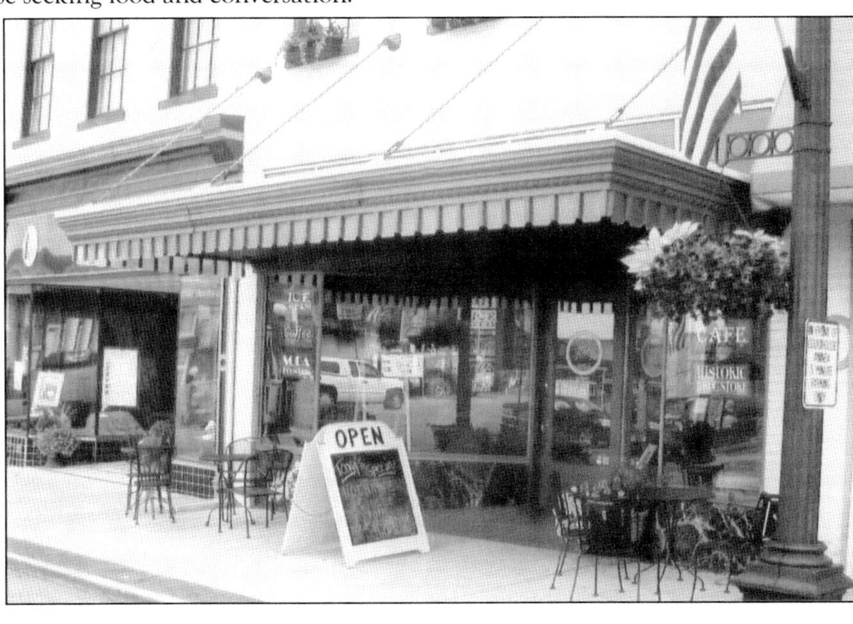

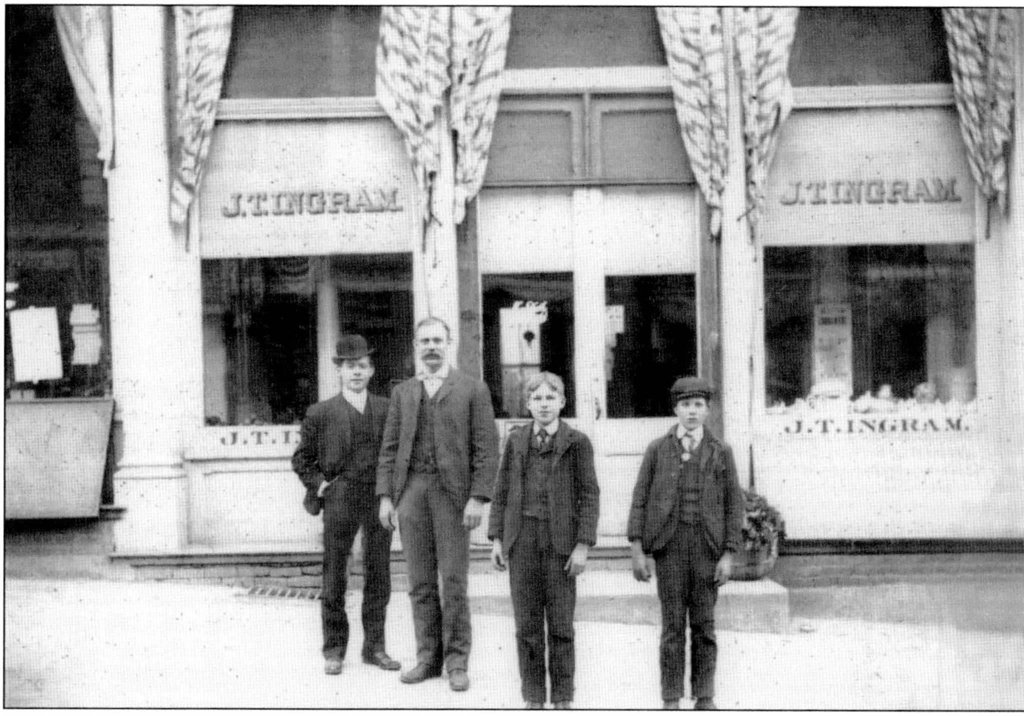

The above photograph shows the outside of J.T. Ingram's grocery during the early 1900s. According to a 1902 newspaper article, Ingram's was "the newest enterprise to throw its doors open to the public." The same article states, "Go to J.T. Ingram's for anything—bakery, confectionery, and groceries. The best line of candies, fruits, and vegetables. Everything fresh and up-to-date." At that time, a free citywide delivery system supplied fresh bread that was hot from the oven to customers. The photograph below shows the rear of the store where butchers did their meat cutting. On the wall behind the butcher are cured hams and buckets of lard.

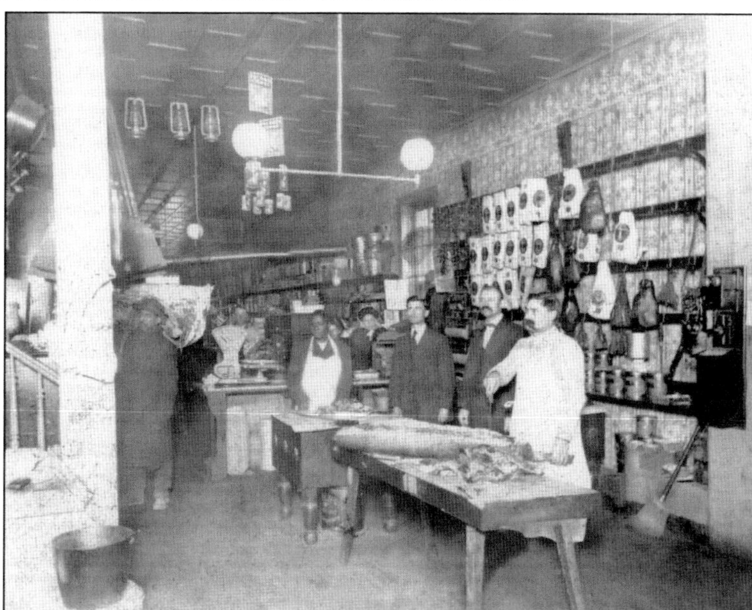

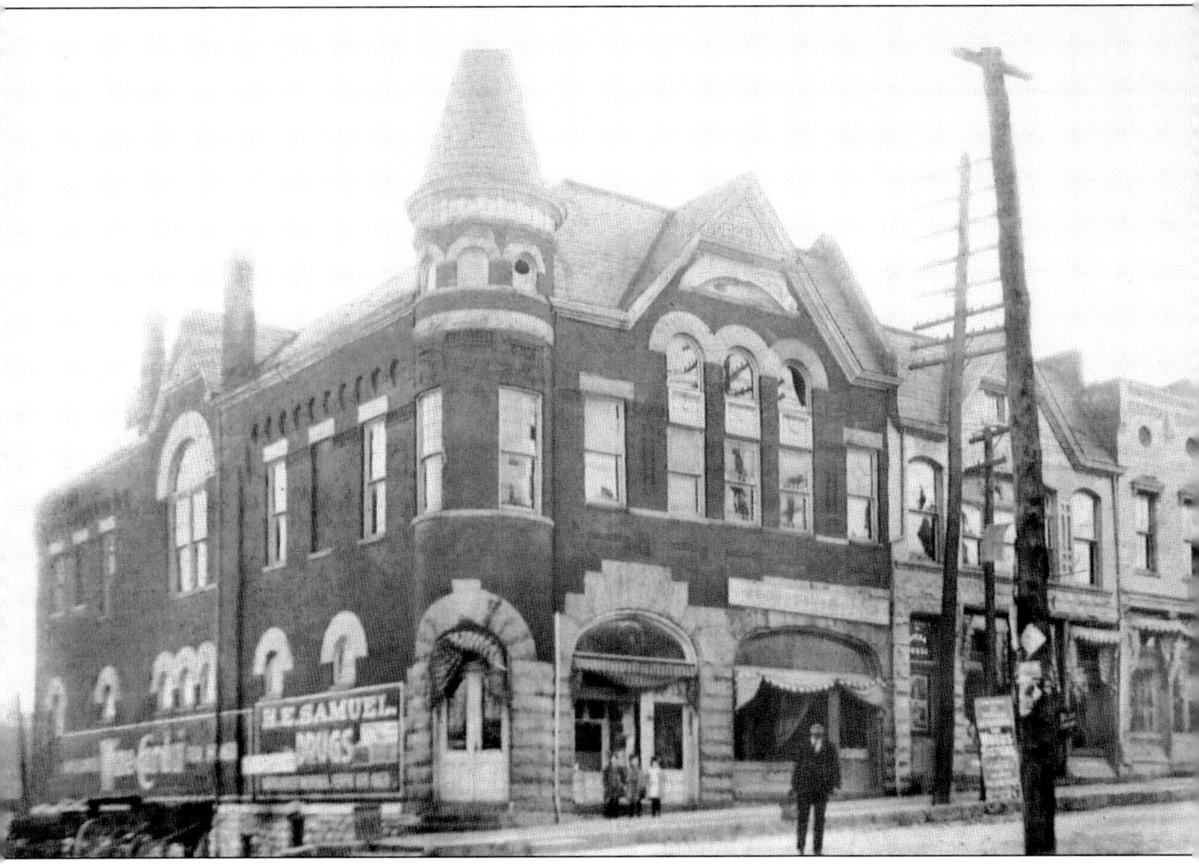

On the corner of East Poplar and Main sits the Blue Front, Main Street's most impressive building. Built in 1887 in the Queen Anne style with Romanesque Revival details of rough stone arches and a corner tower, it gives the street a feeling of substance. Its name was acquired from its best known business, the Blue Front Department Store, which operated there at the turn of the century. James Isenberg and his brother started out with a dry goods store and quickly expanded into a department store that always seemed to be ahead of its time. Among its many innovations was an electric carrier system, which took transactions to a central office where change was made and packages wrapped, and then all was returned to the customer. During the local street fairs, which took place right in front of their businesses, the Blue Front advertised a nursery with "20 nurses in uniform, cradles, and swings" where parents could leave their children. The Blue Front was "throwing open its doors to make the store your home while in town." After 58 years in business, the store closed in 1939.

“Howdy! Harrodsburg, where Kentucky Hospitality had its beginnings, and where the first handshake took place, bids you Welcome.” These are the first lines on an advertisement for the Blue Front Department Store shown here. Known as “Harrodsburg’s Busy Spot,” one of the logos stated, “Invariably Better—Isenberg Brothers, Inc.” This advertisement shows a catalog-like display of women’s wear from different decades between 1780 and 1932.

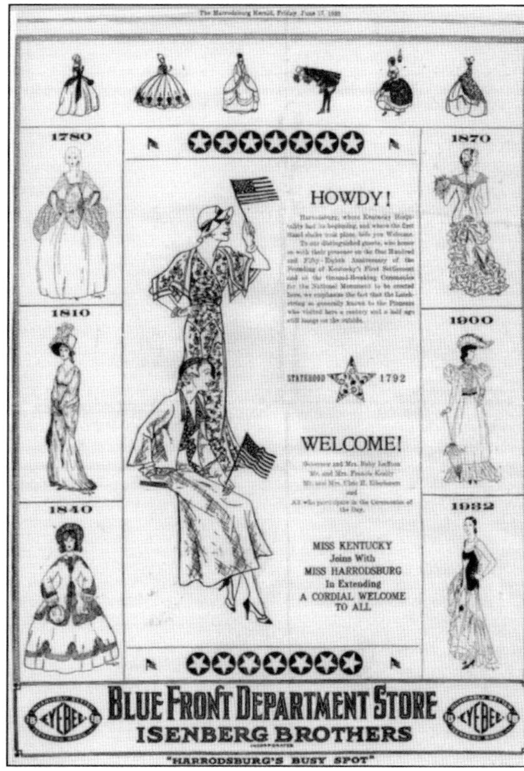

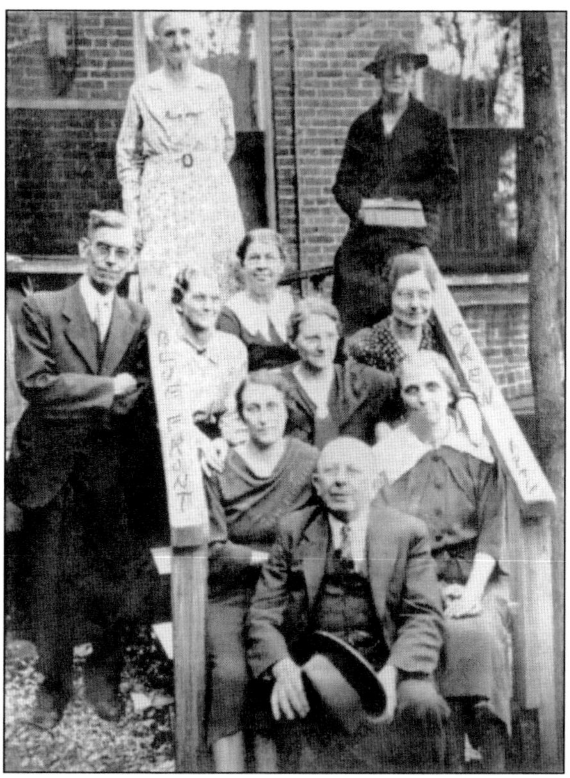

In 1937, the Isenberg brothers sold the Blue Front, and the employees posed for one last photograph. Starting at the bottom of the photograph, they are, from left to right, (first row) Joe McClelland; (second row) Mrs. Alvin Alderson and “Billie” Middleton; (third row) Annie Lee VanArsdall, Lena Ewing, Ann Nelson, and Sue Covert; (fourth row) Mollie Sutterfield and Minnie VanArsdale; and (standing) A.L. Gibson.

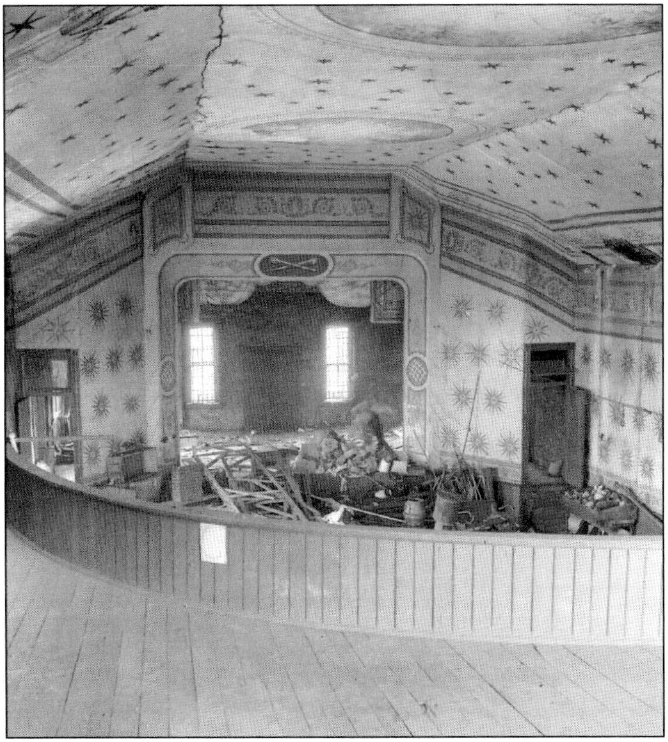

This 1940s photograph of Chenoweth Hall is a sad reminder of the beauty it once possessed. In the foreground is the semicircular balcony overlooking the stage. The regular seats below cannot be seen because old merchandise, fixtures, and other junk were stored upstairs when the Blue Front closed. Below is a close-up of the stenciling done on the walls and ceilings. This is not wallpaper—each stencil was hand painted. Interviewed in 1991, Lucille Graves said, "The Blue Front theater had the most beautiful ceiling and as a child, I remember looking up and seeing the stars on that ceiling." Harrodsburg native Ralph Anderson bought the Blue Front in 1988, and after a lengthy renovation, it was restored to its original glory.

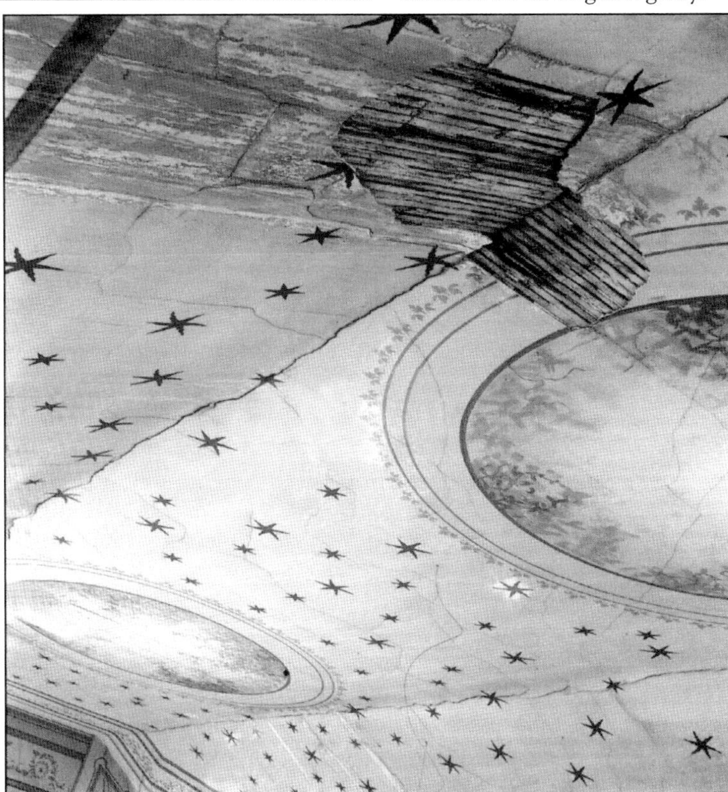

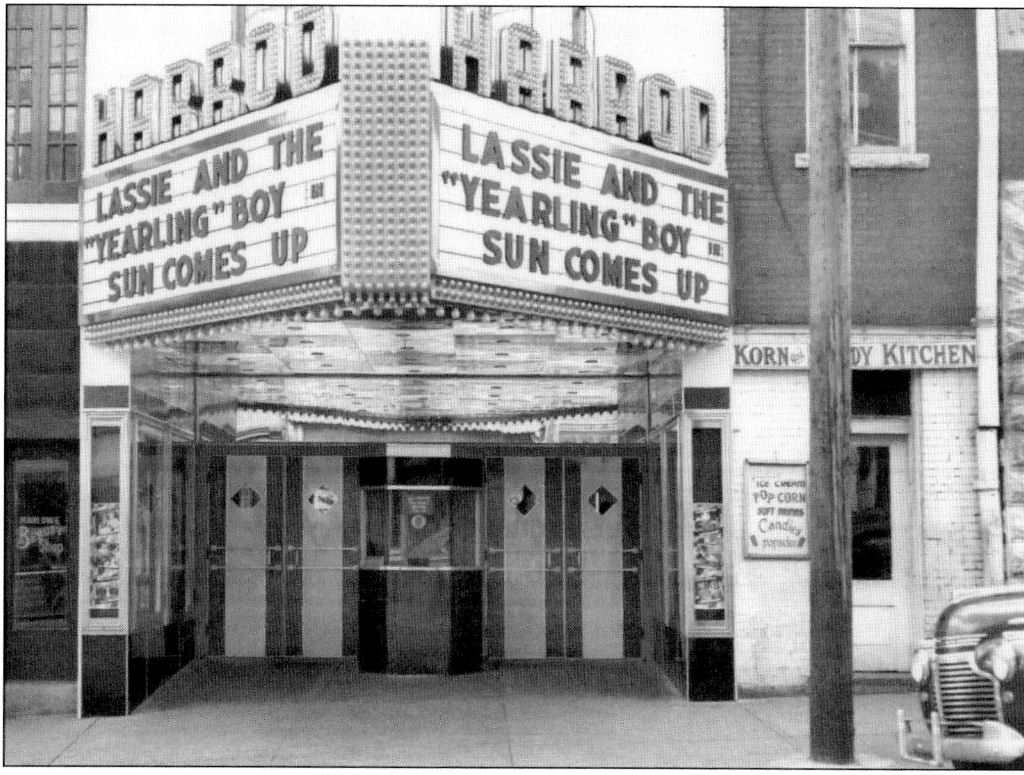

This photograph from the 1940s shows the Harrod Theatre, which had its grand opening in 1940 and operated until 1973. The movie title on its Art Deco marquee was a 1939 release. The theater boasted four restrooms, a lobby and a lounge, a balcony, and seats arranged to provide unobstructed views of the screen.

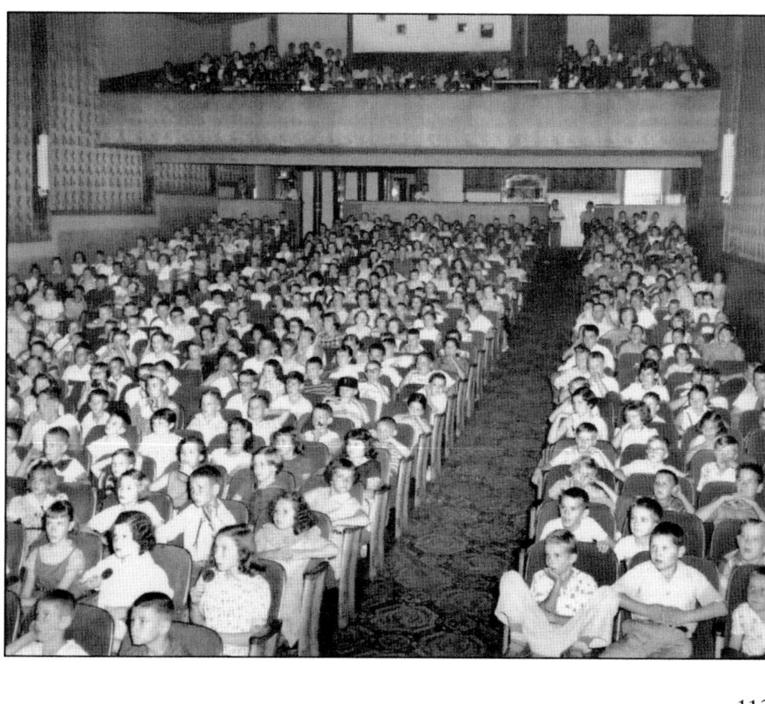

This amazing photograph from the 1950s shows the theater literally packed shoulder-to-shoulder for a Saturday matinee, which was the most popular form of entertainment available for children then. The price was right: between 50¢ and 75¢, depending on the ticket buyer's age. The popcorn was good, and the Saturday movie was always a popular Western or comedy.

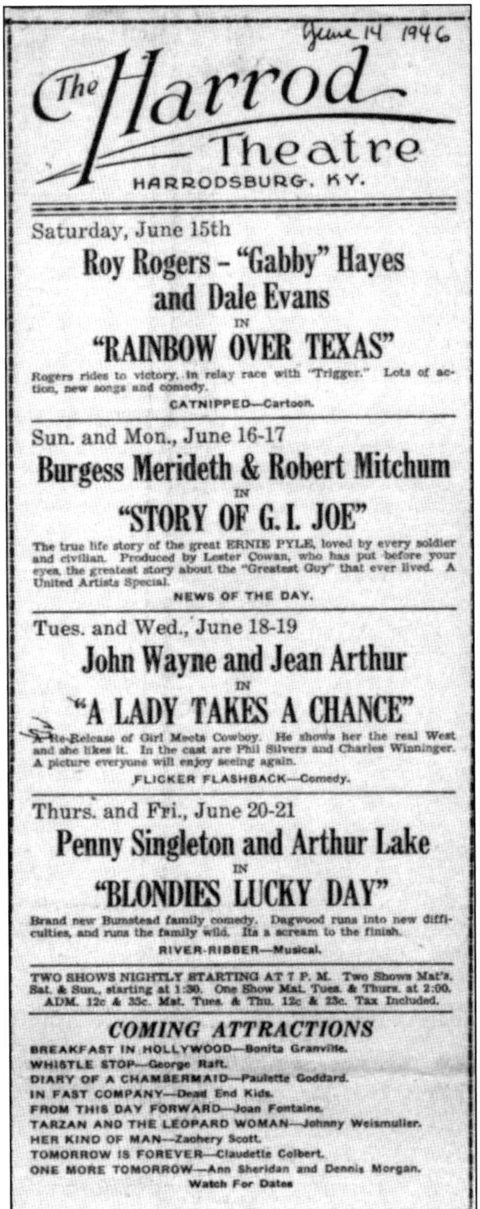

During its 33 years in business, the Harrod Theatre provided both town and county folks with a variety of entertainment in the form of movies and live musical stage shows. An advertisement from 1946 reads, "TWO SHOWS NIGHTLY STARTING AT 7 P.M. Two Shows Mat's. Sat. & Sun starting at 1:30. One Show Mat. Tues. & Thurs. at 2:00. ADM. 12c & 35c. Mat. Tues. & Thu. 12c & 23c. Tax Included." Small towns did not have to wait to see current and popular films and stars. Some features from the 1940s were *Abbott and Costello in Hollywood* (1945), *Rainbow Over Texas* (1946) with Roy Rogers and "Gabby" Hayes, and *That Night in Rio* (1941) with Don Ameche, Alice Faye, and Carmen Miranda. In 1957, *Raintree County*, partly filmed in nearby Danvillle, with Elizabeth Taylor had four showings on Saturday and Sunday at 1:00, 4:00, 7:00, and 10:00 p.m.

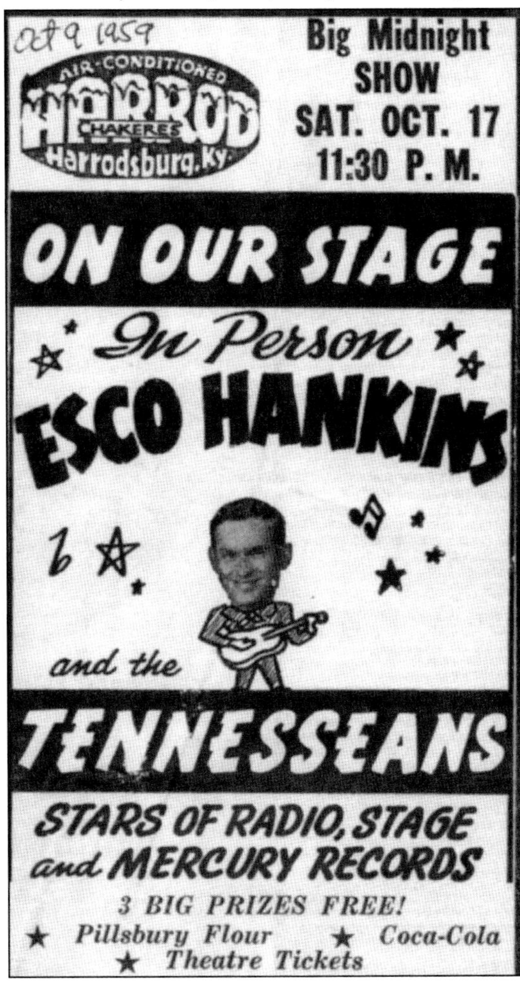

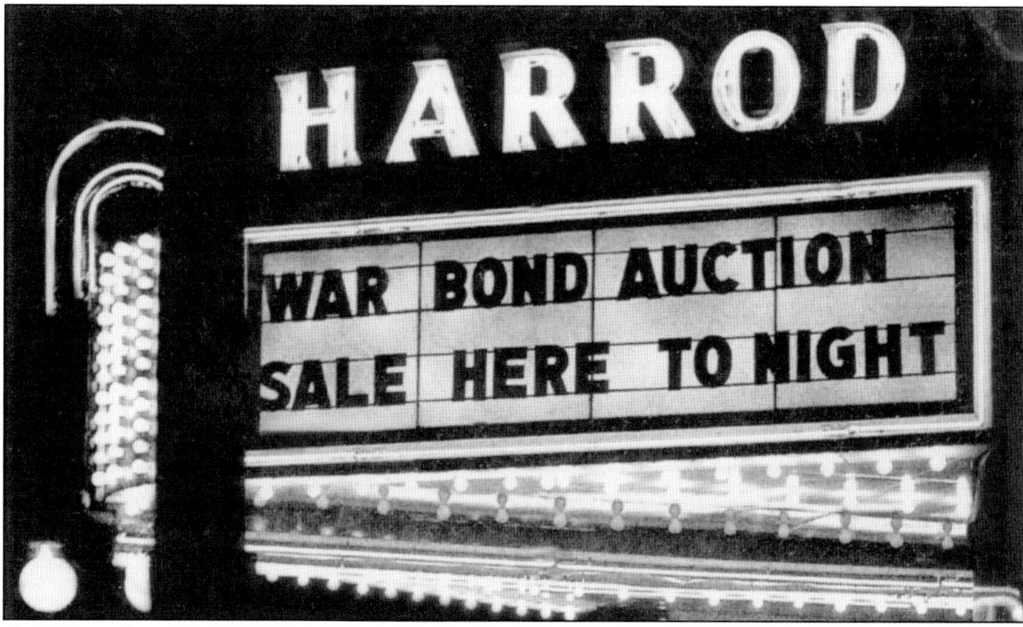

On September 16, 1942, Mercer County made its greatest war effort—the big War Bond Auction, held at the Harrod Theatre. As advertised on the marquee, 175 prizes would be awarded and *The World at War* would be showing on the screen. Mercer County had 1,447 young men in various branches of the armed forces. The photograph below shows every seat filled and Earl Dean, a local attorney, taking bids. Slogans and newspaper advertisements were exhibited everywhere with various sayings: "This war will have to be won by YOU;" "Buy bonds and MORE bonds;" "Uncle Sam will pay YOU to help HIM;" "Bomb A-way with War Bonds;" and "What is money against a boy's life?"

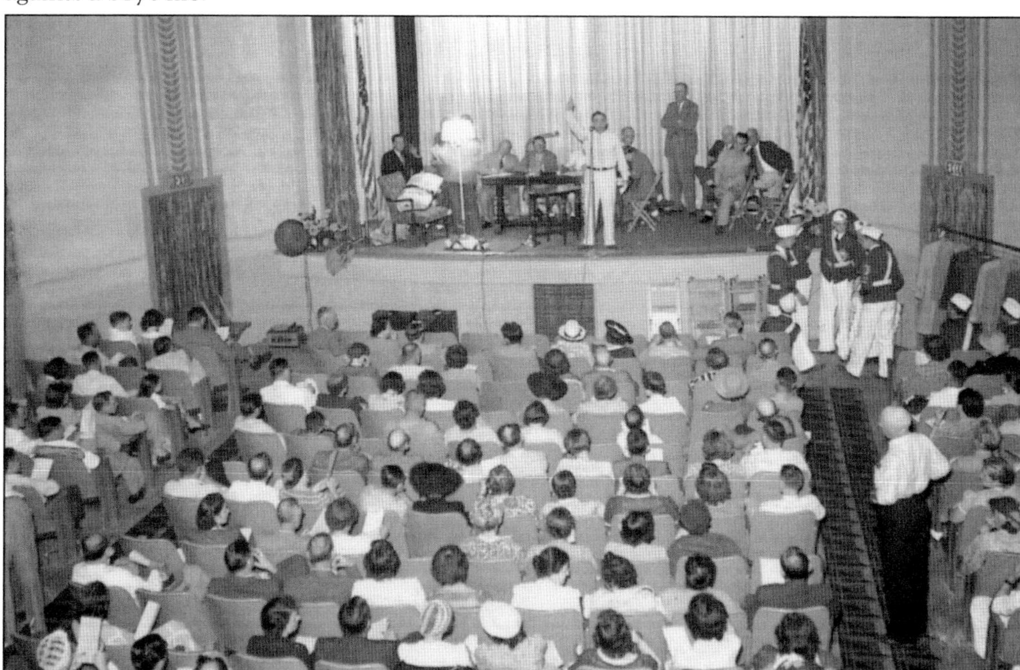

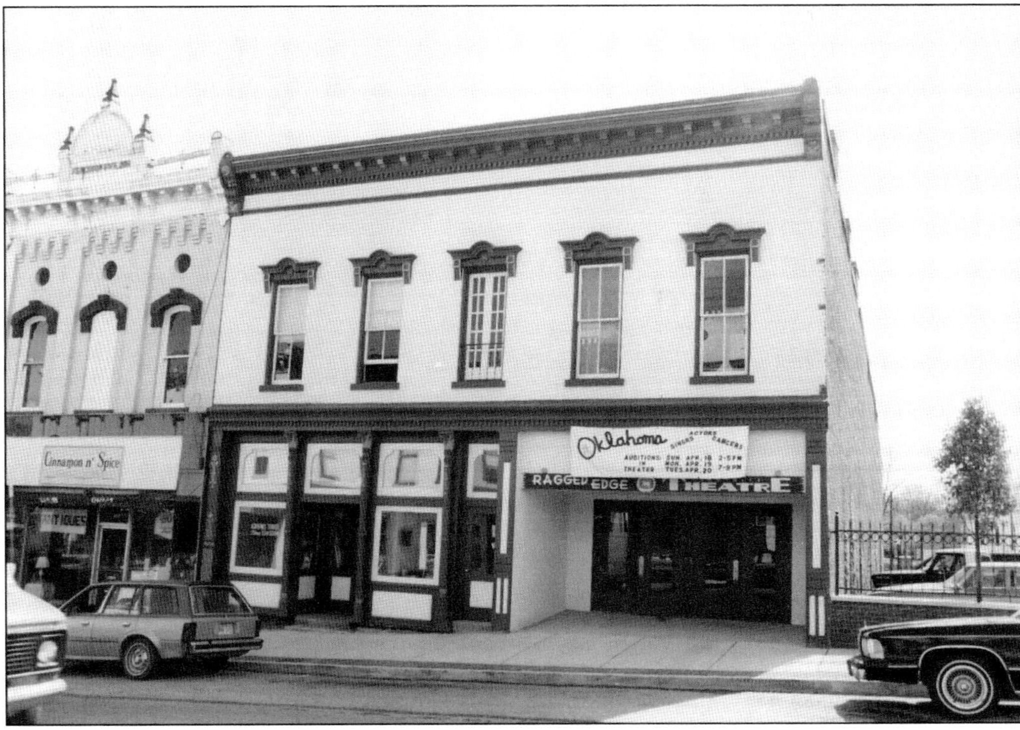

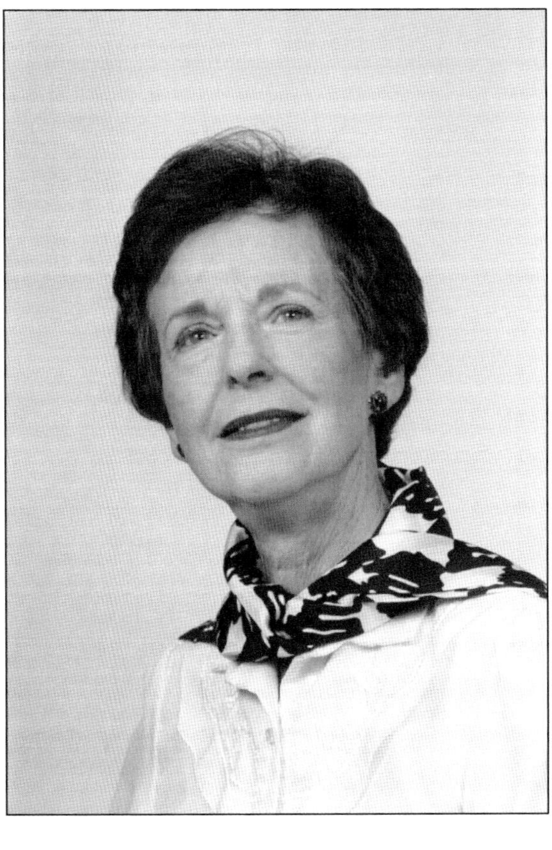

In the above photograph, the Ragged Edge Community Theatre is shown occupying the same building where the Harrod Theatre was located. By 1973, downtown movie theaters were becoming a part of the past as cinemas with large parking lots were opening. The marquee was removed, and the space was used for various businesses. In 1982, Mary Clarence Chelf Jones had returned to her hometown of Harrodsburg after a career teaching voice at the Interlochen Arts School in Michigan. Her dream was to start a community theater. Encouraged by the success of a local production of *Annie Get Your Gun* in 1983, she formed the Ragged Edge Theater Klub.

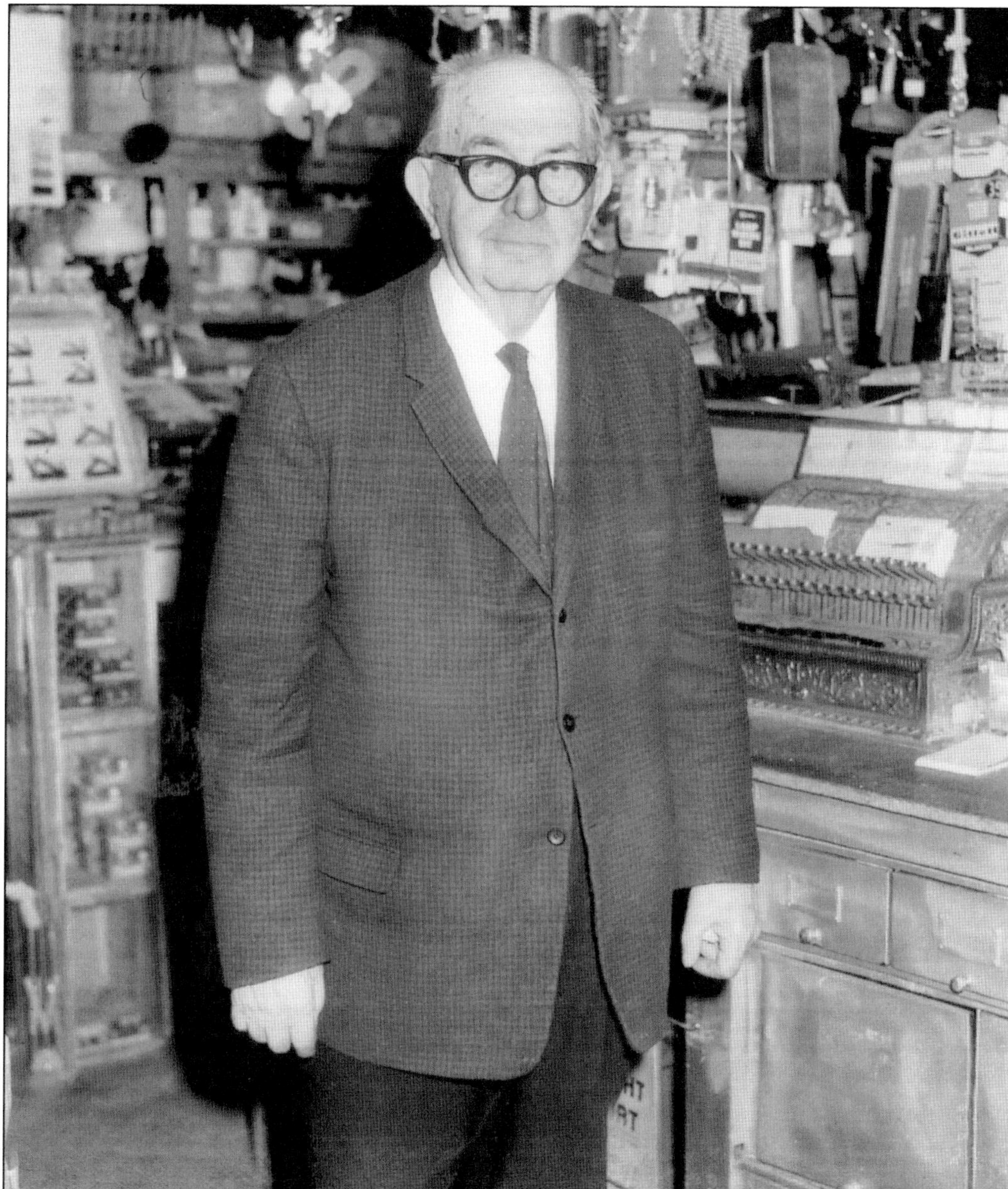

Benjamin Franklin Norfleet is shown standing inside the Norfleet Hardware & Implement Company on East Office Street in 1968. This was one of the most unique hardware stores in central Kentucky. Norfleet carried items dating back to when he started the business in 1934 in addition to stocking modern products. A trip to his store was like stepping back into another time. The saying among his customers was, "If you can't find it at Norfleet's, then it's not available anywhere." Advertisements from the 1940s list the items available: a velocipede (an early bicycle), scooters, sleds, Scout knives, boys' wagons, ice cream freezers, pressure cookers, vases, Libbey-Owens glassware sets, electric heaters, harnesses, lawn mowers, chinaware, scythes, wire fencing, and poultry supplies. Norfleet continued to manage the business from his home after he retired by receiving nightly reports on the day's activities from his daughter. In an interview in 1975, he said he was "continually amazed at the inflationary prices he had to cope with."

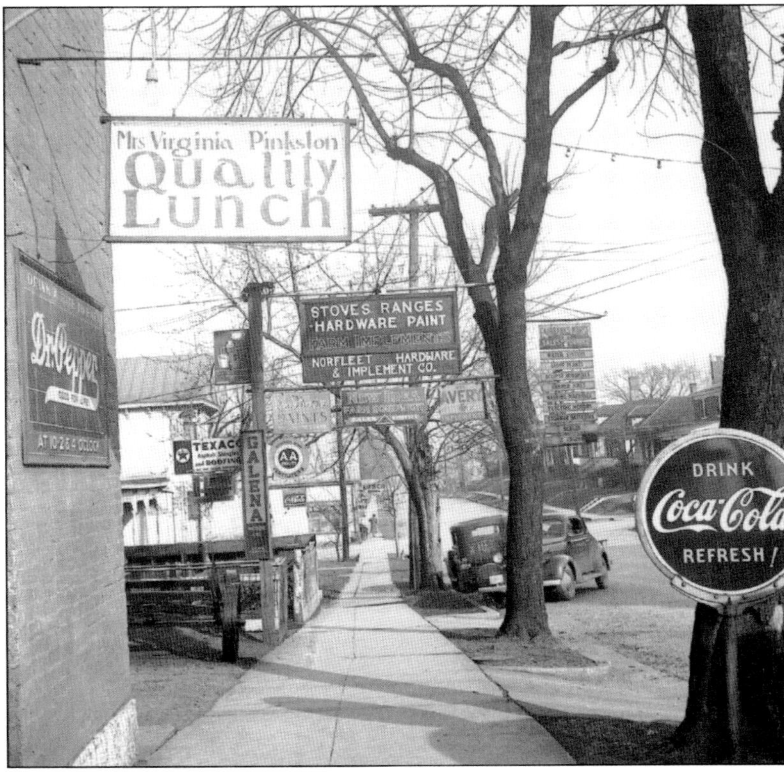

This side of East Office Street was home to two restaurants and Norfleet's Hardware Store. Virginia Pinkston's Quality Lunch was located in the basement of the James Flats Building from the early 1940s until 1947. It was also called Hole in the Wall because the brick wall had to be opened up for a doorway.

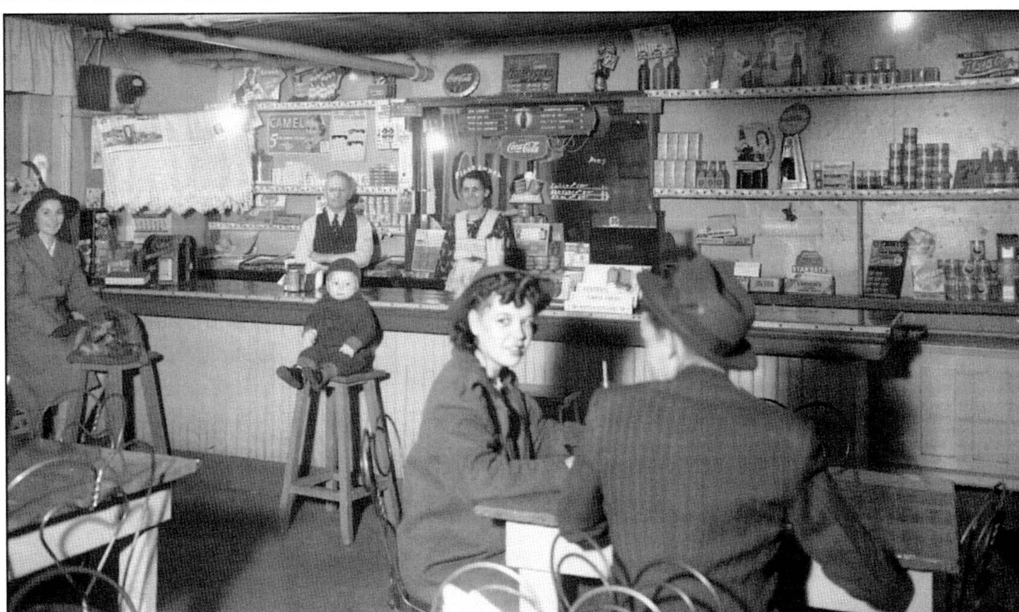

This is an early-1940s view of the Quality Lunch Room. The owner, Virginia Pinkston, is behind the counter and her daughter Kathleen Armstrong is on a stool at the left, with her dog on the stool beside her. Miss Virgie, as Pinkston was called, was a wonderful cook who was known for her hot pork sandwiches. Menu items posted on the mirror at 10¢ each are hamburgers, cheese sandwiches, and roast beef sandwiches.

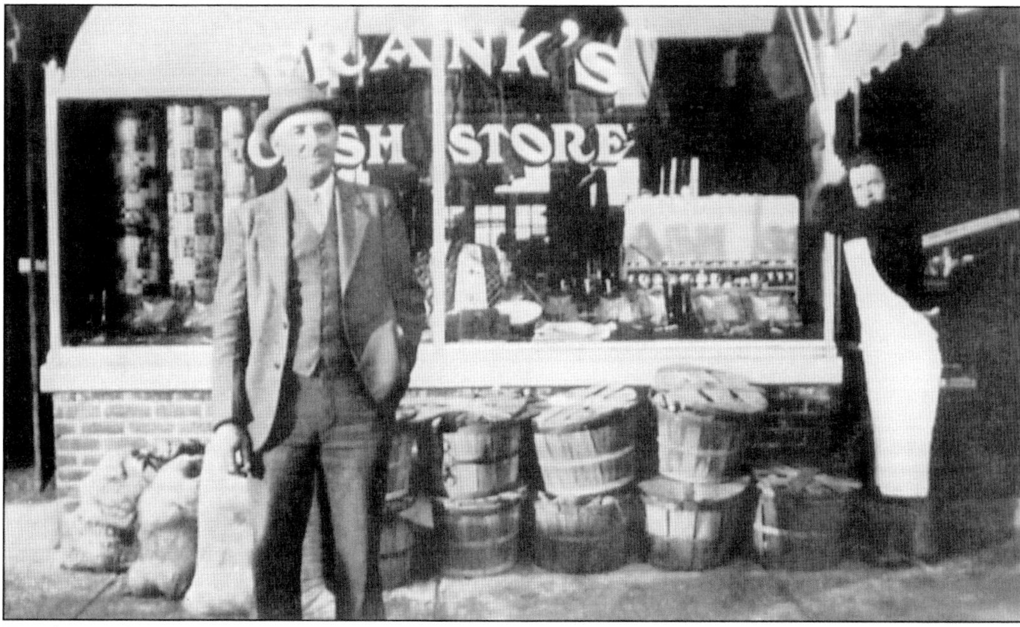

Frank's Cash Store was a typical general store of its day. Everything from produce to farm supplies was available. In the above photograph, Page Bailey is standing in the front of the store he manages while his son Paul is operating the awning. The business was located on the corner of Lexington and Chiles Streets, across from the Ingram Buick Garage. In the below photograph, the employees are, from left to right, Mary Ella West, Paul Bailey, William Bailey, and Page Bailey. Farmers brought in poultry, eggs, and meat; everything was fresh in those days. Mary Ella West was the cream operator. Customers could warm themselves and tell a few tales at the potbellied stove in the back.

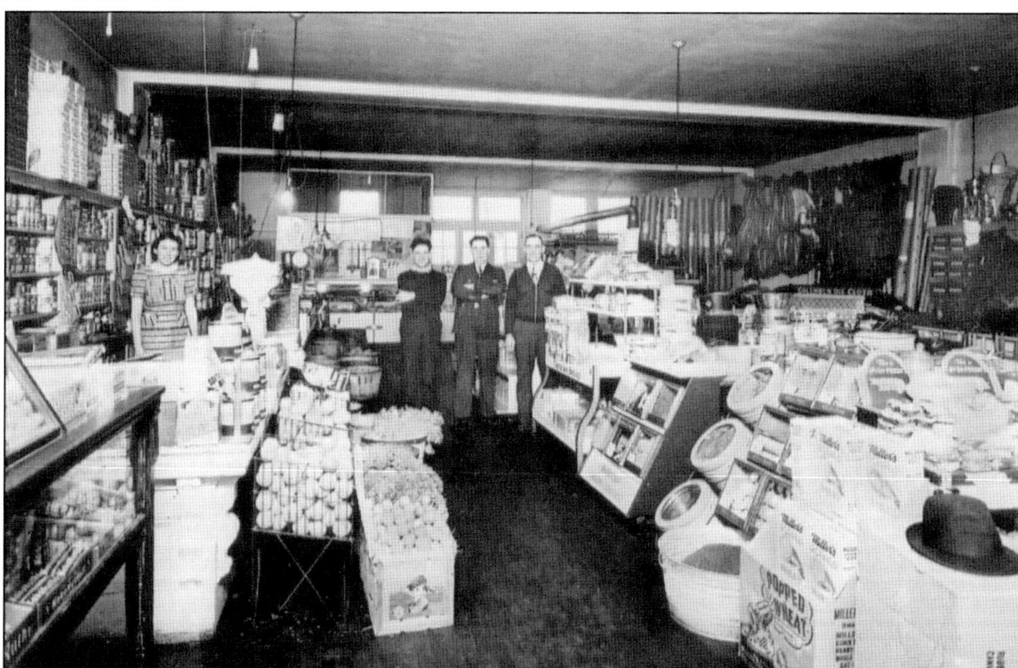

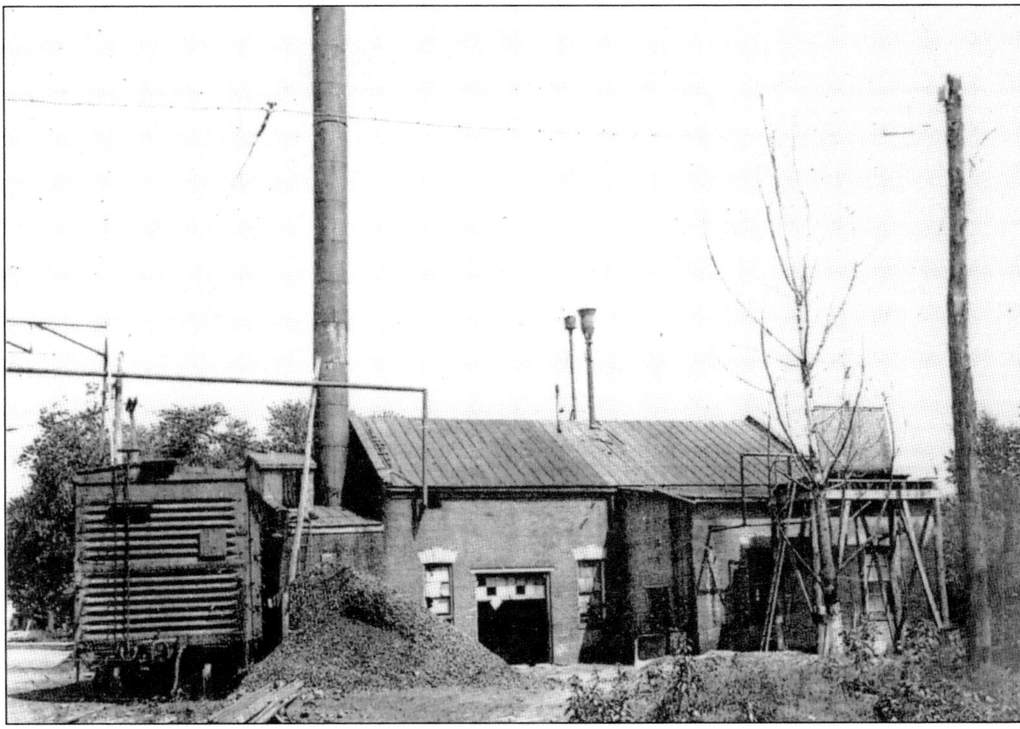

Located on the corner of Chiles and Factory Streets, the Harrodsburg Electric Light Plant, shown during the 1930s, provided the city's electric power before Kentucky Utilities began buying it from the Dix Dam power plant. Steam was produced in three large boilers that operated four generators. At first, the plant only powered lights at night, and electricity was not available during the daytime.

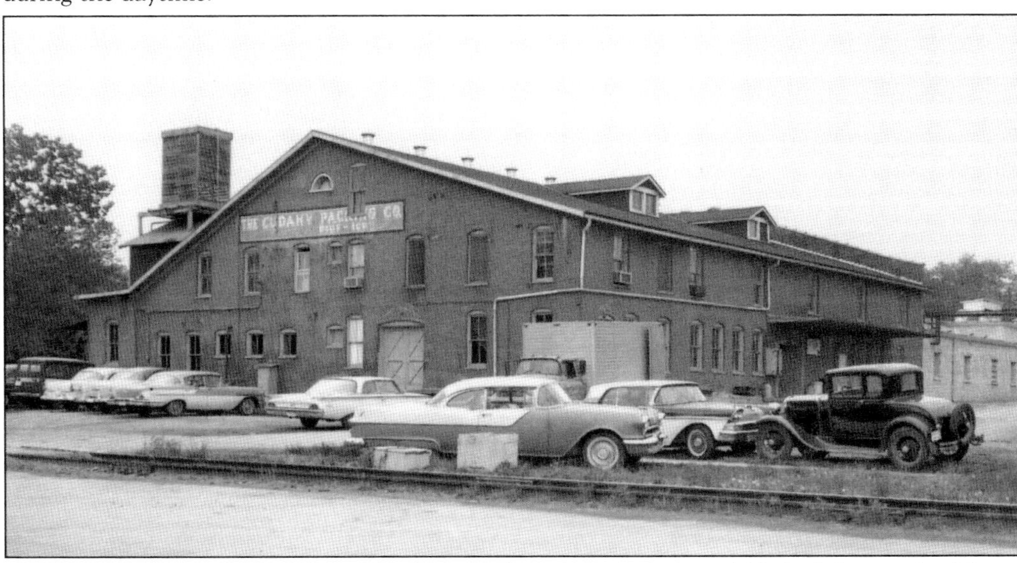

The Harrodsburg Cudahy Plant, which opened in 1942, was one of 25 Cudahys in the United States. Its products were shipped to sales centers all over the country. The local plant made cheese, butter, and ice cream with milk and eggs purchased from local farmers. Also for sale at the plant were 25- or 50-pound blocks of ice for customers' iceboxes.

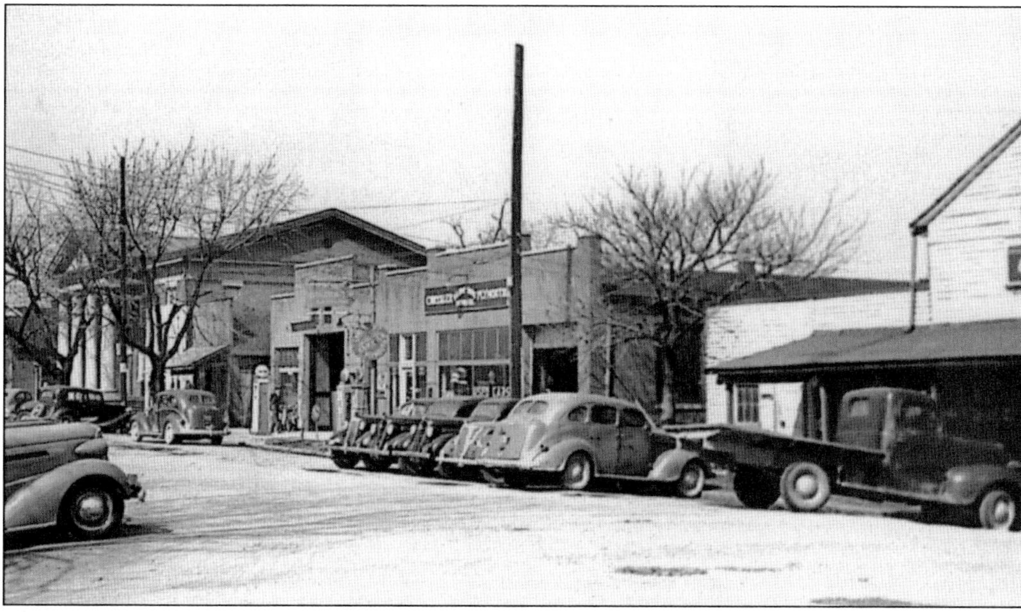

This once busy stretch of Lexington Street now stands empty of retail stores. Only St. Peter's AME Church on the corner is still standing. This photograph from the 1940s shows five businesses, which are, from left to right, the McGlone and Isham barbershop, "Doc" Smalley's tire shop, Dick Corman's garage, Glave Sims's Chrysler-Plymouth dealership, and Teater's grocery.

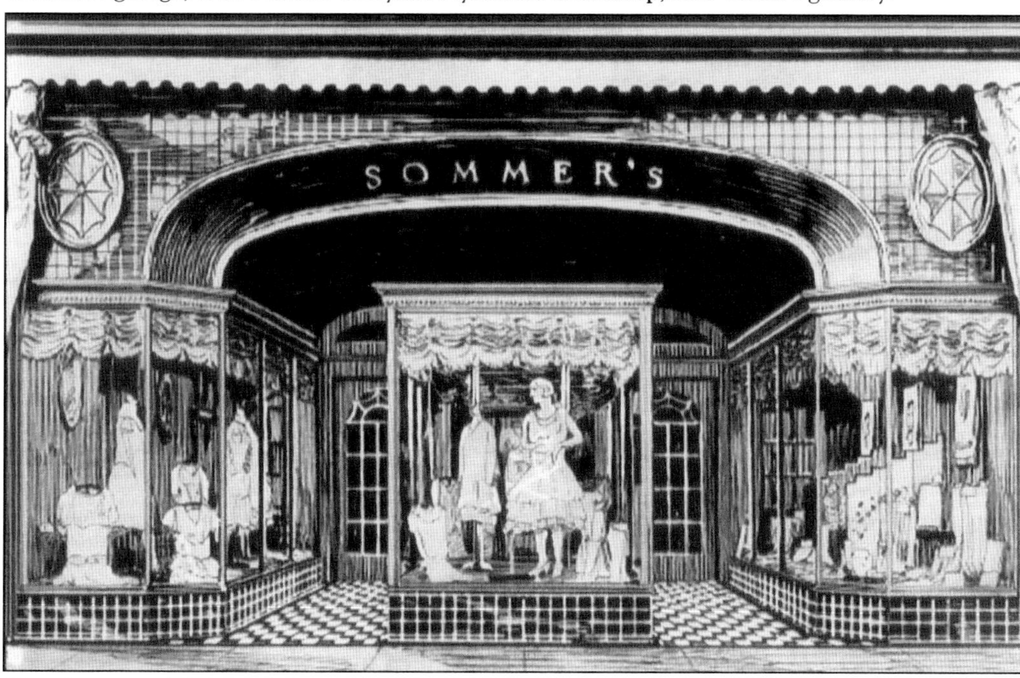

This drawing of Sommer's, a women's department store located on south Main Street, shows an elegant and unusual design for Harrodsburg. The name is possibly German. Immigrating into small towns to look for opportunity was common during the late 1800s and early 1900s. An advertisement from 1930, the year it opened, shows dresses selling for $12.75 and coats for $16. By 1935, its going-out-of-business sale was being advertised.

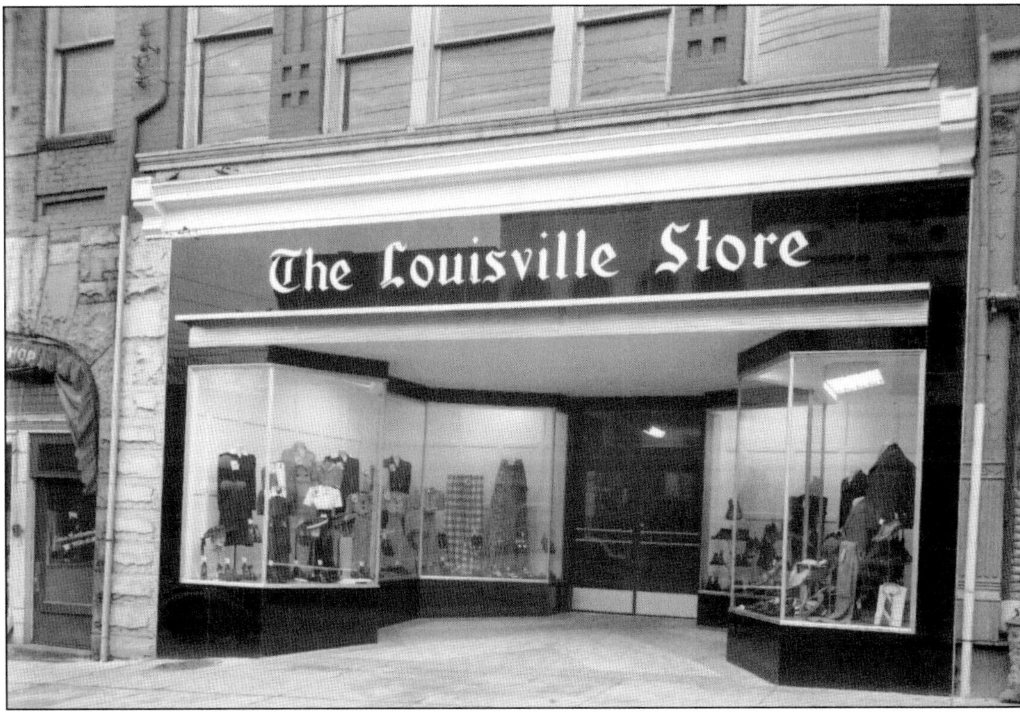

The Louisville Store was another fixture on Main Street that managed to compete successfully and survive for 47 years, from 1941 to 1988. It was one of a chain of similar stores that operated throughout Kentucky. Not fancy, the store was a solid place that sold things that would last: clothing for the family and material for the many women who made their own clothes. The retailer was an authorized dealer for Sportleigh Coats, tailored in Harrodsburg. They sold for $22.95 and were featured in *Vogue* and *Mademoiselle*. In 1970, the store did a complete renovation with a new modern glass front, all new fixtures, and wall-to-wall carpeting throughout. New and more merchandise was added.

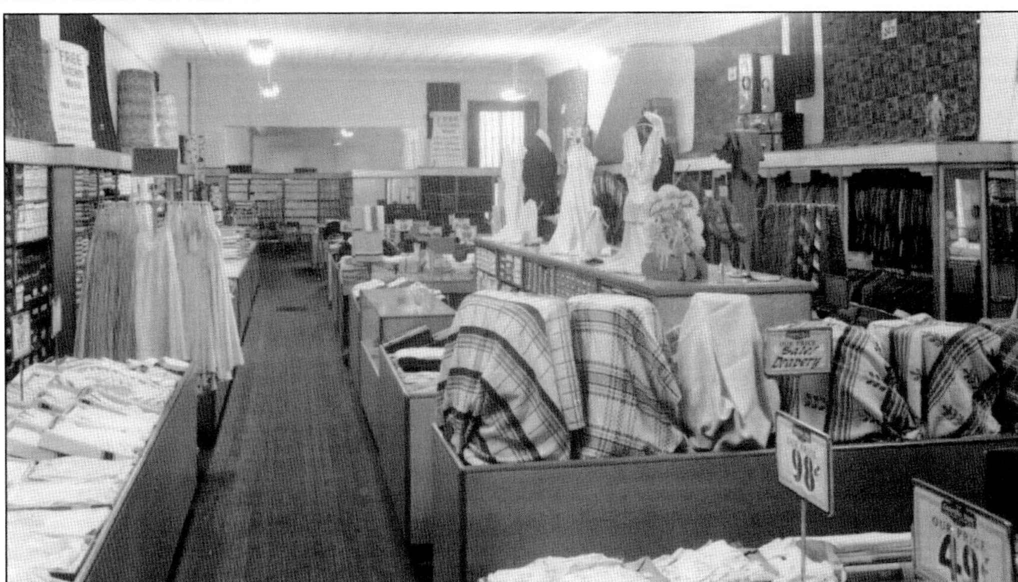

Hoover's Food Store was on Main Street from 1947 until 1969. It was the last grocery on Main Street at a time when people still lived downtown and enjoyed being able to walk to the store. In an interview, Mrs. Hoover said, "We stayed open to nine, 10, maybe 11 o'clock on Saturday nights. People would come in and shop and leave their groceries here, and we would stay until they came and picked them up after the movie."

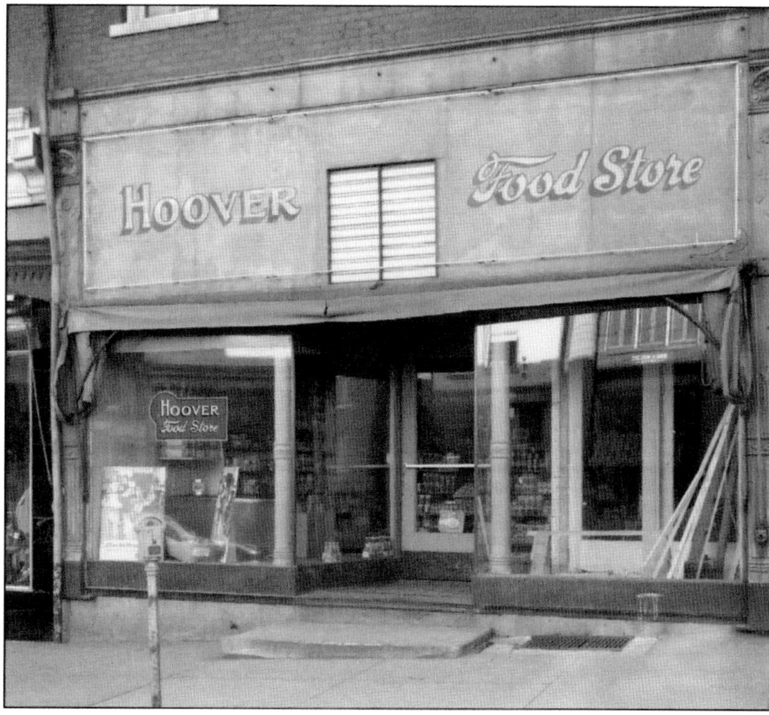

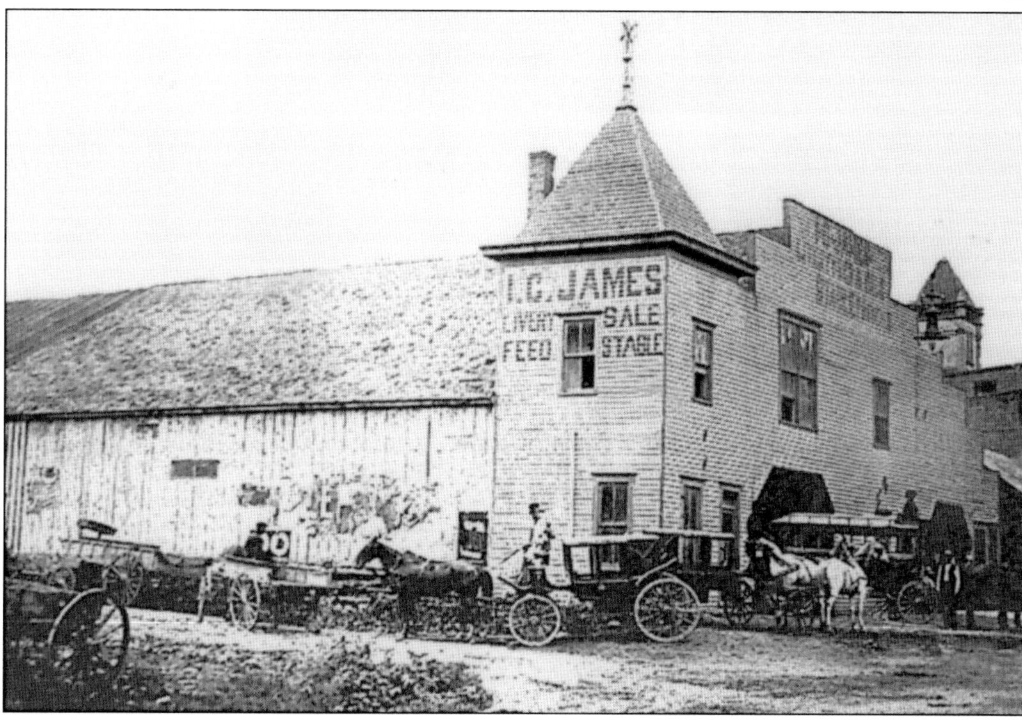

The I.C. James Livery, Feed & Sale Stable, located on the corner of East Office and Greenville Streets, opened in 1882. James had stabling for as many as 250 horses. He was a horseman well known throughout the state, and his stable had the best horses and finest equipment. When cars replaced horses, the building was used as a garage, which burned sometime in the 1920s.

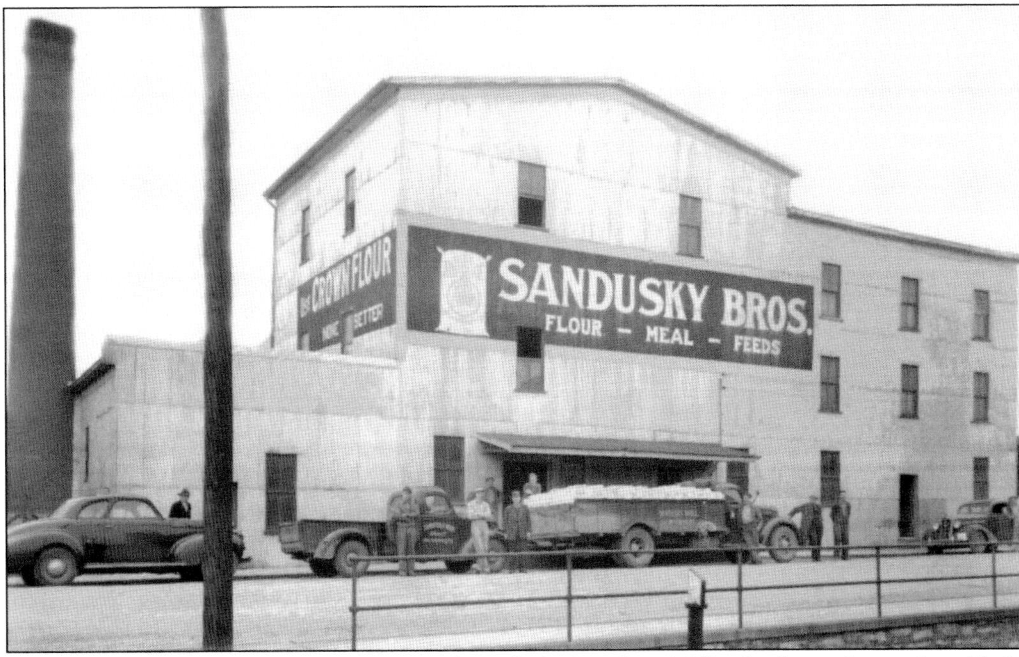

This 1940s photograph shows employees of Sandusky Brothers Mill, which was located on Chiles Street next to Town Creek. The farm supply operation was headquartered there. A mill has been on this site since the late 1800s, and it has been exchanged through many owners over the years. The photograph above identifies the men, but not in order: Hollie Edwards, Ed Massie, Joe Sandusky (in coat at rear of truck), Charlie Johnson, Frank Sandusky, Charlie Edwards, Grover Smith, and Levi Scrogham. In the photograph below, Sandusky employees unload grain shipments at the Harrodsburg depot. Sandusky Mills was one of Harrodsburg's oldest manufacturing operations and was owned and operated by brothers Joe and Frank Sandusky.

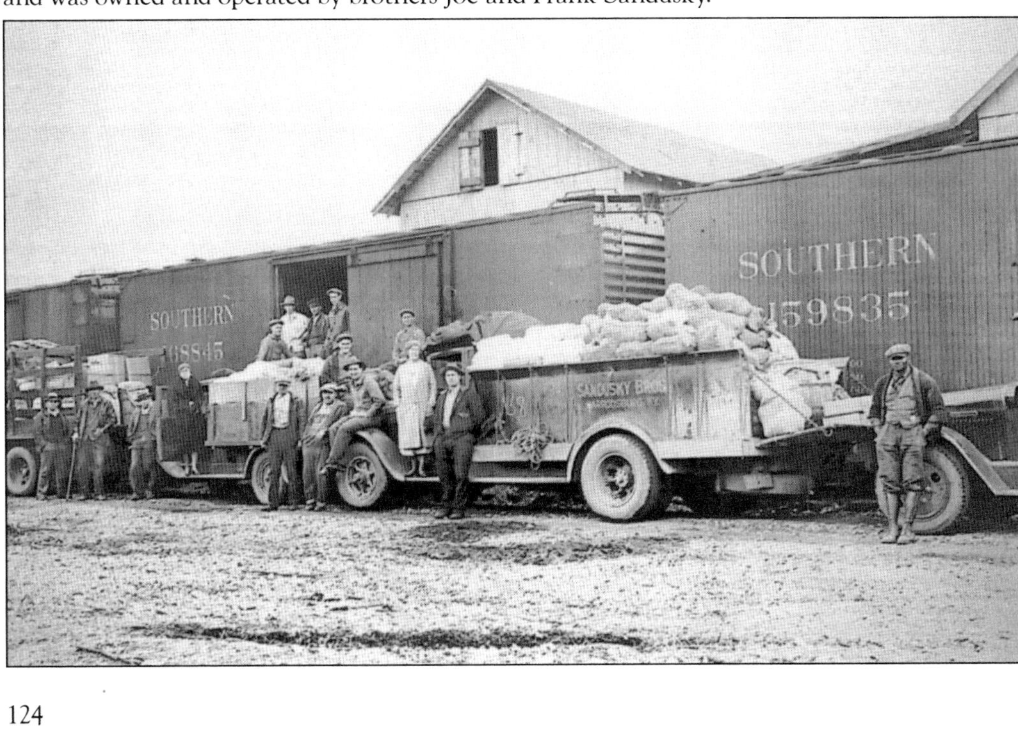

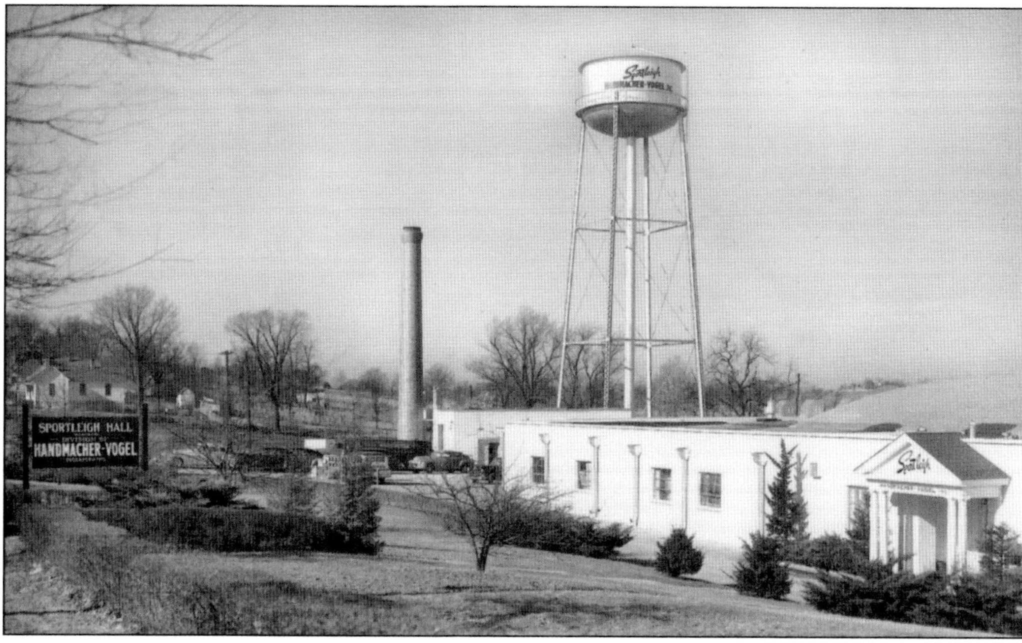

This 1951 photograph (above) shows Sportleigh Hall, a manufacturer of women's clothing and Harrodsburg's largest employer, with close to 450 workers at that time. From 1940 to 1950, its owner was Fred Weissman, who made a success of the factory. Weissman made a donation toward furnishings for the new Mercer General Hospital. He left Harrodsburg in 1950 after a dispute over whether a new, similar industry—essentially a competitor—should be encouraged to locate here. The Mercer Chamber of Commerce was formed out of this dispute. A long row of presses for shirts and coats is shown in the photograph of the factory's interior (below).

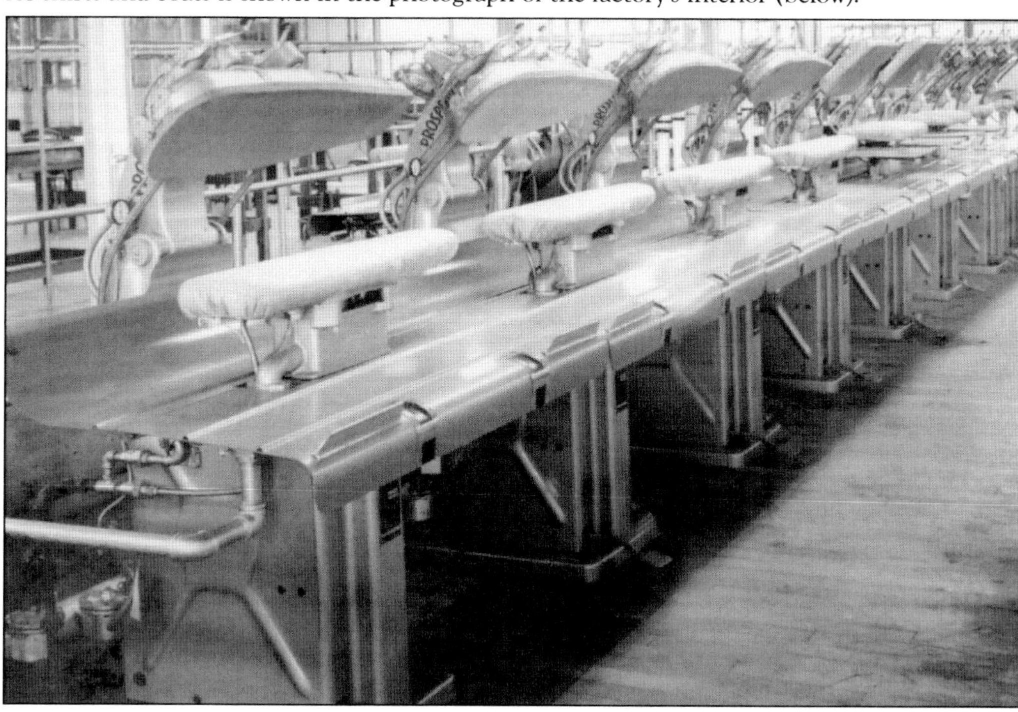

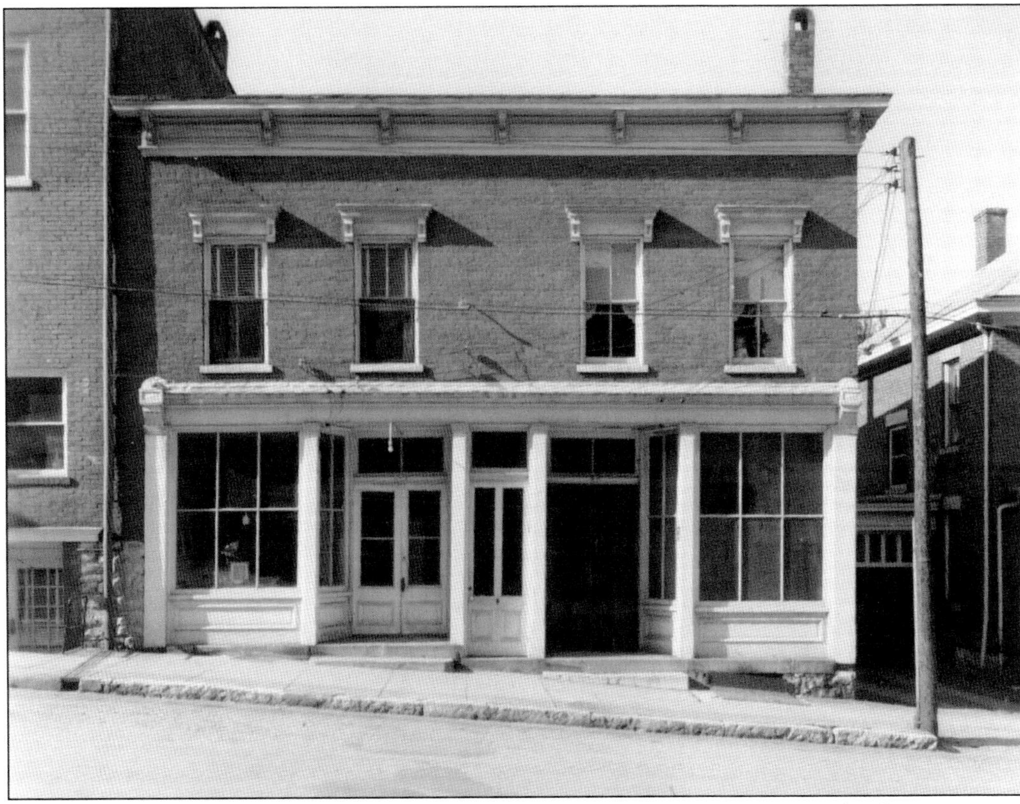

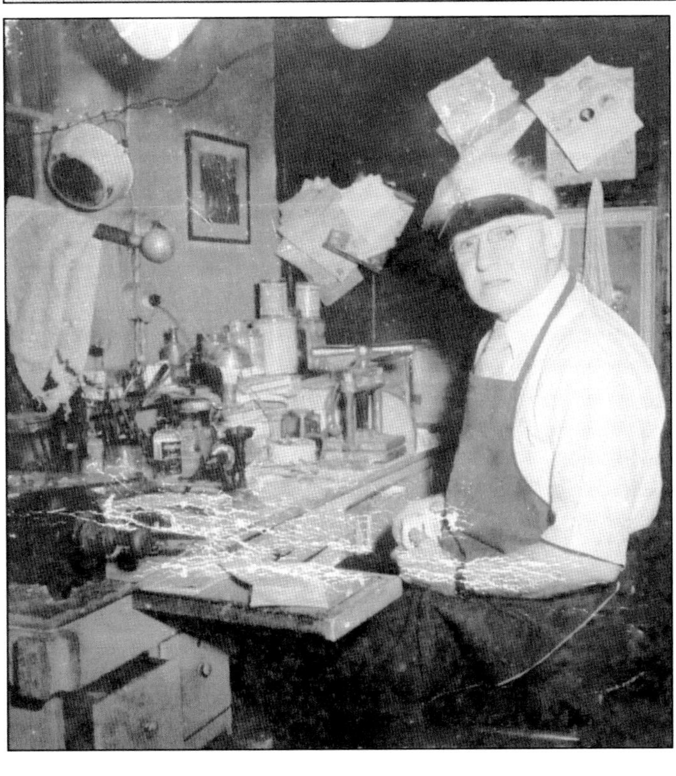

On East Poplar Street is a dignified-looking building (above) from the late 1800s that is virtually the same in appearance as it was then, having survived the fires that occurred around it. It has been home to a microcosm of small-town life. Constructed in the style of the times with ground-level shop space and living quarters above, the building, with its rich and varied history, began as a saloon, and has since housed the post office, a furniture store that also sold caskets, a shoe repair shop, a dental office, several beauty shops, a bookstore, a storefront church, a tropical fish shop, and two photography studios. Dr. A.D. Armstrong (left) bought the building in 1900 for his dental practice.

INDEX

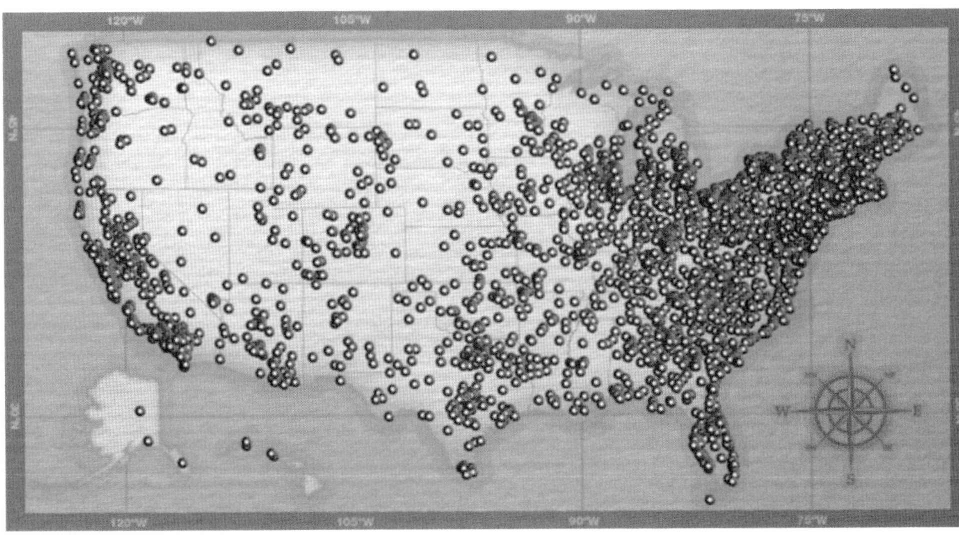